Judge, Jury and Executioner

Judge, Jury and Executioner
Essays on The Punisher *in Print and on Screen*

Edited by Alicia M. Goodman,
Matthew J. McEniry, Ryan Cassidy
and Robert G. Weiner

McFarland & Company, Inc., Publishers
Jefferson, North Carolina

This book has undergone peer review.

Library of Congress Cataloguing-in-Publication Data

Names: Goodman, Alicia M., 1989– editor. | McEniry, Matthew J., 1988– editor. | Cassidy, Ryan, 1984– editor. | Weiner, Robert G., 1966– editor.
Title: Judge, jury and executioner : essays on the Punisher in print and on screen / edited by Alicia M. Goodman, Matthew J. McEniry, Ryan Cassidy and Robert G. Weiner.
Description: Jefferson, North Carolina : McFarland & Company, Inc., Publishers, 2021 | Includes bibliographical references and index.
Identifiers: LCCN 2021032473 | ISBN 9781476682501 (paperback : acid free paper) ∞
ISBN 9781476642949 (ebook)
Subjects: LCSH: Punisher (Fictitious character) | Vigilantes in literature. | Vigilantes in motion pictures. | Antiheroes in literature. | Antiheroes in motion pictures. | Comic strip characters in motion pictures. | BISAC: LITERARY CRITICISM / Comics & Graphic Novels | PERFORMING ARTS / Film / General | LCGFT: Literary criticism. | Film criticism.
Classification: LCC PN6728.P86 J83 2021 | DDC 741.5/973—dc23
LC record available at https://lccn.loc.gov/2021032473

British Library cataloguing data are available
ISBN (print) 978-1-4766-8250-1
ISBN (ebook) 978-1-4766-4294-9

© 2021 Alicia M. Goodman, Matthew J. McEniry,
Ryan Cassidy and Robert G. Weiner. All rights reserved

No part of this book may be reproduced or transmitted in any form or by any means, electronic or mechanical, including photocopying or recording, or by any information storage and retrieval system, without permission in writing from the publisher.

Front cover art © 2021 Shutterstock

Printed in the United States of America

*McFarland & Company, Inc., Publishers
Box 611, Jefferson, North Carolina 28640
www.mcfarlandpub.com*

Table of Contents

Acknowledgments   vii

Introduction
   Alicia M. Goodman, Matthew J. McEniry
   and Robert G. Weiner   1

Section I: Philosophy and Analysis

To Shame Its Inadequacy: The Punisher and His Critics
   Kent Worcester   15

A Tough Pill to Swallow: The Punisher as the Cure for the Ills
of Modern Society
   Ryan Litsey   27

The Long Cold Dark: The Punisher Mindset and Its Dissemination
into the Collective Unconscious
   John Harnett   35

Black and White and Nothing in Between? Some Thoughts
on the Morality of the Punisher
   Anders Lundgren   48

Determined to Punish: Three Case Studies in Punishment
   Matthew J. McEniry   62

Section II: Gender and Feminism

The Punisher as Female: A Thought Experiment
   Alicia M. Goodman   75

Frank Castle, Fanfiction and the Female Gaze
   Elizabeth Jendrzey *and* Meredith Pasahow   91

Takes One to Kill One: *Punisher MAX*'s War on Hegemonic
    Masculinity
        KELLY KANAYAMA   102

Section III: Veteran Studies

Recalling Vietnam in Marvel Cinematic Universe's
    Punisher Storylines
        MIKE LEMON   115

Fighting a Lonely War: Frank Castle and the Domestication
    of Vietnam
        KATHLEEN MCCLANCY   125

Frank Castle's Other War: Meaning, Memory
    and the Vietnam War
        STEPHEN CONNOR   136

Section IV: Politics and Gun Violence

Bullet-Riddled Production: The Punisher's Influence
    on Violence in Decades of Tragedy
        ROB E. KING   155

"When is the right moment to release a TV series about
    a heroic mass shooter?" Contemporary American
    Politics and the Reception of Netflix's *The Punisher*
        MIRIAM KENT   165

About the Contributors   177

Index   180

Acknowledgments

Alicia M. Goodman: I'd like to thank my fellow contributors for their hard work and guidance; I have enjoyed working on the project with all of you. I also must thank Kimberly Grenadier; our conversations about gender theory are always invigorating. Another thank you goes to Kyle Jay for your encouragement and love. Last, to Rob Weiner, your mentorship, feedback, encouragement, and friendship is invaluable; thank you for all that you do—you are a treasure.

Matthew J. McEniry: Thank you to my fellow editors and the essay contributors for your work on this project. We couldn't have done this without you all. Thanks so much to our peer reviewers who helped make this volume more scholarly, accurate, and readable. Finally, a special thanks to my wife Rachel and my daughter Indigo, for these crazy times we currently live in would be much less bright without you two in my life.

Robert G. Weiner: Special thanks to my colleagues in RIO. Thanks to Donell Callender for her support of my work. Laura Heinz for always having an open ear. Thanks to Dr. Ryan Litsey, Joshua Salmans, Lynn Michaels, Mark Todd, Martin Soap, Linus Liberman, G.W. Bridge, Denise Caspell, Dr. Aliza Wong for her support and encouragement. Dr. Robert Moses Peaslee for all the projects we've worked on together. Thanks to the folks in Document Delivery for getting all those Punisher books and more for me. Love and thanks to Marilyn Weiner, Larry and Vicki Weiner, John Oyberbides, Tom Gonzales, and Joe and Geraldine Ferrer. Thanks to my furry friends Victor, Frost, Moon and Kelton. Dedicated to the memory of Lee, Kirby, Little Dude, Wade and Grace. Thanks to my students past and present for teaching me new ways to think about popular culture. Thanks to all the Punisher scribes, artists, letterers, colorists and actors. Thanks for all the great storytelling. Finally, thanks to my colleagues Alicia M. Goodman, Ryan Cassidy, Matthew J. McEniry. Thanks for believing in this project and for your hard work.

Introduction

ALICIA M. GOODMAN, MATTHEW J.
MCENIRY *and* ROBERT G. WEINER

Since the Punisher's (Frank Castle) first appearance in *Amazing Spider-Man* #129 (1974), the character has become one of the most popular icons of the Marvel Universe with numerous series, guest appearances, three feature films, an animated movie, fan films (a notable one, *Dirty Laundry*, featuring former Punisher actor Thomas Jane) and a popular two season series on Netflix. An exceptional collection for a character whose co-creator, Gerry Conway, regarded him as "second tier" (Williams, 2010, p. 12), Conway goes on to state that he was surprised by the Punisher's success and that he was a "much stronger character than I'd originally imagined" (Williams, 2010). It's been estimated that throughout the character's 45+ year career that he has killed a staggering 48,502 people (Conely, 2017). The psychological profile of the Punisher is very complex, but his motives are very clear and simple: "He doesn't just kill people. He tortures, guns down, stabs, and terrorizes anyone he doesn't deem to be an innocent, and his view of innocent/guilty is black and white. Frank Castle is a man with nothing to lose, because he's already lost everything. Now all he has left is his mission" (Conely, 2017).

The Punisher's appearance in #129 is as a vigilante hired by the villainous Jackal, who has convinced the skull-wearing soldier that Spider-Man is the bad guy. The resolution of the issue ends with the Punisher realizing Jackal was deceiving him and vowing to get revenge, leaving Spider-Man alive (Conway, 1974). In *Daredevil vs. Punisher* #2, the Jackal brags to Hammerhead about his interactions with the Punisher: "He's a pure killer. I've stripped away his foolishness. Showed him his true essence. When I met The Punisher he was also nothing. I showed him how to channel his Anger. I gave him direction. Purpose. Molded him into what he is today" (Lapham, 2005). It's not a statement many in the criminal underworld would appreciate. The Punisher would appreciate it even less, as Hammerhead retorts back to the Jackal saying, "I wouldn't brag about that. He might blow your head off one day soon" (Lapham, 2005). The Punisher's origin has been enhanced with the canon story of the death of his family at the hands of various entities. While his wife, son, and daughter's deaths are always the beginning of any given reboot, the perpetrators can differ. His veteran status is also the same through some sort of combat scene which elevates his abilities beyond those of a distraught husband and father. The result is always the same, though, a very angry individual who has a mission of revenge that doesn't stop with the death of his family's killers but spills out into the world of heroes and villains.

Films with popular vigilante killers like *Death Wish* (1974), the Dirty Harry series (1971–1988), and characters like Don Pendelton's Executioner (Mack Bolan) are key influencers for the creation of the Punisher. The Executioner character and his war on the mob (1969) can be seen as the grandfather to Frank Castle and his identity of the Punisher along with his war on criminals (Kraft, 1975, p. 53). The Punisher is an American and believes in patriotism (himself a decorated military veteran), but he is apolitical. He disdains extremist political groups in equal measure. He has no sympathy for extremist right-wing groups, nor does he care for ultra-liberals who are allowing criminals to get away with their actions (Baron, 2007). He doesn't like either political position—he's on his own scale. In fact, the Punisher once saved a flag burner who was trying to make an artistic statement from being hanged, "Because that flag is big—big enough to survive the fool's right to burn it.... No law against flag burning, but there is against assault" (Baron, 2012). The would-be flag burner accuses the Punisher of being a "great white liberal," which is ironic. He tells the would-be performance artist: "My art consists of blowing away crooks" (Baron, 2012).

The Punisher appears with nearly every hero, with teams, monsters, and numerous villains in the Marvel Universe. He has even appeared with Archie and Eminem in special editions. Often, when the Punisher teams up with Daredevil, Captain America, Black Widow (especially in *Avengers Confidential: Black Widow & The Punisher*), Wolverine, or Spider-Man, they (reluctantly) work with him. Castle, on occasion, asks for help from other heroes, but he is cautious because he knows larger superhero teams find his presence uncomfortable. Anti-hero teams like the Thunderbolts often are too tame and disorganized for him, though he tries it out for a few missions by cooperating with Elektra, Ghost Rider, Red Hulk, Red Leader, Venom, and Deadpool. The Punisher quits when Red Hulk refuses to kill Dr. Faustus, instead wanting to flip him for a spot on the team. The Punisher occasionally employs his own sidekick, usually technology and weapons expert Microchip, to enhance his effectiveness between missions. This partnership is difficult as Microchip reflects that "[e]verybody I get close to seems to end up dead" (Remender, 2012). Their working relationship has turned lethal on more than one occasion, seeing Castle kill Microchip due to treachery. Trust is difficult to keep in their line of work. Perhaps one of the most difficult challenges for the Punisher in these teams is to put aside his predisposition to end criminal activities permanently with bullets instead of words and rehabilitation. He often sees the other heroes in the Marvel Universe as naive and putting too much faith in the justice system, especially when he's on the wrong side of it. Despite many attempts, Castle rarely stays in prison long enough for justice to reign in his lethal habits.

There are, however, a few heroes that the Punisher gives his respect to, such as Captain America. The feeling isn't always mutual. Cap has pointed out that his skull symbol is a problem for him explaining: "That skull makes you more than just an Anonymous Nut going out and fulfilling a twisted notion of justice. It changes you from a man into an idea. That skull could inspire people to act like you do. People who don't even know they're being inspired.... Symbols are powerful things, Frank. They're shorthand for big ideas. Advertisements for ideologies. I should know. I've been one for a long time" (Gimple, 2013). The Punisher is familiar with this idea and that's the point. As much as he can respect a symbol of the justice system and patriotism like Captain America, Castle is still going to execute the type of justice he's familiar with. When men choose evil, the skull, death, is their sentence (Gimple, 2013).

The Punisher's worldview is black and white, there is no gray associated with his ideologies. This yields an interesting relationship with almost all the characters he's encountered. They have polarizing opinions about how the Punisher does his work. Black Widow's opinion is the most obvious, stating the "man's a serial killer" (Dixon, 2018, n.p.). Daredevil concurs that although they may share enemies with Castle, the tactics he uses to take them down are vastly different. The Punisher is fighting a war against the mob, the criminal underworld, and anyone he thinks needs to be punished. Daredevil points out his war is "more like his neurosis" (Dixon, 2018, n.p.). General Ross believes the Punisher is a necessary evil, "A lot of good men are alive today because of you, Castle, and a lot of bad men are not" (Way, 2012, n.p.). Spider-Man compares what the Punisher does to losing joy in what they do as heroes, "find the joy in what we are and what we can do. Otherwise, well … down that road lies Punisher town" (Soule, 2016). But Spider-Man is cautious around the joyless vigilante, warning Daredevil: "if you think Castle can be trusted you're not the man without fear, you're the man without sense" (Rucka, 2012). In the most drastic of opinions, Ghost Rider uses his penance stare on Castle, but this yields no results since, despite killing thousands, he feels justified for every life he's taken.

Punisher stories work best when he's solo, such as events where the

Avengers are trying to stop him during one of his rampages. Alone, the Punisher is much more effective as he sets the pace, the rules of engagement, and the method of taking down his target(s). If he teams up with another hero, he's often reduced to "The Disciplinarian," fighting a villain until submission rather than elimination. When Castle goes after gangsters, human traffickers, child pornographers, and drug lords in a lethal setting the stories seem the truest to his character traits. However, while these killings may seem justified because they are getting rid of all kinds of criminals, the Punisher is a murdering fiend. According to a 2005 FBI symposium, the definition for a serial killer is any individual who kills at least two people and doesn't require a cooling off period (FBI, 2005, p. 17). The Punisher is not only a serial killer, he's a mass murderer, which is defined as "murdering multiple people, typically simultaneously or over a relatively short period of time" (Bonn, 2015). The most accurate conclusion is that the Punisher is both of these things, making him a serial mass murderer with a cool off period that is only enforced when he has run out of targets and needs to rearm, reassess, and go hunting once more. Despite this characterization, the Punisher does not see himself as a murderer stating, "Murder is an unjust killing that serves no end" (Edondson, 2015). His purpose is so resolute to his punishment psyche that his killings are always going to have a purpose. They are to achieve justice, to rid the world of the blemishes, and to make sure the injustice he felt never happens again.

Superheroes don't kill as a general rule. Although it is tempting to call the Punisher a superhero or an anti-hero, according to John Romita, Sr., he's more of an anti-villain (Kreuger, p. 29). The Punisher certainly has some characteristics of a superhero in the form of a mission and identity, but he lives in a moral grey area (Coogan, 2005). Killing is usually associated with villainy, no matter what comic universe the characters are situated in. In Noelle Stevenson's (2015) young adult graphic novel *Nimona*, the title character who wants to be a villain sidekick states, after an explosion that caused several shocking deaths: "We're villains! Villains kill people sometimes" (p. 21). In a DC Comics series, Black Lightning admonishes the Blue Devil (who is about to kill a criminal) stating: "you told me you weren't one of the bad guys. Well, bad guys kill" (Andreyko, 2014, n.p.). The Punisher is not a good guy, nor does he see himself as a hero stating, "I'm here to take care of a problem. But let's be clear, I'm no hero…. A guy who does what needs to be done" (Hurwitz, 2017).

The Punisher cultivates a long list of nemeses because of his brutality and aggressiveness toward crime. He chews through a massive amount of henchmen easily, but some villains are successful enough to evade him and become a thorn in his side. Popular criminals such as Jigsaw, the Sniper, the Hood, Recoil, the Russian, Ma Gnucci, G.W. Bridge (though sometimes an ally), and Barracuda are often at the forefront of a series. Of the previous list, Jigsaw is the most frequent occurrence in stories featuring the Punisher. He's very similar to Batman's Joker, he's a matched opposite. The Punisher created Jigsaw by pushing his face through glass, and his tenacity can be attributed through his refusal to allow his disfigurement and pain to prevent him from getting his revenge. The Punisher tries to kill him and has seemingly succeeded on occasion, yet Jigsaw always resurfaces and prepares a new scheme to inconvenience Castle.

Castle has a personal code of conduct for his actions and during the missions he undertakes. He helps and protects the innocents. He's not above helping an elderly person across a busy street. He helps bystanders with car troubles and tries to be a good neighbor. If innocents are in a crossfire, he'll do his best to prevent casualties. He's saved animals including a coyote, shark, and lobsters from a grocery store. However, the Punisher is not perfect and on one occasion has had to kill an innocent woman because he was undercover in a right-wing racist group. The woman was the girlfriend of Stuart Clarke, a sidekick that replaced Microchip (Fraction, 2007). Clarke vowed revenge on the Punisher and used a suit of powered armor to become the villain Rampage in the eventual confrontation (Fraction, 2008).

Perhaps because of the deaths of his family, Castle has an unending devotion to keeping the (not criminal) family unit together. He does believe that some redemption is available for certain members of criminal families, it's a sixth sense he has for those individuals. However, when criminals use family as a bargaining chip or as a tool to achieve a sinister goal, the Punisher doesn't "go easy on men who use family against [him]" (Edmondson, 2010). Writer Robert Crais surmises that Castle's universe requires perfection, harming the bad, punishing evil while the innocent are protected at all cost (Crais, 2017).

The police share an interesting relationship with the Punisher. The leader of a task force designed to take down the Punisher, Detective Soap, points out that "every cop in the department loves him. They're always saying how he does half the job for us" (Ennis, 2000). Often the police don't look too hard for him due to their secret adoration of his methods. As Punisher writer Marc Guggenheim points out, "I think it's generally accepted that Frank Castle doesn't end up in police custody unless Frank Castle wants to end up in police custody" (2017, n.p.). Not all cops believe that what the Punisher is doing benefits them or their reputation. As a partner of a Punisher sympathizer states, "We serve the law. Like it or not that's our job. Castle serves himself…" (Rucka, 2012).

In both a nod to law enforcement officers and the Punisher, Frank Castle has a more violent counterpart in the form of Jacob Gallows from

Punisher 2099. The comic is set in a dystopian future where police protection must be bought from wealth clients. Gallow, a cop himself, goes through the same tragedy as Castle and loses his family to violence. Gallow finds Castle's exploits from the past and models his revenge on the famous anti-hero, becoming the new Punisher. Gallow's methods were much more ruthless and very sadistic, going as far as keeping criminals in basement cells and torturing them for information (Mills, 1990). Frank Castle doesn't revel in the mayhem of Jacob Gallows, even though he can be selfish and at times see his role during missions as less of a justice crusade and more for "extermination" (Edmondson, 2015, n.p.).

Castle isn't afraid of death; he's supposed to be above the weakness of the vessel he's occupying. The Punisher is more than a man in a costume, he's a symbol, a lifestyle, and a prevailing force against persistent evil. He has the confidence to take out any villain he meets. He never waivers in his mission. This is particularly evident when he responds to the villain Face after a lengthy monologue about inevitability and defeat, "you're forgetting one thing, I'm the #@%*& Punisher" (Cloonan, 2017, n.p.). At the same time, the Punisher realizes that these qualities come with consequences. He knows that there is no redemption for himself, even though he does a smattering of good deeds with his punishment. They can't outweigh the massive amount of violence he commits, even if done for the right reasons. The Punisher tries to instill this to a boy whose father was killed by the mob imploring, "stay out of the revenge business, you'd only screw up your life" (Potts, 2008, 42). If he can steer others out of the life path he's walking, perhaps he can feel a little vindicated.

The Punisher has had three official movies made about the character: *The Punisher* (1990), *The Punisher* (2004), and *Punisher: War Zone* (2008). Each of these movies portray Frank Castle in a different setting. They all have their merits, but they also place their own spin on the character. In the 1990 film, the Punisher did not wear his iconic skull and acted more like a hero. The 2004 film saw a grieving Punisher who was methodical and less violent than his comic book counterpart. *Punisher: War Zone* featured a few gory and blood drenched fight scenes, had a proper Micro and included the villain Jigsaw, but they story went off rails after Castle uncharacteristically killed an undercover cop (Mendleson, 2017). Perhaps the most accurate portrayal of the Punisher is Phil Joanau's short film *The Punisher: Dirty Laundry* (2012), starring Thomas Jane reprising his role as Frank Castle. Castle intervenes in a local disruption with brutal efficiency after being goaded into action, showing the audience what the Punisher can do even on his laundry day.

The Netflix *Marvel's The Punisher* (2017–2019) series also differs from the comic character. He's still a veteran, but the wars have been updated to Afghanistan and Iraq. The relationships that he has with people have changed. Karen Page, Billy Russo, Curtis Hoyle, and Micro all have different backgrounds and motivations that drive their interactions with Frank Castle. The Punisher's motivations are diluted, as he stops killing criminals once everyone he thinks is involved with his family's death are dead. In Season 1 he resumes killing once he finds more links to the conspiracy surrounding his family's deaths, and in Season 2 he becomes more of a hero to prevent loss of innocent life. The Netflix portrayal of the Punisher takes some liberties to introduce this character to a wider audience and modernizes a few characteristics, but the overall tone of the Punisher remains focused on brutally punishing his enemies and protecting the innocent (WatchMojo.com, 2018).

The discussions and summary above only scratch the surface of the character's long and complicated history, but hopefully provides the reader some perspective of the depth and complexity of the Punisher. The essays that follow talk about the Punisher from philosophical points of view about morality and justice, some offer critiques about the character through the lenses of gender and feminism, others consider the character's veteran status as focal point of analysis, and still yet, other essays consider the role of politics and gun violence that connects the Punisher's world with the real world.

Kent Worcester's philosophical essay, "To Shame Its Inadequacy: The Punisher and His Critics," positions the Punisher's philosophy of justice based on his interactions with Marvel A-List superheroes. Worcester argues that the Punisher's sense of justice is a critique on Western liberalism and, rather than aligning with the seemingly obvious choice, philosopher Thomas Hobbes, he aligns with Carl Schmitt and his ideas about the "state of exception." Ultimately, this essay constructs the Punisher's philosophy of justice with that of other Marvel heroes.

In "A Tough Pill to Swallow: The Punisher as the Cure for the Ills of Modern Society," Ryan Litsey examines philosophical concepts of justice and what is just in *Marvel's The Punisher* series on Netflix. Using Plato's *The Republic* and Leo Strauss' *The City and Man*, Litsey delves into the different ideas surrounding justice and questions who is more just: the Punisher or the State?

John Harnett, in his essay, "The Long Cold Dark: The Punisher Mindset and Its Dissemination into the Collective Unconscious," explores the disciplined isolation and problematic conviction of the Punisher as an anti-hero, specifically though multimodal and psychoanalytic dynamic depictions of the character. His essay uses Garth Ennis' and Jason Aaron's respective runs on the *Punisher Max* series, as well as the Ennis' four-part mini-series *Born*. Harnett frames his approach against a theoretical

8   Introduction

background consisting of Joseph Campbell's analysis of hero myths, Carl Jung's pairing of a dark herald to the hero's journey, and Fred Parker's exposure of the level of solicitation that exists between the anti-hero and the devil. Harnett concludes the essay by discussing how the Punisher has been disseminated into a collective consciousness and is even used to perpetuate his unforgiving ideology.

Anders Lundgren's "Black and White and Nothing in Between? Some Thoughts on the Morality of the Punisher" is an essay that traces the morality of the Punisher through decades of comic publication. Lundgren questions whether the morality of the Punisher evolves from the character's birth in the 1970s, to the nearly comedic Marvel Knights incantation, to a more recent, darker version of the character in the *Punisher MAX*. This essay goes another step to not only examine the consistency of the Punisher's morality, but also seeks to answer why changes occur.

Matthew J. McEniry's essay, "Determined to Punish: Three Case Studies in Punishment" highlights transformations of character and body that the Punisher goes through to continue to fulfill his life's goal. McEniry analyzes events of *What If … Venom Had Possessed the Punisher?*, *Punisher: War Machine*, and *Cosmic Ghost Rider* to piece together how Frank Castle responded to these situations. In each one, Castle is faced with unique decisions that would be perplexing and strange to the average person. However, he's both focused and determined to continue his crusade to exact punishment on the bad guys. This analysis shows the audience just how far Castle will go in order to fulfill his character's namesake of the Punisher.

Alicia M. Goodman, in her essay, "The Punisher as Female: A Thought Experiment," discusses the various female characters who took on the mantle, such as Cossandra Castle and others who behaved in a Punisher-like fashion. She argues that many of the female Punisher porotypes do not function with the lack of moral compass that Frank Castle has. Goodman discusses concepts of gender fluidity as it applies to the various attempts at giving the Punisher a female counterpart, along with a discussion of female fighting techniques and concludes with the criteria necessary for there to be a true female Punisher.

Elizabeth Jendrzey and Meredith Pasahow's essay, "Frank Castle, Fanfiction and the Female Gaze," examines the Punisher through the eyes of fans, more specifically through fanfiction. This fanfiction has primarily a female authorship and readership. Through the lens of female gaze, Jendrezy and Pasahow present the Punisher in a softer light—one that shows his emotional vulnerability through love for his family and caring for his friends. Their analysis of Frank Castle fanfiction leaves the readers with a sense of how a violent man can also be viewed as a Romantic and caring man too.

In "Takes One to Kill One: *Punisher MAX*'s War on Hegemonic Masculinity," Kelly Kanayama argues that the Punisher is trying to dismantle the very masculine structures he is part of (and inescapable from). Using firsthand interviews with Garth Ennis and analyzing *Punisher MAX: The Platoon* through masculinity studies, Kanayama takes a deep dive into the concept of hegemonic masculinity for the Punisher.

Mike Lemon's essay examines temporality in the extended world of the Punisher. In "Recalling Vietnam in Marvel Cinematic Universe's Punisher Storylines," Lemon considers Netflix's *Marvel's The Punisher* and compares it to its source material. Lemon highlights how the Netflix series updates the Punisher story to have Afghanistan and the American War on Terror as a backdrop and how this change in temporarily works with the story. He also notes that the updates for this series are not totally harmonious with the source material. Focusing on Daniel Webber from the Netflix series, Lemon examines how the adapted and updated storyline separates the Punisher character from his Vietnam veteran identity.

Kathleen McClancy examines the Punisher and positions him in a greater framework of the dichotomies experienced by Vietnam veterans. In "Fighting a Lonely War: Frank Castle and the Domestication of Vietnam," McClancy shows through historiographic examination how the Punisher has changed over time and how that change aligns with evolving attitudes toward the Vietnam War and Vietnam veterans. Paired with the trauma of losing his wife, Frank Castle also faces the trauma of being a soldier and post-war life experiences, and McClancy's essay delves into the character's trauma framed with real-life implications.

In "Frank Castle's Other War: Meaning, Memory and the Vietnam War," Stephen Connor examines the Punisher's connection to Vietnam and how this connection is reflected in contemporary times through attitudes about war in conflict that followed Vietnam. Connor's essay questions how the Punisher comics reinforce attitudes about war and how, in turn, the comics change with evolving sentiments. This essay looks at war, its aftermath, and how these are presented through a Punisher lens.

Rob E. King looks at the Punisher comics and film versions of the character in "Bullet-Riddled Production: The Punisher's Influence on Violence in Decades of Tragedy." King theorizes about the evolution of this character and his relationship to gun violence and vigilant justice. King's essay also considers the relationship between an American consumer audience and gun violence in America.

Miriam Kent's "'When is the right moment to release a TV series about a heroic mass shooter?' Contemporary American Politics and the Reception of Netflix's *The Punisher*" examines the critical reception of the series—both positive and negative critiques. Kent frames what role the

Punisher has in today's political climate through the lenses of gun violence and masculinity. Looking at historical connections between politics and the character and the most recent Netflix adaptation, Kent interrogates cultural complexities of the politicized superhero and contemporary American politics.

These thirteen essays examine different parts of the same complex character. By the end of this book, the Punisher should feel like an old friend—one who is kept at arm's length but is still in periphery; a friend who is there to right society's wrongs, one bullet at a time.

References

Andreyko, M., Keatinge, J., & Robson, R. (2014). *DC Universe presents volume 3: Black Lightning and Blue Devil*. Burbank, CA: DC Entertainment.

Baron, M., Dixon C., & Abnett, D. (2017). *The Punisher epic collection: Capital punishment*. New York: Marvel Comics.

Baron, M., Dixon, C., & Reinhold, B. (2012). *Essential Punisher vol. 4*. New York: Marvel Comics.

Baron, M., Klaus, J., Nocenti, A., Whilce, P., & Friends. (2007). *Essential Punisher vol. 2*. New York: Marvel Comics.

Bonn, S.A. (2015, February 23). *How mass murder and serial murder differ*. Psychology Today. https://www.psychologytoday.com/us/blog/wicked-deeds/201502/how-mass-murder-and-serial-murder-differ.

Cloonan, B., Horak M., & Dillon S. (2017a). *The Punisher vol. 2: End of the line*. New York: Marvel Comics.

Cloonan, B., Horak, M., & Dillon, S. (2017b). *The Punisher vol. 3: King of New York*. New York: Marvel Comics.

Conely, N. (2017, March 30). *The Punisher: 15 people Frank Castle has killed*. Screenrant. https://screenrant.com/people-punisher-has-killed-frank-castle-netflix-series/.

Conway, G. (1974). *Amazing Spider-Man vol. 1*, #129. New York: Marvel Comics.

Coogan, P. (2005). *Superhero: Secret origin of genre*. Austin: Monkeybrain Books.

Crais, R. (2017). Written in blood. In M. Benson, D. Sweircynski, & L. Loughridge, *Punisher MAX: Complete collection vol. 5*. New York: Marvel Comics.

Dixon, C., Barreto, E., & Lilly, M. (2018). *Marvel knights: Defenders of the streets*. New York: Marvel Comics.

Edmondson, N., Blanco, F., & Campbell, J. (2010). Manhunt. In J. Starr, R. Boschi, & D. Brown, *The Punisher MAX: Untold tales*. New York: Marvel Comics.

Edmondson, N., Moritat, & Gerads, M. (2015). *The Punisher vol. 3: Last days*. New York: Marvel Comics.

Ennis, G. (2000). *The Punisher vol. 5*, #2. New York: Marvel Comics.

Fraction, M. (2007). *Punisher war journal vol. 2*, #9. New York: Marvel Comics.

Fraction, M., & Remender, R. (2008). *Punisher war journal vol. 2*, #25. New York: Marvel Comics.

Gimple, S., Texeria, M., & D'Armata, F. (2013). *The Punisher: Nightmare*. New York: Marvel Comics.

Guggenheim, M., & Huston, C. (2017). *Punisher & Bullseye: Deadliest hits*. New York: Marvel Comics.

Hurwitz, G., Campbell, L., & Loughridge, L. (2017). Girls in white dresses. In M. Benson, D. Sweircynski, & L. Loughridge, *Punisher MAX: Complete collection vol. 5*. New York: Marvel Comics.

Kraft, D. (1975). The Executioner speaks out! An exclusive interview with Don Pendleton.

Marvel preview presents: America's greatest crime destroyer! The Punisher, 1(2), 47–58.
Krueger, J. (1994, February). The art of war. *The Punisher anniversary magazine*, 1(1), 24–29.
Lapham, D. (2005). *Daredevil vs. Punisher vol. 1, #2*. New York: Marvel Comics.
Mendleson, S. (2017, December 6). *A comparative study of all three Punisher films*. HuffPost. https://www.huffpost.com/entry/a-comparative-study-of-al_b_149500.
Mills, P., Skinner, T., & Morgan, T. (1993). *The Punisher 2099, #1*. New York: Marvel Comics.
Morton, R.J., & Hilts, M.A. (Eds). (2005). *Serial murder: Multi-disciplinary perspectives for investigators*. Quantico, VA: Federal Bureau of Investigation: National Center for the Analysis of Violent Crime.
Potts, C., Wellington, J., & Lee, J. (2008). *The Punisher war journal: Classic volume 1*. New York: Marvel Comics.
Remender, R., Opera, J., & Romita Jr., J. (2012). *The Punisher by Rick Remender omnibus*. New York: Marvel Comics.
Remender, R., Romita Jr., J., Way, D., & Janson, K. (2011). *Punisher Franken-Castle*. New York: Marvel Comics.
Rucka, G., Waid, M., & Southworth, M. (2012). *The Punisher by Greg Rucka volume 2*. New York: Marvel Comics.
Soule, C., Buffangini, M., & Sudaka, G. (2016). *Daredevil back in black vol. 2: Supersonic*. New York: Marvel Comics.
Stevenson, N. (2015). *Nimona*. New York: HarperTeen.
WatchMojo (2018, January 6). *Top 10 differences between the Punisher TV show and comics* [Video]. Youtube. https://www.youtube.com/watch?v=6IGzWoZL4_I.
Way, D., Dillion, S., & Sabino, J. (2012). *Thunderbolts no quarter*. New York: Marvel Comics.
Williams, S.E. (2010, October). Interview: Gerry Conway: Everything but the Gwen Stacy sink. *Back Issue!*, 1(44), 7–18.

Section I
Philosophy and Analysis

To Shame Its Inadequacy
The Punisher and His Critics

Kent Worcester

In 2011, writer Greg Rucka and editor Stephen Wacker took part in a conference call with bloggers and comics journalists to promote their new Punisher series. During the conversation, Wacker stated that "Castle has killed 48,501 people, counting back to his first appearance" (Manning, 2011). Given that Frank Castle has demolished entire compounds teeming with bad guys, this is an improbably precise figure. But if it is impossible to attach a definitive number to the Punisher's diegetic death toll, the character has most certainly slaughtered thousands of people in limited series, unlimited series, guest appearances, and graphic novels, not to mention movies and Netflix series. It thus seems reasonable to assume that the Punisher is one of the most murderous figures in the history of paraliterature.

Vigilantism is far from uncommon in the Marvel Universe (MU). Writers on comics have designated hundreds of characters as vigilantes, many of whom seek to hand wrongdoers over to the authorities. These costumed adventurers complement rather than supplant lawful authority, even if those in charge are too stubborn to accept their assistance. Their tacit alliance with the powers-that-be helps explain why creators and readers regard Marvel superheroes as legitimate role models. Their methods may be theatrical and extrajudicial, but their actions rarely challenge established norms and institutions.

The Punisher's antiheroic mode of vigilantism points in a different direction. When mainstream heroes encounter Frank Castle they are often struck by the gap between his worldview and theirs. "Castle's impatience *grates* on me," says Dr. Strange (Barbar, 2017, n.p.; throughout this chapter all emphases are in the original source material). But the Punisher takes pride in the "*difference* between me and these 'heroes.'" As he boasts in the third person: when "the *Punisher* takes 'em out, they're out *permanently*"

(Cooper, 1993, n.p.). Or as the Hulk says in a 2012 story, "Something tells me if it lives and breathes, this guy has a gun that can kill it" (Aaron, 2012, n.p.). After nearly half a century of the Punisher's murderous campaign, mainstream heroes have come to recognize that Castle "takes a much more *pragmatic* approach to stopping crime" (Yost, 2013, n.p.)—the words are spoken by the mad scientist Doctor Octopus—than they do. "I just want to rack up a body count!" (Chichester, 1992, n.p.) is a slogan few if any other Marvel personalities are likely to embrace.

The scale and ambition of the Punisher's anticrime violence raises intriguing issues for cultural historians and political theorists. (Relevant secondary studies include Howe, 2012; Palmer, 2013; Worcester, 2012; Worcester, 2016; and Wright, 2003.) An obvious question has to do with the historical context that incubated such an aggressive character. Another concern is the reception the character has received from readers, not only in the mid–1970s, when he was first introduced into the MU, but also in the mid-to-late 1980s, when his earliest series found success in the comics marketplace. This essay addresses a third issue: how other superheroes respond to the Punisher's campaign of anticriminal violence, and how the Punisher frames and defends his actions within the pages of Marvel stories.

Natural Law

Only rarely does the Punisher provide an explicit rationale for his open-ended campaign of anticriminal violence. He usually limits himself to terse observations, such as, "I've got my own war to fight—criminals to destroy. I punish them for butchering my family" (Potts and Lee, 1989, 3). Perhaps his most substantive defense appears in the four-issue miniseries *Punisher: Year One*:

> Sometimes the law is helpless to act, even when it *identifies* the guilty. It follows, therefore, that sometimes it is necessary to act *outside* the law, to *shame* its inadequacy, to pursue a *natural* justice. I'm not talking about *vengeance*. Revenge is *not* a valid motive. It's a tawdry, *emotional* response no better than the act that provokes it. I'm talking about … *punishment* [Abnett, Lanning, and Eaglesham, 1995, n.p.; all ellipses in the original].

This passage, which also features in the 2004 *Punisher* movie, suggests that the Punisher views his campaign as grounded in what the Catholic tradition refers to as "natural law." The concept of natural law assumes that certain rules and constraints are built into the fabric of the universe and that these laws are independent of societal beliefs and norms. Rather than filling the gaps left by law enforcement and the criminal justice system, the Punisher's campaign of violence rests on a conception of natural law that explicitly rebukes the existing political and legal order. The obvious question, for readers and other heroes, is what grants him the right to act as judge, jury, and executioner. After all, the natural law tradition is intended to inform the work of those who write and enforce societal laws rather than those who act outside the legal framework.

Despite his reputation as a man of action, when the Punisher brushes up against other costumed crime-fighters he often feels a need to explain himself. When heroes like Captain America, Daredevil, and Spider-Man engage with the Punisher they tend to highlight the stark differences between their values and his. Yet they each advance distinct claims whenever they push back against the Punisher's brand of vigilantism.

Captain America's pitch focuses on duty, service, and love of country. His approach can be characterized as communitarian and patriotic. It places a strong emphasis on the connections that bind individuals to the community at large. Daredevil, by contrast, is a constitutionalist and an institutionalist. He is a firm believer in the sanctity of the country's founding political documents, such as the Declaration of Independence and the U.S. Constitution, and the value of the public institutions, such as the federal court system, that are based on these documents. As a graduate of Columbia Law School, Matt Murdock seeks to convince Castle that the law is a noble cause. He recognizes the criminal justice system is imperfect but insists it can be made to live up to its ideals. Spider-Man's approach, on the other hand, is neither patriotic nor institutional. Instead, the wall-crawler views the world through a humanist lens. The health and well-being of individuals is his primary focus, and he often reminds the Punisher that innocent bystanders could get hurt as a result of his actions. Spider-Man rarely if ever refers to abstract concepts like nationalism or legalism. He therefore does not try to appeal to the Punisher's sense of patriotic duty or to the importance of observing constitutional norms and practices.

Most of these arguments bounce off Castle's emotional armor. He rejects peaceable forms of vigilantism and pushes back against anything resembling blind optimism. Yet he retains a soft spot for U.S. nationalism, even if he "doesn't hide behind a mantle of patriotism" (Baron and Reinhold, 1989, n.p.). He does not scorn flag and country in the same way that he mocks legalism and humanitarianism. The Punisher takes Captain America seriously, even if he discounts his advice and regards him as naive.

The Punisher and Captain America

When Marvel heroes first meet, they often duke it out. In *Captain America* #241, Captain America and the Punisher are both on the lookout for an "underworld courier" with ties to organized crime. While Steve Rogers intends to take the man into custody, Frank Castle hopes the underling can lead him to "the meeting place of two rival mob bosses" (Barr, 1979, n.p.). The three men end up on a Manhattan rooftop, where Rogers does his best to protect the courier. As the man cowers, Cap and Castle bicker and battle:

> "All right, Punisher—how about drawing a bead on a target who can defend himself?"
>
> "Captain America! I've followed your career for years, sir—and I admire what you stand for—but this is none of your business! Either back off—now—or I'll be forced to deal with you as I would any criminal scum!"

Afterwards, Captain America muses to himself about how, "From what I've read about the Punisher, he's a strange, fanatical crusader who's bent on exterminating all organized crime!" When they meet again, later in the story, the Captain insists that criminals have rights, "just as you do!" The Punisher retorts, "This is a war, and crime *is* the enemy! There's only one way to fight it!" "Wake up, soldier," says Captain America. "You think you're the only one who's ever lost a loved one? Sure, it's a war—but if you fight on their terms, you're no better than they are!" (Barr, Springer, and Marcos, 1979, pp. 14–15, 23, 30).

The contrast between the optimist who wears the flag and the pessimist in black-and-white is both visual and conceptual. Steve Rogers and Frank Castle are both military veterans who fight crime, wear costumes, and look back on midcentury America with fondness. They are fundamentally unalike, however. Captain America has a sunny disposition and an aversion to guns. He is a veteran of World War II, which enjoyed overwhelming public support. The Punisher is a psychologically scarred paranoiac who doesn't "trust people in masks," and who proudly declares that "my luck comes thirty to a clip!" (Chichester, Zaffino, and Texiera, 1992, p. 8). He is a veteran of the Vietnam War, which became increasingly controversial during the 1960s and which is not commemorated as a "good war" in the way that World War II is remembered. "The advantage of working alone," Castle says, "is that everyone else is *fair game*" (Barr and Ross, 1993, n.p.).

Their motivations also diverge. Captain America is a super-soldier whose mission is self-evidently patriotic. The Punisher's very name implies contempt for due process and "self-righteous *prattle*" (Chichester and Zaffino, 1993, n.p.). It may be an exaggeration to say that "the Punisher represents the antithesis of Captain America" (Scott, 2009, p. 125), but their differences are such that even when they are engulfed in battle the Punisher fights alone. In a 1992 Marvel UK miniseries, numerous heroes work to defeat a monster named Charnel, an "alternate reality Baron Strucker." As Castle blasts away at Charnel's minions, Captain America collaborates with She-Hulk, Scarlet Witch, Reed Richards, and others to formulate a plan. In this alternate MU, Charnel kills the Punisher along with many others. "Punisher's war journal *ends*," reads the narrator's box (Abnett and Sharp, 1992, n.p.). But while Captain America perishes with his teammates, Castle dies alone.

Marvel issued a three-part Punisher/Captain America story in the early 1990s that revolves around a government conspiracy to funnel money from drug and arms sales to fund a Latin American dictator who is waging war against neighboring countries. A conspirator uses doctored files and a hapless patsy to manipulate Castle into thinking that Captain America has been smuggling narcotics into the United States. The first issue ends on a cliffhanger as a distraught Punisher snipes Captain America in the chest. In the next issue, Castle learns he was set up. In the meantime, Rogers has managed to recover from his wounds.

"All *wars* begin with some form of *betrayal*," Castle angrily tells Micro, and when he catches up with Captain America, they combine forces. "Figured I owed you!" he tells Steve Rogers, by way of apology. Even as they stand together, their differences are glaring. "Eagle Scout thinks differently," Castle says. "Never understood the stand-up kind. Putting themselves in the spotlight. My *war* stays in the *shadows*." "One thing straight up front," Captain America later says. "I don't like you and I *despise* what it is you *do*! Your methods make me sick!" While Castle wants to get even with the conspirators who deceived him about the "guy ... who wears *flags*," the Captain is looking "for someone to *care* that some of the *good* this country still stands for is being *raped*." "You didn't get all those decorations in just one tour," Rogers pleads; "I just thought ... never mind." "Six tours, G.I. Joe, and *still counting*," replies the Punisher, who is impressed by Captain America's grit and valor, even if he does not quite buy it (Chichester, Clark, and Janson, #2, 1992, n.p.).

In the closing issue's centerfold, the two heroes stand fast as the dictator's U.S.-made planes rain ammo on their position. "Now it's the *stars* and *stripes* fighting a war with the *tactics* of *Nazis*," voices the narrator. After defeating the dictator, they take their battle to D.C., where Captain America smacks around the Attorney General, and the Punisher executes a Justice Department official at point blank range. As the Captain pounds the Attorney General into submission, Castle advises him to "*Lower* the *shield*, man! Just *walk away*! Or you can *never* go *back*." Speaking from experience, Castle notes that:

it's *lonely* as hell once you get here! There's *nothing* ... but the cold satisfaction of *punishment*! Every war I've gone into I've watched the *symbols* behind them all fail in the heat of *battle*. There aren't that many things left to believe in … don't take away one more [Chichester, Clark, and Janson, #3, 1992, n.p.].

Perhaps the best-known Captain America/Punisher meet-up occurs during the *Civil War* series. This post–9/11 story "crossed over into nearly all Marvel titles," and offers "an allegory of the War on Terror and the USA Patriot Act" in which "the government enacts the Superhero Registration Act, a law that requires all superpowered heroes to become licensed agents of the government or risk arrest as outlaws." The superhero community quickly divides into two camps: those who are willing to go public, and those who would prefer to maintain their anonymity. The Punisher sides with Captain America and others who believe that costumes should operate "under a self-directed moral code," as opposed to those who argue that superheroes "need to be trained and properly regulated" (Costello, 1989, pp. 229, 234–235).

The Punisher only plays a supporting role in the *Civil War* storyline, but it is a memorable one. As the Captain and his allies plot to break into the "negative zone prison," where rebel heroes are being held captive, two costumed villains volunteer their support. "You guys ain't the *only* ones scared we're headed for a police state, Captain," explains Goldbug, a master thief. "The super-criminal community's more concerned about Stark's plans than *anyone*," he says. "We just came by to let you know we're here if you *need* us," adds the Plunderer. "Only fair if *Iron Man*'s got super-villains on *his* side, right? Whaddaya say?" Before Captain America has time to respond, the Punisher guns the two men down. "You murderous piece of trash," shouts the Captain, as he punches Castle in the jaw. But the Punisher refuses to fight back. "I wonder why he wouldn't hit *Cap*," asks a hero. "Are you *kidding* me?" replies Spider-Man. "Cap's probably the reason he went to Vietnam. Same guy, different war." "Wrong," retorts Captain America. "Frank Castle is *insane*" (Miller and McNiven, 2014, n.p.). The two wars produced very different kinds of heroes.

The Punisher and Daredevil

The Punisher's attitude toward Captain America is one of begrudging admiration. Daredevil, on the other hand, is "the crimson wimp of Hell's Kitchen" (Potts and Lee, 1989, p. 30). Matt Murdoch's backstory and character logic points in a different direction from Captain America's, and the Punisher responds accordingly. For his part, Murdock concedes that he and Frank Castle will never be friends:

> We've got a healthy mutual *dislike*, based on the contrast in our inherent *beliefs*. My code says every *individual*, no matter his past, deserves a *second chance*. In

his uncompromising *ruthlessness*, nobody stands in his way. Crossing the line of the law is required before the Punisher puts up the crosshairs. Never having gone over, I don't worry about becoming a target—but I can *unnerve* him, putting at odds my relative *innocence* and his refusal to use *lethal force* on the "undeserving" of punishment [Chichester and McDaniel, 1992, p. 9].

If Daredevil irks Frank Castle, Murdoch finds Castle offensive. When the blind lawyer senses Castle for the first time, in a Frank Miller story titled "Child's Play," he thinks, "He's *big*. His heartbeat is *strong*. His movements confident, fluid. He's in excellent shape. And he's a killer." "You have your *methods*," the Punisher tells Daredevil, "and so do I." "Mine don't include senseless brutality," Daredevil replies. Castle tries appealing to Murdoch's desire for retribution: "if we *must* fight let it be as allies. Together we could *terrorize* the underworld—eliminate the enemy we *share!*" But the heroic horned devil spurns his offer. "Whether you kill innocents or criminals, it's *murder*—and that makes *us* enemies, Punisher" (Miller, 1988, n.p.).

Their different fighting styles are suggestive of this philosophical divide. Murdoch uses a club; Castle carries an arsenal. While Daredevil is a master of the fighting arts—quick, fluid, unpredictable—the Punisher is all muscle and gunpowder. "He's *faster* than me," Castle admits. "His boxing *alone* could put down the champ. Then there's *this* junk—Eastern—far, *far* up some high, snowy *mountain-top* Eastern." The accompanying panels show Castle taking a series of hard blows. "It doesn't matter," Castle adds. "I can *take it*. I'm a *rock*" (Lapham, 2006, n.p.). Agility and grace versus blunt force trauma.

When he isn't patrolling Hell's Kitchen, Murdoch spends his time trying to convince others that the system can be made to work. "You can't take the law into your hands," he tells a boy whose sister jumps out a window after ingesting PCP. "The law works, Billy. Just give it a chance." As he later explains, "We're only *human*, Billy. We can be weak. We can be evil. The only way to stop us from killing each other is to make *rules*. Laws. And stick to them. They don't always work. But mostly they do. And they're all we've got" (Miller, 1988, n.p.). Or as Murdoch subsequently asserts, "The Punisher is *wrong*. The courts *work*." As far as Castle is concerned these pleas fall on deaf ears. "You want to waste your time running maggots through the criminal justice merry-go-round, that's your problem," he snarls. "But once I get 'em, they're mine. And I don't waste time. I waste maggots" (Baron and Portacio, 1988, 24).

Daredevil keeps faith with the justice system, and Almighty God. The Punisher holds the view that "anyone can die" (Grant and McLeod, 1993, n.p.). At one time Castle "believed in summer walks and safe, quiet neighborhoods. He believed goodness is its own reward, and America belongs to the people" (Grant and Haynes, 1994, n.p.). After high school he attended seminary but dropped out "when I couldn't shake the feeling that the guilty should be punished before they were forgiven." "There is so much hatred in the world, so much suffering," he tells Father Angus. "How could God allow this to happen?" (Baron and Reinhold, 1989, n.p.).

Yet Castle has been known to espouse an atheist position. In a story from the late 1980s, a stereotypical punk rocker stumbles across an injured Punisher and says to his friends, "Well look at this, there *is* a God!" "No … there … isn't," Castle thinks to himself, as he slips out of consciousness (Potts and Lee, 1989, 26). But in the 1989 *Intruder* graphic novel Castle claims, "I merely carry out His will" (Baron and Reinhold, 1989, n.p.), and in a 1993 *Punisher War Zone* story he concedes he is unlikely to enter the gates of heaven (Abnett and Haynes, 1993, n.p.). "Another man," he says, hedging his bets, "*might* see *His* face up there. Me.… I see nothing but cold stars above" (Rainey and Mayerick, 1992, n.p.).

Daredevil regards Castle as an extremist. "His story will never have a happy ending," he explains; "he is *always* a problem" (Waid and Checchetto, n.p.). Their differences are highlighted in 2002's *Marvel Knights Double-Shot*, which features the characters in back-to-back stories. In "Dirty Job," Murdoch chases down thieves and muggers, and playfully taunts the Kingpin (Haynes, n.p.). By contrast, in "Roots," the Punisher tracks down mob boss Don Signore at the dentist's office, where Castle yanks out his teeth before sending him to the grave. Every panel is rendered from inside looking out, as if a camera had been placed inside the Don's throat. The result is visually arresting but grotesque (Ennis and Quesada, 2002, n.p.).

The Punisher and Spider-Man

If the Captain is an Eagle Scout, and Daredevil meddlesome, then Spider-Man is a "fool" (Grant, McLeod, and Weeks, 1993, n.p.). He might have the makings of "a good soldier" (Harris and Lopez, 2000, n.p.), but he sticks his nose "where it doesn't belong" (Yomtov and Saviuk, 1996, n.p.). When they first meet, the Punisher sizes up Spider-Man as the "kind of scum" who "has ruled this country *too long*" (Conway and Andru, 1974, n.p.). He derides Parker's idealism and rolls his eyes at the claim that "killing anybody, unless in self-defense, is against the law, immoral, and flat-out wrong!" "You live by *your* moral code, Spider-Man, I'll live by mine," Castle sneers (Conway and Buscema, 1988, p. 30). Spider-Man, meanwhile, describes Castle as "*Soldier of Fortune*'s favorite cover boy" (Micheline and Larsen, 1990, p. 19). Spider-Man fails to realize that "every time he puts on that mask … he protects this city's *criminal element* from their own inbred system of selective elimination! Instead of letting them kill each other, he ties them up and delivers them to the *police*, who deliver them to the *courts* ... who put them back on the street! Well, I am the answer to that problem" (DeFalco, Owsley, and Kupperberg, 1987, n.p.).

From Castle's perspective, Spider-Man refuses to grasp that "crime is war. And our side is losing!" (Conway and Buscema, 1988, p. 4). "That's what I don't like about working with you," Spider-Man says. "Too many *bodies*." "That's what I don't like about working with you—not *enough*," the Punisher snaps back (Ostrander, Nauck, and Ryan, 2011, n.p.). As Castle tells himself, Parker is "fast, agile, heart of gold. Saying I'm wrong. Saying I'm evil. Saying all life is precious" (Grant and Haynes, 1994, n.p.). But the fact that Spider-Man has a better sense of humor gives him a certain edge. "You again!" the Punisher exclaims. "What the @#$% do you *want* from me?" "Uh, let me *think*," says Parker. "A spare kleenex perhaps?" (Yomtov and Saviuk, 1996, n.p.).

During a 1980s team-up Parker and Castle find themselves surrounded by white power fanatics. The Punisher captures one of the men and demands to know, "How many of you are there?" "We're saving the world from the inferior races," the man offers by way of a rejoinder. Before the Punisher can fire his weapon, Spider-Man insists that he dial down the violence. "No cold-blooded killing while *I'm* around. I'll web up your buddy and his friend for the police!" "If you're smart," the Punisher responds, "you'll take the kid gloves off and treat these @*!#s with the violence they deserve." Castle takes out most of the would-be fascists but shows mercy to a white supremacist in a wheelchair. The man "assumes I'm going to execute him," he observes. But since "he's not going to do any more harm," I should "let him live," Castle decides. "That Spider-idiot must be getting to me," he thinks (Potts and Ross, 1990, pp. 16, 30).

A year on, Castle and Parker are on the trail of smugglers importing "coffee barrels full of raw cocaine" into New York Harbor. The Punisher readies for battle by testing weapons in a New Jersey warehouse. "Calico M950," he thinks to himself. "Semi-automatic 9mm NATO, 100-round helical magazine. The anti-gunners are gonna love this!" Working together, Castle and Parker find an electronic key card that allows Micro to trace the smuggling ring back to "a special covert cell—of the *U.S. Army*!" "I don't get it," says Spidey. "Seems simple enough," the Punisher shrugs. "The drug lord who's amassing the largest store of illicit substances in world history is ... *the United States of America*!" (Michelinie, 1990, n.p.).

The fact they are going up against military personnel gives Castle pause. "I notice you've stocked up on *non-lethal* weapons," Spider-Man observes. "Already made this month's *kill quota*?" Castle sets him straight. "When I go against the mob, I've no compunctions about using their own methods against them," he explains. "But this is the U.S. Army. *Soldiers*. I used to be one myself and I don't like the idea of slaughtering G.I.s who may think *they're* just doing their *duty*." "My gosh!" Parker teases. "There's a human being under all that macho?" "Yes, I'm human," Castle admits. "It's my greatest *weakness*. But I don't let it stop me. And that's my greatest *strength*" (Micheline and Larsen, 1990, pp. 27, 16, 30).

It turns out that the feds are stockpiling drugs because, as a mid-level government bureaucrat explains, "the economy is tottering, and if it should fall, *gold* would be nothing but lumps of metal! But drugs will *always* maintain their value!" Their aim is to establish a "*cocaine* standard," which Castle finds "sick" but "tricky." Americans are "battered daily with political scandals, increasing crime and poverty. What would this kind of knowledge do to their *morale*?" The two costumed heroes destroy the "powdered bliss" without unveiling the conspiracy. "If I didn't laugh I'd probably cry!" says Parker (Micheline and Larson, 1990, p. 11).

Spider-Man has occasionally fantasized about taking Castle down. "I'm not going to swing by and just let this Punisher dude mow down people in public," he pledges (Bendis and Mark Bagley, 2004, n.p.). Elsewhere, he warns Castle: "I've *seen* you kill people. Okay, maybe they weren't the nicest people—but consider *your* career *over*!" "Hey *watch* it!" he says, as the Punisher shoots at him. "Stay away and it won't be an issue," Castle responds. Like Daredevil, Spider-Man is disturbed by the possibility that he has inadvertently facilitated the Punisher's campaign. "I've let him *escape* too many times," he broods. "All the people he's *killed* because I couldn't hold him ... *never* again" (Grant, McLeod, and Weeks, 1993, n.p.). But the game continues.

Conclusion

The Punisher has argued and fought alongside—and against—numerous superheroes. He has formed temporary alliances with antiheroes like Ghost Rider, Moon Knight, Wolverine, and he has tangled with Cloak and Dagger, Power Pack, and cast members from *The Unbeatable Squirrel Girl*. He has even spent time in the company of Archie and the gang in Riverdale, as well as with DC's Batman, although they did not exactly see eye-to-eye.

The Punisher's most substantive encounters have been with Captain America, Daredevil, and Spider-Man, each of whom use these confrontations to make character-specific cases for socially acceptable forms of vigilantism. Given his lone wolf persona, the fact that Castle regularly ends up in the company of do-gooders like Steve Rogers, Matt Murdoch, and Peter Parker is ironic. Of course, many readers enjoy seeing radically divergent characters interact, and fans are more likely to purchase unfamiliar titles when a favorite character makes a guest appearance. There is a storytelling rationale at work here but a commercial logic as well. Punisher stories debate, mock, advocate for, and puzzle over his campaign with a level of seriousness that is easy to overlook given his flamboyant brutality. At the same time, when Castle defends his actions, he does not expect to convince anyone, except perhaps his extradiegetic audience. He sticks to his guns, in both senses of the term.

References

Aaron, J., & Dillon, S. (2012). *The incredible Hulk*, #8. New York: Marvel Comics.
Abnett, D., & Haynes, H. (1993). *The Punisher war zone*, #17. New York: Marvel Comics.
Abnett, D., Lanning, A., & Eaglesham, D. (1995). *The Punisher year one: Book four*. New York: Marvel Comics.
Abnett, D., & Sharp, L. (1992). *Death's head*, #4. New York: Marvel Comics.
Barbar, J., Murh, J., Broccardo, A., & Standon, D. (2017). *Doctor Strange/The Punisher: Magic bullets*, #2. New York: Marvel Comics.
Baron, M., & Portacio, W. (1988). *The Punisher*, #10. New York: Marvel Comics.
Baron, M., & Reinhold, B. (1989). *Punisher: Intruder*. New York: Marvel Comics.
Barr, M., & Ross, J. (1993). *Killpower: The early years*, #3. New York: Marvel Comics.
Barr, M., Springer, F., & Marcos, P. (1979). *Captain America*, #241. New York: Marvel Comics.
Bendis, B.M., & Bagley, M. (2004). *Ultimate Spider-Man*, #61. New York: Marvel Comics.
Chichester, D.G., Clark, M., & Janson, K. (1992a). *Punisher and Captain America: Blood & glory*, #2. New York: Marvel Comics.
Chichester, D.G., Clark, M., & Janson, K. (1992b). *Punisher and Captain America: Blood & glory*, #3. New York: Marvel Comics.
Chichester, D.G., & McDaniel, S. (1992). *Daredevil*, #309. New York: Marvel Comics.
Chichester, D.G., & Stroman, L. (1992). *Punisher/Black Widow: Spinning doomsday's web*. New York: Marvel Comics.
Chichester, D.G., & Zaffino, J. (1993). *Terror Inc.*, #7. New York: Marvel Comics.
Chichester, D.G., Zaffino, J., & Texeria, M. (1992). *Terror Inc.*, #6. New York: Marvel Comics.
Conway, G., & Andru, R. (1974). *The amazing Spider-Man*, #129. New York: Marvel Comics.
Conway, G., & Buscema, S. (1988a). *The spectacular Spider-Man*, #141. New York: Marvel Comics.
Conway, G., & Buscema, S. (1988b). *The spectacular Spider-Man*, #143. New York: Marvel Comics.
Cooper, C., Case, R., & Bigley, A. (1993). *Darkhold: Pages from the Book of Sin*, #5. New York: Marvel Comics.
Costello, M.J. (1989). *Secret identity crisis: Comic books and the unmasking of Cold War America*. New York: Continuum.
DeFalco, T., Owsley, J., & Kupperberg, A. (1987). *The amazing Spider-Man*, #285. New York: Marvel Comics.
Ennis, G., & Quesada, J. (2002). Roots. In *Marvel knights double shot*, #1. New York: Marvel Comics.
Grant, S., & Haynes, H. (1994a). *The Punisher war journal*, #66. New York: Marvel Comics.
Grant, S., & Haynes, H. (1994b). *The Punisher war journal*, #68. New York: Marvel Comics.
Grant, S., McLeod, B., & Weeks, S. (1993). *Spider-Man*, #34. New York: Marvel Comics.
Harris, J., & Lopez, M. (2000). *Spider-Man vs. Punisher*, #1. New York: Marvel Comics.
Haynes, R. (2002). Dirty job. In *Marvel knights double shot*, #1. New York: Marvel Comics.
Howe, S. (2013). *Marvel Comics: The untold story*. New York: Harper Perennial.
Lapham, D. (2006). *Daredevil vs. Punisher: Means & ends*. New York: Marvel Comics.

Manning, S. (2011, July 8). *Greg Rucka unleashes The Punisher*. CBR. http://www.cbr.com/greg-rucka-unleashes-the-punisher/
Micheline, D. (1990). *The amazing Spider-Man*, #330. New York: Marvel Comics.
Micheline, D., & Larsen, E. (1990). *The amazing Spider-Man*, #331. New York: Marvel Comics.
Miller, F. (1998). *Daredevil and the Punisher child's play Vol. 1*, #1. New York: Marvel Comics.
Miller, M., & McNiven, S. (2014). *Civil War*. New York: Marvel Comics.
Ostrander, J., Nauck, T., & Ryan, M. (2011). *The spectacular Spider-Man*, #1000. New York: Marvel Comics.
Palmer, L. (2013). The Punisher as revisionist superhero western. In C. Hatfield, J. Heer, & K. Worcester (Eds.), *The superhero reader*. Jackson: University Press of Mississippi.
Potts, C., & Lee, J. (1989a). *The Punisher war journal*, #9. New York: Marvel Comics.
Potts, C., & Lee, J. (1989b). *The Punisher war journal*, #10. New York: Marvel Comics.
Potts, C., & Ross, D. (1990). *The Punisher war journal*, #15. New York: Marvel Comics.
Rainey, R., & Mayerik, V. (1992). *The Punisher war journal*, #43. New York: Marvel Comics.
Scott, C. (2009). The alpha and the omega: Captain America and the Punisher. In R. Weiner (Ed.), *Captain America and the struggle of the superhero*. Jefferson, NC: McFarland.
Worcester, K. (2012). The Punisher and the politics of retributive justice. *Law Text Culture, 16*, 329–352.
Worcester, K. (2016). The Punisher: Marvel Universe icon and murderous antihero. In F. Peters, & R. Stewart (Eds.), *Antihero*. Chicago: Intellect.
Wright, B.W. (2003). *Comic book nation: The transformation of youth culture in America*. Baltimore: Johns Hopkins University Press.
Yomtov, N., & Saviuk, A. (1996). *The adventures of Spider-Man*, #1. New York: Marvel Comics.
Yost, C., & Lopez, D. (2013). *The superior Spider-Man*, #22. New York: Marvel Comics.

A Tough Pill to Swallow
The Punisher as the Cure for the Ills of Modern Society

Ryan Litsey

Introduction

We can all imagine ourselves in *that* situation. Something has happened to someone we love. We feel powerless; we want the feeling to go away. What do we do? Do we call the police? Do we call another loved one? Do we get angry and fight back? It is in this moment that you must weigh the pros and cons of action. If you act, you may injure or kill someone. What then: jail or worse? For most, social control and social order are often enough to dissuade action. However, for some, social control is not enough and they must act. It is in that moment of action that they transform into something else; something society does not accept. It is in this cloud of rage and action that the Punisher is born. Many of us can feel similar feelings of the rage, anger and, dare we say, excitement of what we would do to someone who hurt those we loved. What could anyone do to stop us when we have nothing left to lose? How can society come to control such a force? Perhaps control is not the issue when it comes to such an agent of anger. In fact, it may be that the origin of the Punisher may have more to do with society's ills than we thought. The Punisher may be the one that brings punishment to the unjust or he may be the one who is punished with the ills and sins of society by living if fear of arrest and imprisonment. If the Punisher is the receiver of punishment, then he is a character who can return society back to balance even more so than the traditional heroes in their bright colors and their flashy costumes.

Many cultures have proposed such a concept. Some call them sin eaters; the Greeks called them Pharmakos. If the Punisher is to suffer the ills of society, then the question is what ills of society are heaped upon him as he journeys for redemption? The answer comes from understanding the dichotomy between democratic society and the morality of might makes right. Before an understanding of how the Punisher is the embodiment and the cure for the evils of democratic society, it is important to understand the Pharmakos as a construct.

The Pharmakos

The Pharmakos, sometimes known as the scapegoat, served an important role in Greek society and religion. Aside from the common colloquial understanding of a scapegoat, the Ancient Greeks had a very particular ritual surrounding the human scapegoat. One of the first books to discuss the Pharmakos outside of the ancient Greeks was Sir James Frazer's (1951) *The Golden Bough*. Frazer described the scapegoat as both the evil and the cure of society in a material or imagined sense. Whether the evil is physical or not is not the point, but rather the scapegoat serves as "a total clearance of all the ills that have been infesting people" (Frazer, 1951, p. 666). Frazer continued in the discussion of the Ancient Greek scapegoat, in the example of Marseilles, he described a situation in which an individual is selected from society and given room and board at societal expense for one year. The individual is then cast out of the city and by extension society. One parallel that can be drawn initially here is the idea of a scapegoat being maintained at public expense. The Punisher is initially a soldier in the military, which effectively means he is supported by the public expense. When the scapegoat is led from the city, laws and rules of society are suspended for the period in which the scapegoat is being led from society to allow for the citizens to properly punish the scapegoat. The scapegoat also appears in Roman Society as well.

In examining the scapegoat in Roman society Frazer (1951) recognized that during the Saturnalia (scapegoat) festival many of the laws and moralities are thrown aside. This can also have implications when considering the actions of the Punisher as being outside the traditional norms, values, and morals of society. Burkert (1985) also provided a discussion of the Pharmakos.

Burkert's description of the Pharmakos is similar in historical context to that of Frazer, however, Burkert provides very interesting interpretations of events. In describing the purification of Ephesus through the stoning of a scapegoat, Burkert wrote:

> The aggression excited by fear is concentrated on some loathsome outside; everyone feels relieved by the communal projection of the fury born of despair, as well as by the certainty of standing on the side of the just and the pure [p. 83].

Burkert's description highlights a few critical characteristics of the scapegoat. First, the scapegoat is a member of that society. In this case it was a poor beggar. Second, the scapegoat represents the evils of society and gives the rest of the community a straw man to attack and thus assuage their own internal feelings of fear. The case of modern liberal society the fear is the takeover of the strong man. The stoning of the scapegoat is not the removal of the strong man in particular, but rather to serve as a displacement and cure for the dark impulses of the members of a community who would seek to use their own individual freedom to attempt to take over. As Burkert concluded, "The outcast is then also the savior to whom all are most deeply indebted" (p. 84). By literally suffering the slings and arrows of society the Punisher can take on the dual role of embodying the fears of the strong man, while at the same time eliminate other dangerous criminals and allow the community to hunt him in order to assuage the societal fears of the strong man without society having to confront itself with its own limitations.

The Pharmakos can be understood then of being composed of a few distinct criteria. First, it must be a member of society, but somewhat removed. Very much like the soldier of Frank Castle, who when at home lives the American dream. In the Netflix series he is shown to have the perfect family, the perfect marriage, and a house too. However, he is also removed because he is on deployment overseas. Second, the Pharmakos must have the characteristics of the ill as well. The ill in this case is "might makes right." As seen in the Netflix Season 1 episodes of the Punisher, he possesses almost unparalleled military ferocity and determination as evidenced in the third episode of the first season entitled "Kandahar." Third, the Pharmakos must have a moment of exile where they are cast out. It is easy to see this occasion for Frank Castle when his family is brutally murdered. At the time of exile, Frank Castle is no longer a man but the personification of the pharmakon seeking to cure society of its ills. The illness has been alluded above, but a closer examination is necessary.

The Ills of Society

Understanding that the Punisher is the scapegoat for the evils of society, the question is what are the evils of a democratic society? The answer again comes from ancient Greek texts and is a challenge that society in the time of the Punisher still suffers from. The Punisher is both the cause and the cure of the problem of might making right in a democratic society. One of the first examples of the concept of might making right is provided by Thucydides. Writing from 431 to 404 BC, Thucydides tells the history of the

Peloponnesian war, a 27-year war against the Greeks and Spartans. In Book 5 of his epic historiography, there is a section in which Thucydides proposes the might makes right ideology. In the Melian dialogue, Thucydides describes the exchange between the Athenians and the Melians. The Athenians argue:

> When these matters are discussed by practical people, the standard of justice depends on the equality of power to compel and that in fact the strong do what they have the power to do and the weak accept what they have to accept [Warner, 1972, p. 402].

Thucydides may have been an early descriptor of the issue of might makes right; however, he would not be the last.

Socrates addresses the issue as well in Book One of Plato's *Republic*. In the discussions of the make-up of the just society Thrasymachus in the dialogue contends, "I say that the just is nothing other than the advantage of the stronger" (Bloom, 1968, p. 15). Both Thucydides and Thrasymachus raise an important challenge for the democratic society: how can a society balance the freedom of individuals with the strength of those with power or in power? The ancient Greeks were not the only ones to recognize the balance between might and right. In one of his more important speeches to the Cooper Institute, Abraham Lincoln recognized this issue. At the closing of the speech, Lincoln says with emphasis, "Let us have faith that right makes might, and in that faith, let us, to the end, dare to do our duty as we understand it" (Lincoln, 1860, p. 550). The concerns of might over right does not end with Abraham Lincoln. In a letter that Sigmund Freud wrote to Albert Einstein in the 1930s, as part of the discussion around the formation of the League of Nations, Freud is quoted as saying, "You begin with the relations between might and right" (Freud, 1932, Personal Letter). The potential for liberal or democratic societies to fall victim to the strongest is something that has also been discussed within the philosophical literature as well.

Waldron (1987) argued that for liberal societies, "real freedom (sometimes, freedom for the true self) just is submission to and participation in the order of a good society" (p. 131). Waldron illustrates a tension within the liberal understanding of society, which is the balance between the freedom of the individual and the needs and goals of society. At issue is that sometimes the freedom of the individual can come into conflict with the freedom of others. Thus, the concerns with might and right. If a strong individual were to take advantage of the weak, then the bonds of society would begin to fray.

The tension between individual freedom and society is also addressed by John Locke. Locke in his famous *Two Treatises of Government*, writing in the Second Treatise on the origins of political society writes, "The only way whereby any one divests himself of his Natural Liberty, and puts on the bonds of Civil Society is by agreeing with other men to join and unite into a community..." (Laslett ed., 2005, p. 331). Locke was not the only philosopher who recognized the issues of liberal societies. Another insight into this balance between freedom and society was G.W.F. Hegel.

In his work *The Philosophy of Right*, Hegel (1952) address the tensions between the formation of society and the freedom of the individual. Hegel wrote:

> Through the development of civil society, the substance of ethical life acquires it infinite form, which contains itself these two moments: 10 infinite differentiation down to the inward experience of independent self-consciousness, and 20 the form of universality involved in education, the form of thought whereby mind is objective and actual to itself as an organic totality in laws and institutions which are its will in terms of thought [p. 155].

The focus for Hegel in this section is a description of how the individual in society is presented with an opportunity for infinite freedom and the only possibility for ethical behavior. This is a key distinction when considering how the relationship between freedom and society can begin to fracture. If, as Hegel describes, the individual is infinitely able to consider internal differentiation but is ultimately subject to the objectivity of the state, then overtime the strong-willed individual as Thrasymachus described may start to consider themselves superior to the state. If the individual sees themselves as superior to the state not only is that an ethical violation, but also a violation of civil society. Hegel, discussing the role of the state wrote:

> This substantial unity is an absolute unmoved end in itself, in which freedom comes into its supreme right. On the other hand this final end has supreme right against the individual, whose supreme duty is to be a member of the state [p. 156].

The importance of the balance between the individual and the state for Hegel is key to the construction of Civil Society. It is only within the state that the individual has true freedom to behave ethically and relate to individuals in safety. If the state becomes to obsessed about security and protection, then it will inherently breakdown in Hegel's construct since the role of the state is to serve as the objectivity of the mind for the development of ethical society. The state is only a protector and nothing more. The strong man has the potential to view themselves as better able to protect "their" stuff. It is clear in the examples above that liberal society is in a precarious balance between individual freedom and the formation of society.

Understanding the idea proposed above, liberal society is left with an ongoing tension. What happens when the individual of strength begins to impose his or her freedom and will onto the community? To cure society of this illness, there needs to be a Pharmakon. The Pharmakon as demonstrated above is both a part of the disease, but also its cure. This is the role of the Punisher; to punish the strong for violating the will of the consented govern. To understand how the Punisher comes to be the cure for the evils of liberal society it is important to examine the Punisher in context. In this case the first season of the hit Netflix show *The Punisher*.

The Cure for the Evils of Society

The Pharmakon must be a symptom of the disease first in order to be the eventual cure. This is reflected in Frank Castle's origin story as a special ops soldier. A soldier who is literally cared for by American society in the form of the military. A soldier who possess a unique set of skills and ferocity that separates him from other military personnel. Both *Daredevil* and *The Punisher* series are replete with references that further reinforce both the Punisher's membership and exile from society. The quote from Season 1, Episode 1 of the Netflix Punisher series, "One batch, two batch, Penny and a dime" is a line from a book that his daughter loved, and he says it right before he kills someone. He is exiled from society through the murder of his family. At that moment he becomes the Punisher, set on curing society of the ills of might makes right. The understanding of self as a cure is reflected in the courtroom scene in the Netflix show *Daredevil* Season 2 Episode 8 in which the Punisher, in open court, "admits who he is." In the form of testimony before the court, the Punisher admits who he is and claims that he is not sorry. The most telling part of this scene is the courtroom, serving as a proxy for society, literally gasps. This is one of the advantages to the use of a Pharmakon. By embodying both the illness and the cure, society does not have to reflect on the mechanisms that bring about a strong man. Rather society can use the capture of the scapegoat who is the Punisher to assuage their misgivings instead of confronting the root of the problem. The question then becomes who is the true illness? The true illness is the CIA agent William Rawlins.

Rawlins is the embodiment of the ills of society. His might comes not from physical strength, but from historical manipulation of society for personal gain. He is described as from one of the oldest American families. A family as powerful as America itself. He is deeply connected to mechanism of government. Micro, in Season 1, Episode 8 of *The Punisher,* describes Rawlins as:

> He was born at the top of the ladder. The Rawlins's are practically royalty. They're the power behind the throne. They're old, old Virginia money.

Plantations, shipping and industry, arms. I mean, who knows what else they have their hands in [Campos, S1, E8].

The extent to which Rawlins is integrated into society makes him a difficult illness to diagnose. Also, given the close ties to the foundations of American society, to destroy him could potentially call into question the underlying structure of the United States. Rawlins is the embodiment of the evils of the United States; his family owned slaves, he is a high-level government bureaucrat, his code name is Agent Orange (another dark chapter in American history). Finally, when Frank Castle joins the Cerberus group, Rawlins is quoted as saying, "I'm the only authority you will need. I point, you shoot" (Conway & Goddard, 2017). It is at this point that Rawlins takes his position as the strong man seeking to unravel society from the inside. This type of character that is so deeply connected to the fabric of America society can only be eliminated by an exiled scapegoat who possess the ferocity, training and personal characteristics of Rawlins, but is outside of the norms and societal conventions that Rawlins could use to stop his downfall. Rawlins can only be cured by the Punisher.

Conclusion

The Punisher is described as the spirit of vengeance. Some have called him the anti–Batman. These are useful categories for the Punisher, but they overlook the more nuanced role the Punisher has in society. As the scapegoat, the Punisher is able to root out and destroy the more insidious elements of the criminal underworld. Elements of society that seek not to merely commit crime, which can be left to the regular heroes. Rather, the Punisher seeks to destroy those who are the true embodiment of wrong and would seek to destroy society itself from the inside. Those whose might seeks to impose itself on the freedom and individuality of liberal society. These strong men can only be confronted by an exile who is both the disease and the cure.

REFERENCES

Burkert, W., & Raffan, J. (1985). *Greek religion: Archaic and classical (Ancient world)*. Oxford: Blackwell.

Conway, G., Romita, J., Andru, R., Lightfoot, S., LaManna, A., & Kristensen, K. (Writers), & Campos, A. (Director). (November 17, 2017). [Streaming series episode]. Cold Steel. In M. Ambrose (Producer), *The Punisher*. Los Angeles: Netflix.

Conway, G., Romita, J., Andru, R., Lightfoot, S., LaManna, A., & Kristensen, K. (Writers), & Goddard, A. (Director). (November 17, 2017). [Streaming series episode]. Kandahar. In M. Ambrose (Producer), *The Punisher*. Los Angeles: Netflix.

Einstein, A. (1931). The Einstein-Freud correspondence (1931–1932). *Einstein on peace*. http://www.public.asu.edu/~jmlynch/273/documents/FreudEinstein.pdf.

Frazer, J. (1951). *The golden bough: A study in magic and religion.* New York: Macmillan.

Hegel, G., & Knox, T. (1952). *Hegel's philosophy of right.* Oxford: Clarendon Press.

Lincoln, A. (1959). *The collected works of Abraham Lincoln* (R.P. Basler, Ed.). Washington, D.C.: Lincoln Sesquicentennial Commission. https://quod.lib.umich.edu/l/lincoln/lincoln3/1:199?rgn=div1;view=fulltext;q1=cooper.

Locke, J. (2005). *Two treatises of government* (P. Laslett, Ed.). Cambridge, England: Cambridge.

Plato. (1968). *The Republic* (A. Bloom, Trans.). New York: Basic Books. (375 B.C.E).

Thucydides. (1970). *History of the Peloponnesian war* (M.I. Finley, Ed.). (R. Warner, Trans.) London: Penguin Classics. (431 B.C.E.).

Waldron, J. (1987). Theoretical foundations of liberalism. *The Philosophical Quarterly, 37*(147), 127–150. doi:10.2307/2220334.

The Long Cold Dark

The Punisher Mindset and Its Dissemination into the Collective Unconscious

John Harnett

In order to gauge the level of intensity rooted within Frank Castle's subconscious, it is necessary to align the variety of narratives that attempt to shed light on when the defining seed of turmoil was cultivated within it. To that effect, this essay attempts to connect some of the most acute instances of psychological reflection within the mindset of Frank Castle to the type of psychological, mythological, and literary fusion that has colored the enduring legacy of the problematic antihero figure. Given the expansive scope of the Punisher catalogue, the essay focuses on the Punisher's psychological maturation, or degradation, as portrayed in the *Punisher MAX* series and in particular under the guidance of writers Garth Ennis and Jason Aaron, with supplementary input from Gregg Hurwitz's tenure on the title. As this particular narrative arc occupies a predominantly, hyper-masculine sphere this reading does not focus on a more gendered consideration of the Punisher's depiction, other than to intimate that it is largely staged as a reactionary platform from which to initiate, or further validate, a campaign of ultimately hollow vengeance.

The logical start point for an attempted profile of Frank Castle's mindset is his childhood, and to that effect the one-shot story *The Tyger* by Garth Ennis and John Severin attempts to outline his perception of the world as being shaped by the dawning awareness of an inherent impulse in the spirit of man drawn from a seemingly ubiquitous force of nature (Ennis and Severin, 2013). In this storyline, Frank is shown to be an avid reader of poetry as a boy and it is no coincidence that Ennis depicts his fascination for William Blake's poem "The Tyger." In an illustrated collection of poems titled *Songs of Innocence and Experience*, William Blake contrasted the innocence of childhood against a perceived sense of moral corruption which he attributed to the experiential complexities of adulthood and two of his most enduring representations of such contrasting agency were the lamb and the tiger (Blake, 2009). The poem has a visible impact on Frank and in one panel in the comic John Severin locates a confluence of three notable moments in the early development of Frank's worldview. The crux of the poem's philosophical and theological struggle, implied in the line that someone other than God may have created the Tyger, is located above the same style of black and white caption box that synonymously signifies the later Punisher's stream-of-consciousness, and within which he reveals, "I imagined the Tyger" (Ennis, 2013, p. 11). As he does so his facial expression effectively captures someone who has experienced a sense of epiphany as he momentarily disengages from his poetry group and in a brief, two-panel interlude, identifies the source of this awakening when he considers that it is, "Like the caged things at the Bronx Zoo but something more, something that could not be held.... That would not know mercy. Nor remorse, nor even the concept of stopping.... A force made flesh" (Ennis, 2013, p. 11).

Indeed, this influential impression subsequently colors a visit to the museum of natural history where a confrontation with a variety of the world's manifestations of this primal force inspires him to conclude that:

> that day I realized there had always been Tygers. Living in the darkness of our dreams, no less alive for being gone from the physical world. Emerging as it suited them, to stalk, to terrify, to overwhelm completely: Bigger. Badder. Deadlier. Somehow I knew we needed them [Ennis, 2013, p. 20].

So Ennis not only retroactively establishes awareness within Frank of a remorseless "force made flesh" but he nuances it with the formation of an implicit understanding that this force has always been a part of life. This unstoppable "something more" is clearly a precursor to the Punisher's limitless conviction but a further aspect of the poem offers additional insight into the galvanization of young Frank's particular take on justice. When William Blake considers in his poem the origins of an "art" that could be capable of twisting the sinews of the human heart and attempts to fathom the kind of "furnace" that the mind must dwell within to become one with the beast, Ennis tailors an answer suited to the formation of Frank's rigid moral code by proposing that killing is the art and that human immolation signifies his first encounter with the furnace (Blake, 2009). To that effect, at the end of the story young Frank bears witness as his childhood friend and mentor, Private Sal Buvoli (incidentally Frank's first encounter with the military), burns a young mobster by the name of Vincent Rosa to death as a reprisal for Buvoli's sister Lauren's death-by-suicide. This resolutely empowers his developing interpretation of a remorseless and regulating force of nature, and the only word that his mind can ascribe to the horror that he witnesses is "Tyger" (Ennis, 2013, p. 35).

Notably, *The Tyger* opens, and is brought to a close, with the lines "They'll blame it on Vietnam. And they'll be right. And they'll be wrong" (Ennis, 2013, p. 2/48) and the ambiguity in that final line is faithfully served by the window into his childhood that the short story opens. However, in order for his dark perspective to fully manifest it required an unobstructed conduit of release and an environment wholly conducive to the proliferation of unchecked appetite, and in war Frank found both. Joseph Conrad set an intriguing literary precedent for such conditions in *Heart of Darkness* and his description of the psychological impact that the primacy of an alien, or "savage," setting can have on the unprepared mind could as easily be read as an insight into the effect that the hellish mud hills and humid, trap-riddled, jungles that constituted the backdrop of the Vietnam War had on Frank's experience of:

> the savagery, the utter savagery, (that) had closed around him,—all that mysterious life of the wilderness that stirs in the forest, in the jungles, in the hearts of wild men. There's no initiation either into such mysteries. He has to live in the midst of the incomprehensible, which is also detestable. And it has a fascination, too, that goes to work upon him. The fascination of the abomination [Conrad, 2002, p. 106].

Indeed, one sequence of panels in the Punisher story *The Platoon*, by Garth Ennis and Goran Parlov, captures a telling conversation that Frank has with a Sergeant Dryden on his first tour of Vietnam during which he is questioned about his motivation for wanting to sign up for a second tour. In response, Castle can only stare blankly into space and admit that war, "Answers something in me, that's all" (Ennis, 2018, p. 68). So even before the voice of the abomination calls out to him in kind, people had already begun to notice Castle's propensity and appetite for war. This is precisely the "dark promise" that the military's upper echelon in Vietnam (the "brass in Da Nang") detect in him in the *Punisher MAX* mini-series entitled *Born*, again by Ennis and Parlov, which results in his reassignment to the covert world of special forces operations where accountability is not uncommonly prone to redaction from the pages of history—conditions which are quite conducive to the further development of the personified "Tyger" that Ennis attempts to tap into (Ennis, 2003, Vol. 1, p. 7).

It is this off-grid and absolute immersion into the darkest shadows of war that leads Ennis to stage the arrival of Castle's Dark Herald thus:

> There is a great beast loose in the world of men. It awoke in dark times, to fight a terrible enemy. It stormed through Europe, across the far Pacific, and crushed the evil that it found there underfoot. But when it was victorious, when

the crooked cross and the rising sun were done with, the Great Beast's keepers found that it would not go back to sleep. So the Great Beast must be fed: and every generation, our country goes to war to do just that [Ennis, 2003, Vol. 4, p. 1].

Although the terrible enemy that Ennis is referring to here is temporally located in the Second World War, it is not inconceivable that the dark times he mentions imbue a primeval timelessness to the concept of a generational Great Beast. Indeed, when the Beast does finally begin to entice Castle it briefly hints at the extent of its tenure in the world when it cryptically reveals, "Let's just say we're in the same line of work, Frank. And I've been at it a lot, lot longer than you" (Ennis, 2003, Vol. 4, p. 22). As such it falls squarely into the domain of myth. According to mythologist Joseph Campbell, the initiation of the hero's quest will involve the influence of a knowledgeable herald or omniscient watcher. He explains that such a:

> herald or announcer of the adventure (often dark, loathly, or terrifying) is a beast, representative of the repressed instinctual fecundity within ourselves, and yet, the hero and his ultimate God—are understood as the outside and the inside of a single, self-mirrored mystery [Campbell 1993, p. 40/53].

There is much to glean from this observation in the context of how Castle's initial dark promise for combat evolves into a form of subconscious fortification by way of a dissociative/authoritative "voice" in his head dominant enough to bestow upon him the conviction needed to perpetuate his endless campaign. Campbell also offered that "the unconscious sends all sorts of vapors, odd beings, terrors, and deluding images up into the mind" which are "dangerous" but "fiendishly fascinating too (representing the) destruction of the world that we have built and in which we live, and of ourselves within it" (Campbell 1993, p. 8). The "fiendish fascination" identified here by Campbell is arguably of a type with the "fascination of the abomination" that Joseph Conrad maintained lies waiting to be discovered in the darkest heart of an incomprehensible domain—after all, where better to find the Devil than Hell itself (Conrad 2008, p. 106). Thus, by ascribing an overall sense of instinctual legacy to the source of this voice by way of tapping into the concept of mans perpetual tendency towards war, as well as the implicit biblical connotations that arise through the adoption of Blake's Tyger, the mythic resonance of the Punisher's inception is convincingly harbored.

In an approach similar to Joseph Campbell's uncovering of the archetypal foundations of hero myths Carl Jung also highlighted an underlying darkness, or potential for destruction, synonymous with the appearance of tutelary guides. He identified the source of this Othered voice as the subconscious manifesting as what more primitive cultures would have regarded as Evil. Jung stressed a notable aspect of this manifestation that suitably aligns with the gradual descent of Frank Castle's mind into an abyss of subliminal coercion when he cautioned that:

> The dark side of the Self is the most dangerous thing of all, precisely because the Self is the greatest power in the psyche. It can cause people to "spin" megalomaniac or other delusory fantasies that catch them up and "possess" them. A person in this state ... loses all touch with human reality [Jung 1968, p. 234].

The sense of detachment from humanity implied in this observation suitably addresses the impenetrable darkness that reaches out to Castle. Just like Conrad's Mr. Kurtz, "his soul was mad. Being alone in the wilderness, it had looked within itself ... and it had gone mad" (Conrad, 2002, p. 174). Interestingly, Castle's radio officer in the aforementioned *The Platoon*, strikes a similar tone when he reflects on the fact that their survival required, "forgetting everything you'd ever been taught about the very idea of civilisation," to the point where, "You had to kind of let the Devil in the door" (Ennis, 2018, p. 33). Effectively, Castle had begun letting the Devil in the door once he had been introduced to the evocative force of nature that dwelt in Blake's poetry. This conceptual submission to darkness is disturbingly portrayed in the *Born* storyline. Set against the backdrop of the closing stages of the Vietnam War, at one point it depicts a General Padden arriving in Firebase Valley Forge, where Castle has been stationed, to conduct a surprise inspection and during his discussion with Frank he makes strong indications that American involvement in the Vietnam War is about to end, to which Castle responds with a discernible expression of brooding disapproval (Ennis, 2003, Vol. 1, p. 18). Further opening the door for the Devil to enter his life, he dramatically exhibits early warning signs of the detachment from human reality that Jung attributed to the dark side of the self and responds to this update from his commanding officer by positioning the general directly in the line of active sniper fire (Ennis, 2003, Vol. 1, p. 19). The act is not an isolated one and in the aftermath of a North Vietnamese Army ambush later in the story Castle summarily executes a fellow soldier, Punisher-style, for raping a captured and wounded enemy combatant (Ennis, 2003, Vol. 2, p. 18). Indeed, the motivation is even carried over to the point where Castle is later shown to be on the verge of removing the pin from a grenade intended for the indecisive Colonel Ottman, another of his superior officers (Ennis, 2003, Vol. 3, p. 9). Tellingly, it is after such incidents that the voice from within, or the "Beast" as Ennis offers, begins to coil its way around Castle's perception of reality and goads him to acknowledge how good it feels to murder when it observes, "I know you love this.... When did you ever feel so alive? So full of fierce black joy?" (Ennis, 2003, Vol. 1, p. 21). As a result, the reader is drawn to question to whom this seemingly Othered voice belongs and to consider who, or what, is trying to lay down the enticing parameters of a tailor-made Faustian pact. For instance, the conditions of Mephistopheles' offer in Johann Wolfgang von Goethe's *Faust: A Tragedy in Two Parts* center on an arrangement whereby the insatiable Heinrich Faust is bestowed with everlasting life until presented by Mephistopheles with a form of pleasure so sublime that he finally admits that he is satiated, at which point his soul becomes forfeit and is claimed by the demon (Williams, 2007, p. XVII). Contrastingly, the equivalently Machiavellian beast or demon in Castle's life, be it subconscious or otherwise (or otherworldly), presents him with a subversive propitiatory appeal to insatiable appetite by offering him a war that never ends in exchange for an undisclosed but ominous price to be carried forward to a later point in time:

> That urge you have, to give every motherfucker in the world exactly what they deserve? ... I can fix it so you can do this forever, Frank. There'll be a price to pay, but you can keep on going and never have to stop.... A war that lasts forever, a war that never ends, but you have to say the word, Frank [Ennis, 2003, Vol. 4, p. 15].

So whereas Faust is promised a life of cumulative pleasure until he comes upon an aspect of it that fully satisfies him, Castle is offered a life of enduring horror in exchange for the one thing redemptive enough to pull him back from the brink of a soulless existence. Jung observed that in spite of the inherent danger that surrounds the dark herald the hero can ultimately draw great strength and renewed conviction from its protective and advisory role (Jung, 1968, 112). This is demonstrated in the *Born* storyline by way of Castle being the sole survivor of the eventual Valley Forge assault in Vietnam, a point that the Beast makes sure he acknowledge when it clarifies for him that it is, "Not every day you beat two dozen men to death and soak up seven bullets, is it?" (Ennis, 2003, Vol. 4, p. 20). However, the aforementioned detachment from human reality that Jung also identified as a consequence of engaging with such a dark agent is validated by the eye witness account of one Sergeant W.J. Torrance. Indeed, Torrance's impression of the man that is left standing in the battle's aftermath reads as someone who has stared too long into the jaws of death, as he recalls, "You've heard of a thousand yard stare? This guy had a million mile one. He'd seen forever. He'd been somewhere else, and I don't know, sometimes I wonder if he'd maybe had a pretty good fucking conversation with someone he met there" (Ennis, 2012, Vol. 10, p. 107). In the hands of artist Darick Robertson, Frank is very much depicted as having concluded just such a conversation as he vocalizes the word "Yes" to the Beast's offer in a frameless panel, almost as if the conventional boundaries of page layout are transcended in order to suggest the enduring consequences his decision will have (Ennis, 2003, Vol. 1, p. 15). The reader is confronted with a face of maniacal conviction that reflects the spreading flames all around him and the moment perfectly captures the epiphanic impact elicited by the intimate commune he now shares with the spirit of the Tyger he became so enamored with as a boy in Blake's poetry. The effect is a well documented one in literary and philosophical discourse and is suitably articulated by Friedrich Nietzsche who likened it to "the shock of an earthquake," whereby:

> the soul is all at once convulsed, torn loose, torn away—it itself does not know what is happening. A drive and impulse rules and masters it like a command; a will and desire awakens to go off, anywhere, at any cost; a vehement dangerous curiosity for an undiscovered world flames and flickers in all its senses [Kolocotroni, Goldman, and Taxidou, Eds. 2004, p. 18].

Indeed, the vehement drive that would go on to become the Punisher's *modus operandi* is palpably rendered by the artist's depiction of a blood-spattered Castle whose eyes have seen forever. Effectively, he is now doubly empowered, both by the subconscious manifestation of a Mephistophelean herald and the clinically detached mindset of the special forces operator, all that he is missing is a concretizing reason to live, something that only death can grant him.

In his introduction to Gregg Hurwitz and Laurence Campbell's *Girls in White Dresses* author Robert Crais points out that "Pain is the nitrous-fueled, blown-Hemi, 454-cubic-inch, All-American engine that powers Frank Castle (and) the ghosts of Castle's wife and children forever fuel his guilt at being unable to protect them" (Crais, 2017, Introduction). Notably, in the *Born* storyline, once he agrees to the Beast's offer there is an inevitable finality to its parting reminder to "Just enjoy what you've got for the short time you'll have it" as Frank tightly clutches his family to him and is depicted with an expression not usually attributed to his stone-faced exterior, a look of fear (Ennis, 2003, p. 22). Yet, ironically, it is the fear of emotional attachment which induces the release that Frank ultimately desires from conventional life and which pushes that all-American engine to full throttle. The dark promise that the war fans into a consuming ideology leaves room for nothing else in his life. Arguably, one of the most tragic aspects of the Punisher narrative is the problematic ambiguity surrounding his attempts to articulate to his wife the psychological turmoil caused by the war and the possibility that in his tortured inability to do so he inadvertently, or perhaps knowingly, walked his family into the firing line in order to sever the connection to what remained of his own humanity. This clinical, and ultimately dehumanizing, mindset is powerfully rendered in *Valley Forge, Valley Forge*, the closing chapter to Ennis and

Parlov's run on the *Punisher MAX* series, where, according to the mother of one of the men who died under Castle's command in Firebase Valley Forge in Vietnam, "the trouble with men like that is they get a taste for conflict. They don't want to stop. They sometimes make things happen that otherwise wouldn't" (Ennis, 2012, Vol. 10, p. 62). Indeed, in *Punisher MAX: Bullseye,* Jason Aaron probes this concept to its deepest psychological extent by framing a story in which the psychotic assassin, Bullseye, decides that the only way he can kill Frank is to climb inside his mind to the point where he becomes a chilling parody of him (Aaron and Dillon, 2011). Consequent to a perverse re-enactment of Frank's family's murder Bullseye sets about infiltrating Castle's hardened psychological profile. To this effect, he deconstructs the seemingly implausible scenario that one of the military's most proficient combat veterans would have been wholly unaware of the danger that lied waiting in Central Park on the fateful day that his family was cut down. Detaching from his own immediate surroundings Bullseye asks himself:

> If you were already the Punisher in all but name, the question becomes ... why didn't you see it coming? ... All those times you avoided death in the jungle, so why did it get the jump on you then? You got them killed, Frank. Your wife. Your kids. You let them die right in front of your eyes. How could you let that happen? [Aaron, 2011, Vol. 2, p. 99].

By way of the suggestion that it takes a psychopath to fully relate to the Punisher's sociopathic drive he methodically locates Castle's most intimate source of guilt and completely deconstructs his apathetic detachment with the whispered revelation into Frank's ear that:

> You were sitting with your wife, right before the shooting started.... You leaned over and said something to her.... The last words she ever heard out of your mouth.... I know what you said to her Frank.... You said ... I want a divorce. Didn't you? Didn't you, Frank old buddy? [Aaron, 2011, Vol. 2, p. 130].

The orchestration of this interaction on the page is a celebration of the innovative manner in which the medium of comics can initially withhold, then strategically disclose, a powerful emotional impact. The words "I want a divorce" are depicted in a font so small that one literally needs a magnifying glass to make them out (Aaron, 2011, Vol. 2, p. 130). Just as Bullseye had to go to extreme efforts to probe Castle's mind so too must the reader be made to put in extra effort to see what he found there. The reader is also served up another crucial depiction of Frank's facial expression, this time rendered by the much regarded *Punisher* artist Steve Dillon. Following on from the look of epiphany depicted on his face in *The Tyger*, and on to the expression of maniacal release displayed in *Born*, Bullseye's psychoanalytic conclusion induces a state of complete paralysis in Castle and achieves something that no opponent has managed to do, bring the Punisher's crusade to a complete dead stop. Consequently, as the state of paralysis induced by Bullseye's revelation gradually begins to dissipate, the sense of guilt and scorn that Frank heaps upon himself is magnified to a disproportionate level as he comes to acknowledge that:

> The thing that haunts me now isn't the moment they died.... It's the moment right before that, when I had everything ... and I threw it all away. There was a time when I wished I'd died with them that day. But I know the reason I survived. It wasn't so I could seek revenge in their name. So I could wage my little war. It was so I could suffer. What I deserved was pain. Years of it. No rest. No joy. A lifetime of punishment [Aaron, 2012, Vol. 3, p. 91].

As such the very act of remembering is a source of renewed suffering for the soldier who failed to accomplish the most important mission of all, protecting his family. Accordingly, even though his past represents a consistently fresh site of pain it can also be tapped as an indomitable source of motivating intensity. Castle never allows himself reprieve from the role he played in his family's tragic outcome, and he is unable to stop apologizing to them long after their passing:

> I'm used to apologizing to dead children. I've been doing it for years. I tell my own kids I'm sorry for getting them killed. Sorry for walking them into an ambush. Sorry for failing them in every conceivable way. Sorry for the way I've chosen to honor their memory. But most of all, I'm sorry they were ever born in the first place [Aaron, 2012, Vol. 4, p. 55].

However, there is a measure of progression within the scope of his afflicted mind from such consistent regret to a grim acquiescence to the consequences of sustaining a personal war, "My world was like an abattoir. Everyone it touched it cut to ribbons, whether they were good or bad" (Ennis, 2012, Vol. 9, p. 97). Given his conclusive assessment of the impact he has on those around him, even potential friends or lovers, there is a cold logic to his decision to utterly detach and seek solace in the only thing he was ever good at, carrying out his mission, and it is the manner in which he applies himself to it that elects him to the apex standard of the medium's predators.

While his time in Vietnam allowed him to fully explore the dark appetite that burned within him it also demonstrated a level of professionalism and efficiency that many under his command came to believe would be the only thing capable of getting them safely through the war. Indeed, one of those men, Stevie Goodwin, points out that "[h]is dedication to his men is total. Not from love—that word and he do not belong together—but from the same determination to do his job correctly that informs his every action" (Ennis, 2003, Vol. 1, p. 7). Thus, in the theater of war he exemplifies the mindset that military schooling strives to impose. Notably, although the Beast never addresses Frank directly after his return home from Vietnam there is a point much later in his endless campaign where he discloses a recurring dream that contains the implication that the Beast's influence has been so resolute that he has become one himself:

> There's a dream I have from time to time. And in the dream I don't stop. I kill the soldiers and the hitmen, the extortioners and racketeers, the dark old fucks who send them out to fight. I hold the trigger down until they're gone.... But I don't stop. The innocents are watching, just like always. The slack-jawed thousands, gazing at the beast. My family lie red and shredded in the grass. I face the crowd and bring the weapon to my shoulder. If my world ends, I tell them, so does yours. The recoil starts and I wake up. It's just a dream, I always tell myself [Ennis, 2012, Vol. 4, p. 64].

The dream is the embodiment of complete release and indiscriminate fury in which collateral human damage isn't just accidental it is intentional. Yet, in spite of the crippling guilt that colors his memories and an impulsive subconscious attraction to the kind of raw hunger underlying such dreams it is essential for Castle to section away his pain and suppress such unregulated passion in order to dispatch each target with clinical and systematic efficiency. As Robert Crais puts it, "Castle's moral place in the universe requires perfection ... his is and must be a flawless vengeance" (Crais, 2017, Introduction).

Consequently, his incursive penetration of the criminal underworld becomes an extension of the same presence of mind and strategic analysis that he honed on the battlefield. This concept of an isolated figure that becomes consumed by an obsessive self-justified crusade has a strong literary, cinematic, and comics-based foundation. From the Creature in Mary Shelley's *Frankenstein* to Travis Bickle in Martin Scorcese's *Taxi Driver* to Ogami Itto in Kazuo Koike and Goseki Kojima's *Lone Wolf and Cub*. In Fred Parker's commentary on this anti-heroic archetype in the aptly titled *The Devil as Muse* he argues that what such protagonists have in common is that they are:

> charismatic yet profoundly isolated figures, exiles or outlaws from conventional society, alienated by a combination of their superior nobility of mind and some obscure act of crime or transgression in their past. Their consciousness is withdrawn, inflamed, and brooding; the pain they carry within is never fully communicated, but expressed in part by the attitude of disdain, severe and superb, which they show to human weakness in others as in themselves, and also to the littleness of life itself, its weakness to sustain their desires. They are *fallen* beings—or so at least they experience their existence—but tremendous in their fallenness: they can neither altogether regret what they have become, because of the dark knowledge which they now possess, nor reconcile themselves to their

condition, but vibrate between the poles of grim acquiescence and unappeasable rebellion. It often seems to be the intensity of this consciousness itself that constitutes their alienated self: consciousness not only *of* but also *as* alienation [Parker, 2011, p. 113/114].

In the tradition of the classic Byronic hero Parker describes the fallen and inherently flawed outsider who in spite of their outcast state exudes an inflamed and superior nobility of mind that lionizes them as tremendous to behold. Given the tremendous quality Parker attributes to such figures they are received with a combination of apprehension and admiration. As Mr. Kurtz's widow reflects in *Heart of Darkness*, "It was impossible to know him and not to admire him" (Conrad, 2008, p. 183). So too does Castle's impact on the collective unconscious of those occupying the Punisher's world range from fearful awe to professional admiration to poignant empathy. Reflecting on his time as Castle's partner the weapons expert Microchip captures Castle's force of nature approach when he explains that "[h]e thinks like a soldier. He treats war like what it's supposed to be: the total destruction of the enemy" (Ennis, 2013, Vol. 1, p. 38). Additionally, when a special forces unit are tasked to apprehend Castle they instantly recognize one of their own and their assessment of their target leaves them in no doubt as to how formidable he is in spite of his advanced age:

> He gathers intel, then keeps hitting targets 'till the opposition's finished.... He's systematic, ... He takes each organisation apart piece by piece.... We're not kidding ourselves about his capabilities.... He's one of us: he knows how special forces units operate, even what you might call tribal customs [Ennis, 2012, Vol 10, p. 29].

Indeed, their commanding officer, Colonel Howe, who himself was inspired to sign up to the specialized unit after being rescued from a Vietcong POW camp by Frank, succinctly conveys Castle's work ethic when he observes that "[h]e never goes off-duty, is the difference" (Ennis, 2012, Vol. 10, p. 84).

Given this nuanced accrual of literary and psychological influence coupled with an enduring sense of torturous survivor guilt it may well be that a figure like Frank Castle occupies a position just beyond the perimeter of conclusive analysis or judgment, as the most enduring literary, cinematic, and comics antiheroes do. As intriguing as it is to try to map where in his own mind one of the medium's most enduring antiheroes is coming from it is also inevitable to wonder where he might have ended up if events had played out differently for him. This possible alternative Frank is hinted at by the ones who knew him best, those who served and fought with him before he signed over to the darkness of special forces operations. Gathered together in an empty bar long past serving hours in a hushed act of remembrance it is former Sergeant Dryden, the man that Castle first revealed his dark appetite to, who explains to the same writer that composed the fictional *Valley Forge, Valley Forge: The Slaughter of a U.S. Marine Garrison and the Birth of The Punisher* that:

> Frank Castle saved the life of every man in his platoon. Some of them he shielded with his own flesh and blood you understand how important that is? You see how much more important it is, than first kills, an' the Punisher, an' all the other answers to the mystery you people always wanna know? You see the kinda man he coulda been? [Ennis, 2018, p. 117].

Within the fictional framework of the Punisher universe it might be nice to consider this alternative Frank Castle and what he might have been, one that came home from the war and grew to learn how to leave it behind. But to do that is to underestimate the inescapable lure of the Tyger that he devoted his life to as very much the dark equivalent of a spiritual calling. And it is in his own words, even after discovering that he had become a father and a family man once again that we see him briefly consider opening that doorway back into the light. However, such consideration is fleeting, an expendable liability in a mind full of war, and not even a second chance at redemption is enough to counteract his implacable resolve to occupy the heart of society's darkness and to right every wrong he sees:

> That was the real problem ... a day would come when I'd read the paper, or watch the news, and see something needing to be done. The sun slipped away behind me, the last sliver seeming to pause on the horizon, then succumbing to the black. And I drove on through the shadows of America, through the long, cold, dark night that I've made of my life. [Ennis, Vol. 9, p. 121].

This essay has attempted to ascribe a psychological and mythological undercurrent to the mannerisms of one of comics' most brutal protagonists, and by doing so, has highlighted the enduring appeal of a character that may initially be perceived to lack depth. In deference to such mythic foundations, when Joseph Campbell meditated on the inexorable hold that myth has over the human psyche he concluded that the turning point of each narrative resides "at the bottom of the abyss" wherein can be found "the voice of salvation" (Campbell, 1991, p. 44). However, the enduring fascination with Frank Castle stems from the fact that his voice of salvation is equally his voice of damnation, thus playing on the archetypal binary division and internal schism that typifies our attraction to the conflicted antihero figure in general. It was noted in the beginning of this essay that when Frank visited the museum of natural history as a child he deduced that the cycle of life had always included Tygers, and concluded that "somehow we needed them" (Ennis, 2013, p. 20). So too is it with stories about conflicted, controversial, and ambivalent figures like the Punisher. Residing/operating on the fringes of society, stalking his prey with calculated patience and finally striking with methodical efficiency he comes to embody the symbolic Tyger that called out to something in him that is never fully revealed. And it is left to the readers, viewers, and critics of his problematic legacy to discern shape and meaning from the long cold dark of self-torment that he continues to draw strength from.

REFERENCES

Aaron, J., & Dillon, S. (2011a). *Punisher MAX: Bullseye*. New York: Marvel Comics.
Aaron, J., & Dillon, S. (2011b). *Punisher MAX: Frank*. New York: Marvel Comics.
Aaron, J., & Dillon, S. (2011c). *Punisher MAX: Homeless*. New York: Marvel Comics.
Blake, W. (2009). *William Blake: The complete illuminated books*. London: Thames and Hudson.
Campbell, J. (1993). *The hero with a thousand faces*. London: Fontana Press.
Campbell, J. (1991). *The power of myth*. New York: Anchor Books.
Conrad, J. (2008). *Heart of darkness*. Oxford, England: Oxford University Press.
Ennis, G., Larosa, L., Fernandez, L., Braithwaite, D., Parlov, G., Medina, L., & Chaykin, H. (2005–2013). *Punisher Max* (Vols. 1–10). New York: Marvel Comics.
Ennis, G., & Parlov, G. (2018). *Punisher: The platoon*. New York: Marvel Comics.
Ennis, G., & Robertson, D. (2003). *Born: Max comics*. New York: Marvel Comics.
Ennis, G., & Severin, J. (2013). *Punisher: The Tyger*. New York: Marvel Comics.
Goethe, J.W. (2007). *Faust: A tragedy in two parts*. London: Wordsworth.
Groensteen, T. (2013). *Comics and narration*. Jackson: University Press of Mississippi.
Hurwitz, G., & Campbell, L. (2017). *Punisher MAX: The complete collection vol. 5*. New York: Marvel Comics.
Jung, C. (1968). *Man and his symbols*. New York: Dell Publishing.
Kolocotroni, V., Goldman, J., Taxidou, O. (Eds.). (2004). *Modernism: An anthology of sources and documents*. Edinburgh: Edinburgh University Press.
Parker, F. (2011). *The devil as muse*. Waco: Baylor University Press.

Black and White and Nothing in Between?

Some Thoughts on the Morality of the Punisher

Anders Lundgren

> Sometimes we see a man so profoundly indignant at a great outrage, which he has experienced or perhaps only witnessed, that he deliberately and irretrievably stakes his own life in order to take vengeance on the perpetrator of that outrage.
>
> —Arthur Schopenhauer, *The World as Will and Representation* (1819)

The career of most successful fictional characters waxes and wanes. In comics an interpretation by adept creators can bring a character back from obscurity. An adaptation into other media may lead to heightened public awareness. To take one such example, by 2018 it was safe to say that more people than ever knew of the Punisher. Coming off the first season of his own show on Netflix, Marvel's deadliest vigilante was in high demand. His publisher was of course more than happy to oblige. Among the titles made available were *Punisher MAX: The Platoon* (Ennis & Parlov, 2018). Set during the General Offensive and Uprising of Tet Mau Than 1968, more generally known as the Tet Offensive, a tipping point when the war turned in favor of North Vietnamese forces, audiences were introduced to one Lt. Frank Castle during his inaugural tour in Vietnam. The framing device here is that journalist Michael Goodwin meets up with the surviving members of Castle's first command. Through their remembrances of the man, Goodwin tries to ascertain where Lt. Castle ended, and where the Punisher began. A quick note on names: Though he was given the name Francis Castiglione at birth, this was later changed to Frank Castle. Different circumstances and reasons for the name change have been given (Sodaro, 2012, pp. 2–3).

A very different comic was the limited series *Cosmic Ghost Rider*, written by Donny Cates with art by Dylan Burnett. The series illustrated how Frank Castle, through a series of increasingly bad decisions, went from being the Punisher to donning the mantle of Ghost Rider, received cosmic powers from Galactus, and in the end became the servant of Thanos. It is no understatement to label these depictions of the character as worlds apart. *Punisher MAX: The Platoon* takes place on Earth-200111, a version of our planet nearly devoid of superpowered beings, in contrast to Earth-616 where most of the Marvel stories are set.

An essay discussing the morality of a fictional character benefits from bearing wildly diverse depictions such as these in mind. As part of the Marvel Universe since the 1970s, Frank Castle/the Punisher has been subjected to many interpretations by a myriad of writers and artists. Additionally, as the examples above illustrate, various adaptations in other media and the concurrent push and pull from comics to film and back again have led to further tweaks. New tiles are constantly added to the mosaic that by necessity and design constitutes the makeup of any long-lived character owned by a publishing entity rather than a single creator. In all of this, can you still find core traits, or are the only constants of the Punisher the inconsistencies of his portrayal? Can a discussion about morality even be fruitful in a case such as this? An unforgiving attitude towards violent criminals is definitely part of the character make up no matter who is writing the script. Depending on the views of different writers, this can then be cast in a positive or negative light as will be demonstrated in the discussion ahead.

In the Beginning

The Punisher captured the zeitgeist of the decade in which he was created. The early 1970s gives us many examples of the gritty urban hero. The film *Dirty Harry*, in which hard-nosed San Francisco Police Department Inspector Harry Callahan was introduced, premiered in 1971. Starring Clint Eastwood in one of his signature roles, the film was loosely based on the hunt for the all-too-real serial killer calling himself Zodiac. Don Siegel's movie offered the cathartic ending reality did not deliver. Gerry Conway cites both *Dirty Harry* and Don Pendleton's *The Executioner* novels about a Vietnam war veteran fighting organized crime as his two main sources of inspiration when he created the Punisher (Arndt, 2015, p. 34).

The 1972 novel *Death Wish* by Brian Garfield portrays the transformation of mild-mannered New York Certified Public Accountant Paul Benjamin into an unhinged and violent man after an attack by muggers leaves his wife dead and his daughter in a catatonic state. In 1974 it was turned into a film starring Charles Bronson. From Garfield's point of view, Michael Winner's adaptation took so many liberties with the source material that it inspired him to write the follow-up novel *Death Sentence* in 1975. Garfield felt that, unlike his book, the film was not clear in depicting the protagonist's precarious mental state, and furthermore turned his indictment of vigilantism completely on its head (Vlastelica, 2018). Garfield's very negative reaction to how his work was interpreted is one illustration among many of the hostility that was heaped upon both *Dirty Harry* and *Death Wish*, along with extremely generous box office receipts that turned the films into the first installments of long-lived franchises. "The movie's moral position is fascist. No doubt about it," as Roger Ebert so succinctly put it in his review of *Dirty Harry* dated January 1, 1971. *Death Wish* gets a similar verdict (Ebert, 1971/1974). These well-known examples of the vigilante genre are only a fraction of what was a genuine staple of the movie repertoire throughout the decade.

In many ways the critique and success of these two films are analogous to the response the Punisher has met since his introduction. He is popular and polarizing in almost equal measure, sparking debate whilst instrumental in selling a lot of comics. One possible interpretation is that even many of those that vehemently opposed his habit of killing instead of capturing violent criminals found stories about him interesting to read. Consequently, during the peak of his popularity, lasting roughly from the late 1980s to the mid–1990s, the Punisher had at one point five different publications to his name: *The Punisher, The Punisher War Journal, The Punisher Magazine, The Punisher Armory*, and *The Punisher War Zone*. Furthermore, he was featured in several releases that were part of Marvel's graphic novel line, various specials, and made numerous guest appearances in other titles.

Most likely nobody foresaw his future success when the character made his debut as a secondary villain in one of Marvel's most popular books at the time. Readers were first introduced to the Punisher through the striking cover to *The Amazing Spider-Man* #129 (1974 February) by Gil Kane and John Romita, Sr. Depicted against a stark yellow background we see a black clad skull-emblazoned character with Spider-Man in the sights of a high-powered rifle. The 19-page story shows the Punisher working for the Jackal, also making his first appearance here, to deliver on what the cover promised. The Punisher comes across as a somewhat erratic and gullible individual, quite far removed from the cold, calculating instrument of retribution we know him as today. One thing is made perfectly clear from the start however—the Punisher's willingness to use lethal force in dealing with those he perceives as evil. There is very little in the way of a rationale presented for his modus operandi in this first appearance, apart from a little speech-making in one of his confrontations with Spider-Man. When asked about the line of reasoning behind the Punisher's actions during an interview conducted in the late 1980s, Gerry Conway had this to say:

> My intention with the character was always to make him ... how can I put it? A complex character; complex because he saw the world in black and white terms. [...] The Punisher's view of the world is a simple one—there are good people and there are bad people, and the bad people deserve to die [Mougin 1989, p. 6].

While it was certainly a novel idea to feature a hero with a black and white view of the world dispensing capital punishment in a Marvel context, it was not without antecedents elsewhere in comics. After leaving Marvel in 1966 due to numerous disagreements, prolific cartoonist Steve Ditko went on to work for other publishers. Two characters he created are relevant to the discussion. The first one is Mr. A, who was introduced in an eponymous story printed in Wally Wood's underground comic *witzend* #3 (1967 January). This publication was designed to be an outlet for creators to try ideas and concepts that might be frowned upon in the mainstream. In Ditko's story, we meet Rex Graine, a no-nonsense newspaper reporter not content with fighting corruption and crime through his journalistic endeavors, who also moonlights as the titular vigilante. Mr. A appears in a white business suit, with steel gloves on his hands, and an expressionless metal mask covering his features. With this character Ditko made one of his boldest statements, a comic that without restraints gave voice to the objectivist philosophy he adhered to. Objectivism was developed by writer Ayn Rand and first presented in her novels *The Fountainhead* (1943) and *Atlas Shrugged* (1957). In the simplest of terms it is a system driven by logic, extreme individualism and moral absolutes. As interpreted in the comics of Ditko this is an attitude towards life that does not suffer shades of gray in any way, shape, or form.

The second relevant character is the Question, the secret identity of TV reporter Vic Sage. Developed simultaneously with Mr. A, the Question made his debut as a backup feature in the revived title *Blue Beetle* #1 (1967 June). Displaying the same flair for menswear and masks, in his case a completely featureless one, the Question leaves a blank calling card that when touched shows a smoky question mark. The character is presented as a fairly unforgiving crime fighter, but since his exploits were published by mainstream company Charlton Comics, they had to be deemed acceptable by the regulatory body the industry had set up the previous decade. The Comics Code Authority was a self-regulating (i.e., self-censoring) initiative started in 1954 by various publishers in response to the heated debates about comics and their supposed connection to juvenile delinquency, leading to senate hearings and public book burnings in the early 1950s. Its power started to wane in the late 1960s and it has been defunct since January 2011. This meant that the Question, while still a vigilante, was more likely to expose criminals and turn them over to the authorities than to act as judge, jury and executioner. Ditko did not hold back when writing Mr. A however. The underground comic that featured his stories was beholden to no one, and the creators seemingly took pride in overstepping the boundaries laid out by the Comics Code Authority. Consequently Mr. A is often seen killing violent criminals while laying down the objectivist law in no uncertain terms. With his deeds and half-black half-white calling cards he embodied the same basic principles that the Punisher would express through sartorial choices and actions rather than words a few years later.

To his detractors, Mr. A represents the superhero as a soapbox. Looking at the verbosity of any given page this is certainly an understandable position, even to one who has no objections to what he is saying. Ditko retained the rights to the character and continued to self-publish Mr. A throughout his life with no deviations from the objectivist path he originally set out for his creation. The Question, on the other hand, was made under work-for-hire conditions and owned first by Charlton Comics and later by DC. While some creators have portrayed him in a way that paid homage to what Ditko first envisioned, he has gone through different iterations and character developments that even have him question the legitimacy of his formerly unambiguous moral positions. The different routes taken by Mr. A and the Question illustrate undiluted vision versus compromise, creator ownership versus work-for-hire.

Comic-book history is of course full of characters that change with the times. The Punisher exists under the same conditions as the Question, and unlike Mr. A has not been the mouthpiece of what could be defined as one persistent philosophy. Garth Ennis' run on *Punisher MAX* may be the most fully realized when it comes to consistency of outlook and the depiction of the protagonist. But even his stories range from the somber and true to life portrayal of human trafficking in *Punisher MAX: The Slavers*, to the ultraviolent slapstick of *Punisher MAX: Barracuda* (Ennis 2006). The latter reading almost like an extremely bloody Popeye comic at times. While certainly still staying true to the basic characterization of its protagonist, this thematic range sets it apart from the single-mindedness displayed by Ditko's Mr. A. Whether a writing style that admits a wider range of moods and plurality of opinion is good or bad is up to the individual reader.

Zeitgeist

The aforementioned books, films and comics were not created in a vacuum but arose from a general feeling of unease. So, while some people leveled harsh criticism at the accepting, even celebratory, depictions of miscreants terminated with extreme prejudice, to others this was more a welcome change of pace. To put things in perspective, it is an established fact that in the early 1970s a galloping economic crisis led to widespread urban decay in the U.S. In its wake came an increase in violent crime that the forces of law and order were seemingly unable or unwilling to combat. Examples of this deplorable state of affairs were to be found in for instance New York, home town to both Marvel and the Punisher. Between 1965 and 1975 many things had taken a turn for the worse. 500,000 jobs in manufacturing had been lost, most of them between 1969 and 1975. The yearly murder rate had gone up from 681 to 1,690. Rapes and break-ins had more than tripled. Car thefts and assaults had more than doubled. The recorded amount of robberies was ten times higher. The city was teetering on the edge of bankruptcy with no signs of help coming from outside. When Mayor Abe Beame, in an effort to remedy this situation, announced pay cuts and massive layoffs, one of the replies from the city's workers was the writing and distribution of a now infamous pamphlet entitled "Welcome to Fear City." Handed out at airports and other routes into the Big Apple, this publication sported a Grim Reaper on the cover and contained "A Survival Guide for Visitors to the city of New York." Urging tourists to among other things "Stay off the streets after 6 P.M." and "Remain in Manhattan," the text signed by the Council for Public Safety is emblematic of this volatile period in New York's history (Baker, 2015).

The Vietnam War and its repercussions both domestically and internationally also played a big role in the general American anxiety of the time. Even those not directly supporting the growing anti-war movement began to doubt the validity of the undertaking following the Tet Offensive, the success of which led to the gradual withdrawal of American troops until the end of U.S. involvement on August 15, 1973. While not a part of how the Punisher was initially presented the conflict has over time come to be integral to understanding him. The military training and experiences in country provide the basis for his combat proficiency as well as numerous plots, recurring characters and villains. It should however be noted that Marvel's notorious sliding time scale (in short, characters rarely grow older, basically staying the same age as when they were first introduced) and different versions of the character have also made the Punisher a veteran of other combat zones. An example is the 11th series (begun in 2016) by Becky Cloonan, Steve Dillon and Matt Horak, in which the Punisher took part in an operation in an unspecified desert country. *Punisher Noir* (Tieri & Azaceta, 2009) has the First World War as a backdrop to the story. Again, the specifics may change, but the character remains the same.

Difference and Repetition

The social and cultural climate during the years leading up to the creation of the Punisher are vital to comprehending the character and why he came to resonate strongly with his audience. Reactions to his first appearance were so enthusiastic that he returned to the pages of *The Amazing Spider-Man* just a few months after his debut (Sacks, 2014, p. 127). More or less reluctant team-ups where the Punisher interacts with superheroes from the Marvel Universe exemplify a recurring storytelling mode during the character's long history. Typically during these encounters, a fair amount of time is spent on the clash between different outlooks and codes of conduct. In the simplest of terms, the ethos of letting the punishment fit the crime is contrasted with a belief in the justice system, rehabilitation and second chances, no matter what the offence. In some of these stories there are occasionally bizarre twists to the Punisher's deadly way of handling things. To escape the criticism of characters like Captain America, Daredevil and Spider-Man, the Punisher at times reverts to softer ways of fighting crime—for example by using "Mercy Bullets"—non-lethal sleep-inducing ammunition. For Marvel, toning down the Punisher's killing of his opponents was a strategy to escape the attention of the Comics Code Authority. (Arndt, 2015, p. 34.) Make no mistake, criminals still wound up dead when he showed up, but the deaths were not depicted in excessively graphic ways. Since that time the violence has gradually increased to a level where these days anything goes.

The other main approach to writing the Punisher is best exemplified by the stories printed in *Marvel Preview* #2 (1975 August). Clearly aimed at an older audience and beyond the reach of certain regulatory bodies, this black and white magazine presented decidedly harsher narratives in which superheroes are nowhere to be seen. Closer in tone to the popular men's adventure books that inspired the character, it is no great surprise that Don Pendleton (creator of the Executioner that inspired Conway when he came up with the Punisher) is the subject of an interview in this particular issue. It is also within these pages that we Social Media, Surveillance and Social Control for the first time get, to witness what propelled the Punisher into his war on crime: the death of his wife and two children at the hands of mafia hitmen. This trauma is henceforth a central motif that is repeated whenever the character makes an appearance. The killing of Castle's family is often mentioned in an introduction, some lines of dialogue, or relived in the form of a flashback. Different writers have put their own spin on the original event, adding and subtracting to keep it relevant and raw. While based in the realities of comics publishing, where you work from the assumption that any given issue or graphic novel can be a reader's first contact with the characters therein, the temptation to put this into a larger philosophical context is impossible to resist.

Compelled by the violent deaths of his wife and children to engage in an endless war on criminals, the man formerly known as Frank Castle is a perfect embodiment of an idea espoused by German philosopher Friedrich Nietzsche—that of the eternal return (Nietzsche, 2001, pp. 194–195). In layman's terms, this concept means that all of existence repeats itself endlessly. Of his own accord and through the vagaries of Marvel, Frank Castle is trapped in a cycle of violence with no end in sight. He has fought every type of crime and terrorist organization throughout the world. The long running partnership with computer hacker Micro had the stories sliding over into something resembling a sitcom at times, albeit with a whole lot of killing between gags. Micro was created by Mike Baron and Klaus Janson and introduced in *The Punisher* #4 (1987 November). The character assisted with intelligence gathering and money laundering, and served as quartermaster in many subsequent narratives.

Occasionally there have been storylines that break from the tedium of killing mobsters and drug dealers. There was a time when the Punisher had experimental regenerative surgery after his face was carved up by the villain Jigsaw. The resultant change in skin color had him posing as African American Frank Rook and teaming up with Luke Cage to make South Side, Chicago, free from crack-dealing gangs. Both characters had at this time temporarily relocated from their native New York due to various work-related complications. Prompted by Cage to refrain from killing their opponents, this was yet another illustration of Punisher's modus operandi being questioned by the superhero set (Baron et al., 1992). The "Eurohit" storyline turned Punisher into a globetrotting figure going up against high-tech villains together with an extended family of associates, neither of which would have felt out of place in a James Bond film (Abnett, Lanning & Braithwaite, 1992 & 1994). In two other instances of physical transformation the Punisher has also been a superpowered hitman for the heavenly host (Golden, Sniegoski & Wrightson, 1998), and turned into the hulking creature Franken-Castle (Remender et al., 2010). None of these proved permanent, but were followed by a return to New York and the status quo ante of fighting street-level criminals. At the end of the day, the Punisher stories are variations on a comparatively limited theme.

As touched on earlier, the Punisher was not popular with everyone, so when Steve Grant, after some years of lobbying, got the chance to write the first mini-series, one of the things he had to do was address Bill Mantlo's spiteful interpretation seen in the pages of *The Spectacular Spider-Man* a few years prior. Viewing him as nothing but a heavily armed lunatic, Mantlo presented the Punisher randomly shooting people with no apparent concern whether he hit the wife beater or his victim, a guy missing the waste basket due to a gust of wind or a cabbie accidentally running a red light to get out of the line of fire (Mantlo & Milgrom, 1983, pp. 3–6). Grant sorted this out through a conversation revealing that somebody had slipped drugs into the Punisher's food during a stay at Ryker's Island penitentiary (Grant & Zeck, 1986, p. 6).

When Garth Ennis took over after Golden and Sniegoski, the regrettable episode with the angels was quickly addressed and tossed aside (Ennis & Dillon, 2000, pp. 20–21). In the case of Ennis, you can also see a distinct progression from the darkly humorous tone in his issues of the *Marvel Knights* run (August 2001–February 2004) to how he portrayed the character in *Punisher MAX* (March 2004–October 2008), though not entirely without relapses to the earlier style as exemplified by the previously mentioned *Barracuda* narrative. To reiterate, in the latter series the action moves from Earth-616 to Earth-200111, although some characters and events seemingly carry over from one version of our planet to the other. As an opening salvo, Ennis and artist Lewis Larosa take the opportunity to revisit that fateful picnic in Central Park, with the death of Castle's family described in graphic detail. Throughout the rest of the series Ennis goes on to address a number of characters and storylines that have previously featured in the Punisher comics, giving them a harsh makeover. For instance, the grisly murder of a guard dog at the estate of Mafia Don Cesare (Ennis & Larosa, 2004, p. 9) can be seen as a severing of the ties with some of the more cutesy stuff previous writers put in there. Such as the Punisher's dog Max, whose apparent euthanasia at the hands of his master (Baron & Haynes, 1991, p. 16) was met with such a reasonable and strong reaction by readers that this was later retconned as emergency surgery that saved the dog's life and saw him return in a later story. (Dixon & Kwapisz, 1993, p. 5). It should also be noted that when the Punisher of Earth-616 relocated to Los Angeles he adopted a coyote that was given the name Loot (Edmondson & Gerads, 2014). Once an idea, like in this instance a vigilante and his dog, has been introduced into an ongoing story you can be quite certain that someone will comment on it or use it in a future installment. As with most forms of literature, superhero comics are written in dialog with what has come before. The rest of that first *Punisher MAX* arc reads like an ultraviolent reply to Chuck Dixon's story "Countdown," which jumped between different Punisher titles in the mid-1990s (Dixon 1995). In Ennis' version, the attempt to rein in the Punisher ends with Micro getting a point-blank shotgun blast to the head (Ennis & Larosa, 2004, p. 23). So when viewing these comics through the lens of Nietzsche's ideas one does well to speak with Gilles Deleuze:

> And what would eternal return be, if we forgot that it is a vertiginous movement endowed with a force: not one which causes the return of the Same in general, but one which selects, one which expels as well as creates, destroys as well as produces? [Deleuze 1994, p. 11]

The rejection of older ideas at odds with what a new writer hopes to achieve during his time with the character is in the case of the Punisher stories, as noted earlier, almost invariably a violent process. If looking at the fictional Marvel Universe as a whole, the creation, destruction and production of characters and entire worlds are needless to say par for the course and an integral part of the constant reinvention that has kept it going for decades. This concluding section will continue the discussion on how this impacts the depiction and views on the Punisher.

Cop? Butcher? Thug?

While he has certainly not been the subject of as wildly different interpretations as some other comic-book heroes, the divergences in behavior are marked enough for this reader to see several versions of the Punisher existing side by side as different writer and artist teams put their own sensibilities and ideals to bear on the same basic formula. When attempting an overview of the comics published about the Punisher, the amount of inconsequential dross you see is staggering. Maybe this is what it is like to be a religious person or an unswerving patriot? To still see the ideal despite all the questionable actions performed in the name of what you believe in. A world where actions always have consequences. Boomerang ethics. What you give out is what you should get back. The way the Punisher is depicted ranges from a handsome athletic guy of Italian-American descent, a freakishly muscled brawler who foregoes shaving and has a nose that has obviously been broken more than once, and, when stabs at realism are called for, a banged-up but still towering older man. See, for example, Jim Lee's, John Romita Jr.'s and Lewis Larosa's respective interpretations in the early issues of *The Punisher War Journal* (1988), *The Punisher War Zone* (1992), and *Punisher MAX* (2004). The way he looks often correlates with how he acts. Tactical and exact in his application of force, or the exact opposite. As the title of one collection put it, a *Barbarian with a Gun* (Dixon & Buscema, 2008). Reading early reactions, it is obviously a description some deem accurate. Letters published in *Marvel Super Action* #1 in 1976 make connections between the conflict in Vietnam and what the Punisher is doing, with the bottom line being that his actions are morally wrong. One individual urges Marvel to change the character—a suggestion the publisher clearly did not heed (Goodwin, 1976, pp. 3–4). Academic analyses of the Punisher comics tend to stem from a similarly critical stance. He has among other things been diagnosed with Antisocial Personality Disorder (Getzfeld, 2008, p. 167–168) and labeled a radical conservative racist (DiPaolo, 2011, p. 131). More sympathetic readings do exist, and one of them states that:

> His unblinking rage permits him to look past the veil of the social contract. From the Punisher's standpoint, humanity never left the state of nature. Part of the reason why he is so angry is because the rest of us are so naïve [Worcester, 2012, p. 340].

Those that try to see things from his perspective are however few and far between. Writer Matthew Rosenberg's letter of comment in his first 2017 issue of *The Punisher* makes it obvious that little has changed over the years (Rosenberg, 2017, p. 22). Deadly vigilantism is generally not more palatable to an audience today than when the Punisher was first introduced. If we broaden the perspective and include reactions to the Netflix show, this becomes even clearer. In a somewhat typical review, Charles Pulliam-Moore (2017) compares the Punisher's executions of the people who murdered his family to the actions of then recent mass-shooters. Following that line of thought the assumption would be that by giving violent men violent ends you become like them. This is debatable. When taking up his role as the writer of the first ongoing series it seemed as if Mike Baron had been making a list, checking it twice, and deciding on just who deserved to die. Within a year the Punisher had killed analogues for Nguyen Ngoc Loan, Jim Jones, Charles Manson, and Pablo Escobar. Loan is infamous for his public execution of Viet Cong officer Bay Lop. Jones for the mass suicide of his congregation at the People's Temple in Guyana. Manson was instrumental in the killing of Sharon Tate and many others. Escobar was the king of Colombia's cocaine trade. In what way is freeing the world of guys like these comparable to shooting innocent people at an outdoor concert? An argument that gets aired often is that once you start paying people back in kind the situation will invariably spin out of control and you end up with death squads in the streets—as in the Philippines where President Rodrigo Duterte's war on drugs and open support of extrajudicial killings caused some to call him "The Punisher," an honorific the wealth of evidence regarding his questionable ethics would suggest he does not deserve (Lamb, 2017).

Much has been said to the effect that what makes the Punisher interesting is that he performs his tasks without the benefit of superpowers. A recurring theme is a variation on the slightly tiresome trope of the hero fighting his dark twin, in the form of other vigilantes and organizations with a similar mission statement. Unlike them he is equipped with an incorruptible moral compass and the dedication to put in the time to ascertain that his targets are actually legitimate and that his hits will not result in undeserving people getting hurt. In today's murky world that may seem to qualify almost as a superpower. His convictions are so strong that when led to believe he has been the cause of innocents dying, it has driven him to the brink of suicide (Hurwitz & Campbell, 2008, p. 13). This uncompromising nature is part of why writer Steven Grant in a very eloquent piece identifies the Punisher as an existentialist:

> That's sure the Punisher as I conceived him: a man who knows he's going to die and who knows in the big picture his actions will count for nothing, but who pursues his course because this is what he has chosen to do [Grant 2001].

Does this come through in the comics he has written about with the character? If one were feeling extremely generous one could find a little bit of Danish existentialist philosopher and theologian Søren Kierkegaard meets the 1985 film *Commando* in titles like *The Punisher: Return to Big Nothing*. This graphic novel drawn by Mike Zeck displays the artist's usual oversized, heavily muscled character design. Grant gives a lot of space to the protagonist's interior monologue, detailing who he used to be, his now dead dreams, and the zeal fueling his relentless campaign against criminals. The depiction of the long conflict between the Punisher and the sadistic gunnery sergeant turned violent malefactor Gorman does carry a tone suggesting kinship with both *Commando* and the personal choice and commitment essential to Kierkegaard. In some parts, the Punisher's interior monologue hints at a possibly grandiose view of his war on crime, reflecting a religious side that turned up in some portrayals around this time. Shortly before he snaps the neck of a Cambodian drug dealer with his bare hands, this is what passes through his mind: "I am the flood, washing clean the earth. I am the wind that blows away the dust" (Grant & Zeck, 1989, p. 54). Other examples are to be found in the first film adaptation starring Dolph Lundgren. A few of his soliloquies describe how he talks to God asking if "What I'm doing is right or wrong" (Kamen & Goldblatt, 1989). In the graphic novel *The Punisher: Intruder* there are flashbacks depicting his time at the seminary and subsequent break with the church (Baron & Reinhold, 1989). This is another facet of the character that might benefit from further study. It also bears additional testimony to the existence of several parallel versions, not just in terms of different continuities but also when it comes to the depiction of his ideology and motivations. In *Punisher MAX*, doubt, religious or otherwise, does not enter the equation, and in its place there is a focused pursuit of people defined by their acts of cruelty.

What the Punisher is doing might be justified given the above examination. The time some people spend on empathizing with perpetrators of rape and murder, claiming that they in light of their troubled upbringing or socioeconomic status are in fact as much the victims as the people they have made to suffer is staggering. And while this author is all for society using various efforts to make existence meaningful (even though this should really be up to the individual) and taking care of people who due to difficult circumstances are about to lose their way in life, this should all stop when a person chooses to victimize others. A lot of discussions about the Punisher echo the views of Bill Mantlo, who depicted him as nothing but an armed thug lacking both empathy and morals—as if the Punisher did not go after human traffickers and their ilk, who ruin lives and do not care about anybody else. Like singer-songwriter Boyd Rice once put it: "Would you want to spare such a rabble, if there was at hand a sure way of destroying them? That is for you to decide" (Rice, 1990).

REFERENCES

Abnett, D., Lanning, A., & Braithwaite, D. (1992). *The Punisher*, #64–70. New York: Marvel Comics.
Abnett, D., Lanning, A., & Braithwaite, D. (1994). *The Punisher annual*, #7. New York: Marvel Comics.
Arndt, R.J. (2015). "We were given the gift of serendipity": Gerry Conway on his first half decade-plus at Marvel, DC & elsewhere. *Alter Ego*, 3(131), 3–44.
Baker, K. (2015, May 18). *Welcome to Fear City—The inside story of New York's civil war, 40 years on.* The Guardian. https://www.theguardian.com/cities/2015/may/18/welcome-to-fear-city-the-inside-story-of-new-yorks-civil-war-40-years-on.
Baron, M., & Haynes, H. (1991). *The Punisher*, #57. New York: Marvel Comics.
Baron, M., & Janson, K. (1987). *The Punisher*, #4. New York: Marvel Comics.
Baron, M., McLaurin, M., Haynes, H., & Mayerik, V. (1992). *The Punisher*, #59–62. New York: Marvel Comics.
Baron, M., & Reinhold, B. (1989). *The Punisher: Intruder*. New York: Marvel Comics.
Conway, G., & Andru, R. (1974). *The amazing Spider-Man*, #129. New York: Marvel Comics.
Conway, G., & DeZuniga, T. (1975). *Marvel preview*, #2. New York: Marvel Comics.
Deleuze, G. (1994). *Difference and repetition*. New York: Columbia University Press.
DiPaolo, M. (2011). *War, politics and superheroes: Ethics and propaganda in comics and film*. Jefferson, NC: McFarland.
Ditko, S., & Glanzman, D.C. (1967). *Blue Beetle*, #1. New York: Fox Comics.
Dixon, C., & Buscema, J. (2008). *The Punisher: Barbarian with a gun*. New York: Marvel Comics.
Dixon, C., & Kwapisz, G. (1993). *The Punisher war journal*, #59. New York: Marvel Comics.
Dixon, C., & various artists. (1995a, June). *The Punisher*, #103. New York: Marvel Comics.
Dixon, C., & various artists. (1995b, June). *The Punisher war journal*, #79. New York: Marvel Comics.
Dixon, C., & various artists. (1995a, July). *The Punisher war zone*, #41. New York: Marvel Comics.
Dixon, C., & various artists. (1995b, July). *The Punisher*, #104. New York: Marvel Comics.
Dixon, C., & various artists. (1995c, July). *The Punisher war journal*, #80. New York: Marvel Comics.
Ebert, R. (1971). *Dirty Harry*. Roger Ebert. https://www.rogerebert.com/reviews/dirty-harry-1971.
Ebert, R. (1974). *Death wish*. Robert Ebert. https://www.rogerebert.com/reviews/death-wish-1974.
Edmondson, N., & Gerads, M. (2014). *The Punisher*, #2. New York: Marvel Comics.
Ennis, G., & Dillon, S. (2000). *The Punisher*, #1. New York: Marvel Comics.
Ennis, G., & Larosa, L. (2004, March). *Punisher MAX*, #1. New York: Marvel Comics.
Ennis, G., & Larosa, L. (2004, July). *Punisher MAX*, #6. New York: Marvel Comics.
Ennis, G., & Fernandez, L. (2006). *Punisher MAX vol. 5: The slavers*. New York: Marvel Comics.
Ennis, G., & Parlov, G. (2006). *Punisher MAX vol. 6: Barracuda*. New York: Marvel Comics.

Ennis, G., & Parlov, G. (2018). *Punisher MAX: The platoon*. New York: Marvel Comics.
Garfield, B. (1972). *Death wish*. Philadelphia: David Mckay.
Garfield, B. (1975). *Death sentence*. Lanham, MD: M. Evans.
Getzfeld, A. (2008). What would Freud say? Psychopathology and the Punisher. In R.S. Rosenberg (Ed.), *The psychology of superheroes: An unauthorized exploration* (pp. 163–174). Dallas: Ben Bella Books.
Goldblatt, M. (Director). (1989). *The Punisher* [Film]. United States: New World Pictures.
Golden, C., Sniegoski, T., & Wrightson, B. (1998–1999). *The Punisher*, #1–4. New York: Marvel Comics.
Goodwin, A., & DeZuniga, T. (1976). *Marvel super action*, #1. New York: Marvel Comics.
Grant, S. (2001, July 26). *Issue #104*. CBR. https://www.cbr.com/issue-104/.
Grant, S., & Zeck, M. (1986). *The Punisher*, #1. New York: Marvel Comics.
Grant, S., & Zeck, M. (1989). *The Punisher: Return to big nothing*. New York: Epic Comics.
Hurwitz, G., & Campbell, L. (2008). *The Punisher*, #63. New York: Marvel Comics.
Lamb, K. (2017, April 2). *Thousands dead: The Philippine president, the death squad allegations and a brutal drugs war*. The Guardian. https://www.theguardian.com/world/2017/apr/02/philippines-president-duterte-drugs-war-death-squads.
Lester, M.L. (Director). (1985). *Commando* [Film]. United States: Silver Pictures.
Mantlo, B., & Milgrom, A. (1983). *The spectacular Spider-Man*, #82. New York: Marvel Comics.
Mougin, L. (1989). *David Anthony Kraft's comics interview super special: The Punisher*. New York: Fictioneer Books.
Nietzsche, F. (2001). *The gay science*. Cambridge: Cambridge University Press.
Pulliam-Moore, C. (2017, November 14). *Netflix's The Punisher is a brutal humanization of Frank Castle that can't face its own demons*. io9gizmodo. https://io9.gizmodo.com/netflixs-the-punisher-is-a-brutal-humanization-of-frank-1820323091.
Remender, R., Moore, T., & various artists (2010a). *Franken-Castle*, #17–21. New York: Marvel Comics.
Remender, R., Moore, T., & various artists (2010b). *The Punisher*, #11–16. New York: Marvel Comics.
Rice, B. (1990). As for the fools [Song] *On music, martinis and misanthropy* [Album]. United Kingdom: New European Recordings.
Rosenberg, M., & Vilanova, G. (2017). *The Punisher*, #218. New York: Marvel Comics.
Sacks, J. (2014). *American comic book chronicles: The 1970s*. Raleigh, NC: Two Morrows.
Schopenhauer, A. (1966). *The world as will and representation vol. 1* (E.F.J. Payne, Trans.) New York: Dover. (Original work published 1819)
Siegel, D. (Director). (1971). *Dirty Harry* [Film]. United States: The Malpaso Company.
Sodaro, R.J. (2012). *Punisher: The official index to the Marvel Universe*. Chelsea, MI: Sheridan Books.
Tieri, F., & Azaceta, P. (2009). *Punisher noir*. New York: Marvel Comics.
Vlastelica, R. (2018, March 6). *Neither Death Wish film dares to grapple with the anti-vigilante stance of the novel*. AVClub. https://www.avclub.com/neither-death-wish-film-dares-to-grapple-with-the-anti-1823498155.
Winner, M. (Director). (1974). *Death wish* [Film]. United States: Paramount Pictures.
Wood, W. (Ed.). (1967). *witzend*, #3. New York: Wallace Wood.
Worcester, K. (2012). The Punisher and the politics of retributive justice. *Law Text Culture*, 16, 329–352. https://ro.uow.edu.au/cgi/viewcontent.cgi?referer=https://www.google.com/&httpsredir=1&article=1299&context=ltc.

Determined to Punish
Three Case Studies in Punishment

MATTHEW J. MCENIRY

The Punisher (Frank Castle) is a simple character with simple motives. He has a black and white outlook on life and morality. Anyone who strays too far from this moral code eventually ends up in his sights. He is not a typical superhero; his methods are far blunter and more direct. He is a soldier in a much different war of his own making. He is a weapon that is needed but not often utilized. He's not a team player, in fact Steven Grant explained that he wanted the Punisher "to be the absolute pariah of the Marvel Universe. He doesn't like to minimize his control of a situation..." (Novick, 1994, p. 11). Control is what the Punisher craves because the one constant of his origin story is that control was taken away from him. Whether he's a soldier from Vietnam or Afghanistan, the loss of his family was out of his control. He wasn't able to save them like he saved the men he had fought with, he couldn't see the ambush coming, and he was left helpless and alone. That event transformed him into the anti-hero that appears in the comics today. It made sure that the one constant trait that he desires above all else is the ability to punish those that hurt the innocent.

The Punisher's version of punishment is usually swift and deadly. Co-creator Gerry Conway points out that "he was the first modern comics 'hero' who ever made a name for himself by pulling a trigger" (Conway, 1994, p. 9). This overwhelming urge to punish, however, has allowed the Punisher to find himself in unique circumstances in various storylines. This essay looks at the Punisher's role as the host for the Venom symbiote, and how Frank Castle uses it for punishment and vengeance through absolute control. This control is very different from the other two soldiers who once bonded with the same symbiote, Flash Thompson and Lee Price. Yet another story to be analyzed is Castle's involvement with Hydra and his acquiring of the War Machine armor which highlights his desire for redemption through power and punishment. Finally, Frank Castle's psyche will be tested and driven to the brink of madness as the Cosmic Ghost Rider because of his desperation to inflict punishment on the cosmic beings who killed everything he wanted to protect. These three unique stories offer an intense look into the will of the Punisher's legacy and character.

The Venom symbiote has had two official hosts that were soldiers in the Iraq War. Flash Thompson was a heroic Army veteran (*The Amazing Spider-Man* #574) who used the symbiote as a military asset (*The Amazing Spider-Man* #654 & #654.1), a secret Avenger (*Secret Avengers* #23), and a Thunderbolt member (*Thunderbolts Vol 2* #1). Thompson would be hunted down by the FBI using anti-symbiote weaponry to recover the symbiote, but only managed to separate it from him and send it into a feral state (*Venom* #150). Venom did not immediately return to Flash because of its shame at enjoying the feelings of being bloodthirsty and angry (Costa, 2017). However, it would remember the actions and persona of Flash by wanting to remain a hero and do good in the world. Lee Price was an ex-Army Ranger who was haunted by his internal demons (*Venom Vol 3* #3). When Venom found Price, he regretted the decision, this was not a heroic soldier that he had chosen, but someone who abused his power for their own benefit. Lee made Venom a prisoner by removing the partnership of a symbiote and host and focusing mainly on what he wanted to accomplish. Venom was explicitly clear that it did not enjoy that type of control being exerted (Costa, 2017b). His motivations would eventually lead him to attempt to create a power vacuum and become the leader of a powerful criminal syndicate. Lee would continue to ignore Venom's feelings and voice, using his own painful memories to silence the arguments from the symbiote. When Venom tries to use these memories against him, Lee threatens to "lock you somewhere that'll do real damage" (Costa, 2017c). Lee eventually loses control of Venom because the symbiote desires to be a hero once again, "Lee causes too much needless death" (Costa, 2017d). But he's resistant and insists that he's stronger than Venom, only when the symbiote shows him that he's broken inside, the real reason why he killed his parents, and why he's afraid & alone does Lee relent and find himself in custody (2017d).

This version of Venom is not the one that we see in the issue *What If? ... Venom had possessed the Punisher?* The version that attaches to Frank Castle at the church where Spider-Man gets rid of the symbiote is much more about getting vengeance than being heroic. Even though Venom may have heroism in its DNA after its time with Spider-Man, Castle's will is stronger (Costa, 2017a). Castle finds that Venom responds to his thoughts and finds he is in control. At first, he believes it to be a S.H.I.E.L.D. suit. He employs its shapeshifting abilities to get closer to his targets. He finds out that it shoots webbing but complains that it doesn't do any damage. Castle has inspiration and wonders aloud, "If it can do webbing—can it do bullets?" (Busiek, 1992). Now he has mastery over symbiotic bullets. His "methods grow more brutal and vicious with each passing day" (such as killing mobsters that surrender), but unlike Spider-Man, "he doesn't seem to care" (1992). The reader sees that the Punisher is taking a back seat to the symbiote, as it's putting him to sleep and controlling the narrative at night. This is clear when Micro starts to tell Castle about the possible dangers of this living suit followed by his being smashed against a crate for his concern by an angry Venom. Soon, a confrontation between Spider-Man and the Punisher occurs during one of these night episodes and Venom is about to kill the web crawler. The Punisher stops this using his will and prevents the symbiote from getting his revenge. The Punisher regains control over the suit and doesn't have any idea how it got away from him (1992).

Although he's faced with the possibility, he's no longer in control presently, he ignores those thoughts and goes out to hunt Tombstone, a new Kingpin associate. The Punisher succeeds in defeating this villain by biting his head off and, despite a defense mounted by Typhoid Mary and Daredevil, manages to throw Kingpin out a window to his death. Daredevil knows that something is amiss with the Punisher, as he is able to detect an accelerated heartbeat and slurred speech (1992). Castle is tired and losing control to the symbiote. Castle doesn't go back to rest, but "he prowls the city, the alien manipulating and distorting his hunter's instincts, channeling them toward one specific target—Spider-Man" (1992). However, when the target isn't found the symbiote must bend to the Punisher's highly directed mind and goes back to hunting criminals (1992). Eventually, Spider-Man, Daredevil, and Moon Knight mount an offensive against the Punisher and using a sonic gun disable the alien menace. This is the moment that Castle has been waiting for and is able to bargain with the symbiote for control.

> "It's real simple: Obey my orders—do everything I tell you, instantly—and I'll let you live. Don't—and I'll kill you. Even if I have to kill myself to get you. One time offer—take it or leave it" [1992].

The symbiote is reluctant at first, but it can see the breadth of what Castle is capable of and makes a choice. The Punisher confirms this by saying:

> "My war's nothing if I'm not in control. I'm nothing. And my war is more important to me than my life. It can see into my mind. It knows I'm serious. It doesn't have complete focus. It wants Spider-Man dead, but it also wants life, adventure, the thrill of the hunt. It makes the right choice" [1992].

To end the confrontation and any further argument, the Punisher states, "It's over; It works for me now" (1992). The other heroes must take his word for it, because they don't have the guts to kill him. The issue ends with the narrator asking the reader if they could believe that the Punisher tames Venom and turns it into an instrument of, if not justice, then vengeance.

Between these two stories of exerting control over the Venom symbiote, we can see that Frank Castle is overwhelmingly stronger in will and mind than Lee Price. Though ruthless in his own sense, Price is haunted by the memories of his childhood and his attempts to be stronger than the symbiote are only attempts. Venom gets out of his mental prison several times during Price's six-issue arc and each time is punished severely for it. The final time that Venom defies his host is for a reunification with the heroic Spider-Man, and even though it is ultimately a trick, it's for the betterment of the symbiote. Price threatens to kill it, but it's an empty gesture because Price does not want to die either. This is especially evident when he is faced with death many years later at the hands of Carnage (Cates, Ahmed, Taylor, 2019). Frank Castle's resolve is absolute, he has a war that he is fighting and is committed to the cause. All his effort would be wasted if he wasn't in control, he shows Venom his resolve and the symbiote, as angry at Spider-Man and wanting revenge against him, realizes that it would rather serve than die. The Punisher of the world of "What If?" is able to punish his enemies through vengeance and control—something Lee Price was incapable of accomplishing.

Transitioning back to the current Earth-616 timeline (this is the official timeline of the Marvel comics universe overall), the 2017 series *Secret Empire*, introduces a Punisher that is working for the evil organization Hydra. Frank Castle is devoted to a soldier he's looked up to his entire life, Captain America. This time an evil version of Steve Rogers, the symbol of American patriotism and democracy, has been turned into the Supreme Commander of Hydra. Faced with a moral quandary, the Punisher is offered "a safer world—an army to wage the same war I've been fighting my whole damn life. A way to finally win it" (Spencer, 2017a). When other heroes ask him how he could be on the wrong side, he says he's never been on their side. He states, "He's right [Rogers] about you all. You were too weak. Too afraid to do what had to be done. Hydra will, though. I've seen it" (2017a). The Punisher is wholly convinced that Hydra's methods will give him a world that is better, free from the scum that he's been pursuing since the death of his family. There's also some naivety in his beliefs, an idealism that Hydra will do right by the world. He wants Hydra's version of the world too badly and overlooks some of Hydra's worse traits. When it all comes crashing down and the Hydra version of Steve Rogers is imprisoned, Castle sets out on his own and starts to kill Hydra agents to attempt to redemption. Reflecting on his past decisions he says:

"I've made plenty of mistakes in this life. Too many to count. This here might be the worst of them though. I was tricked—manipulated by the one man I thought I could trust. Now it's time to make things right" [Spencer, 2017b].

Watching from the shadows, Nick Fury sees an opportunity that will give Frank Castle the means and abilities to punish a new target and allow him to seek his own redemption. He directs the Punisher to steal the War Machine armor and take out the military leader, Petrov, in a country going through a power struggle of sorts—Chernaya (Rosenberg, 2018a). Outfitted with one of the most powerful pieces of tech in the world, the Punisher goes on a mission to take out rogue S.H.I.E.L.D. agents, eliminate Petrov, and perhaps gain some goodwill. It doesn't necessarily go quite to plan.

His mission begins by saving a few isolated citizens as he gets used to his new armor and weapon systems. He starts to liberate re-education camps to draw out the important pieces of the mission and ends up fighting ex-S.H.I.E.L.D agents clad in similar Stark suit technology. The first challenge the Punisher faces is this duel with overwhelming odds and a young agent is overconfident, mocking him with, "You should've known not to use equipment you aren't trained on. But I guess old people forget that stuff" (Rosenberg, 2018b). The Punisher retorts with, "You young guys never learn. Equipment doesn't matter. Only thing that matters is…. A willingness to do what the other guy won't" (2018b). With those words the Punisher mashes his fingers through the agent's skull. It is a gruesome panel that highlights the lengths that the Punisher will go for the mission. He is not going to give up when faced with adversity. He won't be labeled an old man not fit for fighting. He is entering in this new world of high-tech with a sense of determination and focus, not showing off like the agents he has been tasked to take down. However, despite his attempts to escape the ambush, he is faced with a life-threatening situation at the bottom of the ocean.

The third issue of the story shows fishermen bringing up the suit and the Punisher quickly needing to get to land because "I've got people to kill" (Rosenberg, 2018c). Ever the driven individual that needs revenge, Castle has only one thing on his mind as he finds someone to repair "his" armor. Already thinking of it as his has some interesting effects on how others will treat him later. As writer Matthew Rosenburg states, "We gave him the War Machine Armor, but he's not becoming War Machine. He could never. War Machine is James Rhodes, a hero, an Avenger, something to aspire to. Frank is simply The Punisher, nothing more and nothing less" (2017a).

As Castle becomes more attached to the abilities and enhancements of this armor, audiences will see his actions become more radical, aspiring to a superhero, but in the end it's not out of a heroic destiny but out of necessity. Castle takes the fight to Petrov's men, systematically taking out high ranking members of his cadre. Despite Fury ordering him out of the country, due to Petrov's claims that he has control of the country's nukes, Castle refuses because the mission is not yet complete. He goes to Petrov's speech to the world to punish him, killing most of his men, eliminating the ex-S.H.I.E.L.D. agents, stopping a launched nuke and cutting up Petrov, who has his own suit of armor, by exposing weak points in his armor with a knife. Mission completed, Frank Castle is labeled a terrorist because of his wanton destruction and killing of a recognized world leader. Due to his high profile in the world, he heads back to where he can do the most good—New York City (Rosenberg, 2018d).

The Punisher's time spent in New York City is not welcomed by most of the heroes, including an angry Captain Marvel. She fights the Punisher early in the series, preventing him from killing some heavy hitting criminals. After escaping that confrontation, he must face Daredevil's scrutiny on his return. Both highlight his involvement in Hydra and how they have not forgotten—no one has. In response to a retort by the Punisher about him cleaning up the streets in her dead boyfriend's armor, Captain Marvel states, "Were you this righteous when you were murdering people for Hydra? When the fascists took over, some of us fought … but you couldn't get in line fast enough. You @#$% traitor!" (Rosenberg, 2018e). Daredevil also points out that new opportunities Castle refers to is a weak ploy, "You worked for Hydra, Frank. Maybe they tricked you or offered you something you needed, but that doesn't change it. You backed the bad guys. Even by your rule book, that has to have consequences, right?" (2018e).

Both Captain Marvel and Daredevil point out characteristics that are true, but the Punisher believes that the armor is a chance for redemption in his mind. It's true, he took the offer from Hydra to inflict punishment on those who deserved it, but they also tricked him in how they presented the facts. The Punisher doesn't like being in situations where he feels weak or foolish, it's obviously something he has to own up to, but it's a difficult road and every hero in New York is going to let him know how difficult. More heroes team up to take down the Punisher, track him to his hideout, and confront him in a battle where he escapes and leads them on a chase across the city.

Eventually, he confronts Nick Fury who warns him that he's a danger to everyone around him, "how long until you accidentally [blow up a school]? Firing missiles all over the place" (Rosenberg, 2018f). Fury reminds him that before the armor heroes could ignore the guy with a gun because superheroes existed in the world. But now that he has an equalizer, he can no longer be ignored. The other heroes want to see the tables turned on Castle. Fury tries to get this point across by saying, "You joined Hydra, you %$#@. There's no gray on this. Nobody wants to see you get the benefit of the doubt. You're the bad guy. They want to see you punished" (2018f). Castle responds, "But now with the armor I can.... I want to fix it" (2018f). But Fury only sees the solution being him turning himself in, an ending that Castle does not envision for himself. He doesn't want to believe that he had been naïve or corrupted by Hydra. Castle believes that if he eliminates enough of the Hydra organization, he can avoid the punishment he is due. He has been doing that since the dissolution of Hydra, he figures he can continue it with much more success now that he is a walking tank. He will continue to use the armor as an equalizer for him as long as he's able. He wants to hunt the rest of Hydra for redemption.

In a confrontation with Baron Zemo, he is nearly killed, but saved by a group of heroes. Revealing his plan to kill the rest of Hydra, Black Widow and Bucky subdue the other heroes and team up with the Punisher to accomplish this task (Rosenberg, 2018g). This leads to the prison where the Supreme Commander Rogers is held, and they break in. Captain Marvel and other heroes have followed the Punisher but are distracted by released prisoners and their attention is divided. Iron Man confronts the Punisher in armor with familiar lines, "I had my way, you wouldn't even be allowed to look at anything of Rhodey's. You're a serial killer. You backed Hydra" (Rosenberg, 2018h). Castle creates a situation that Stark must deal with immediately and is free to pursue Zemo's helicopter. Zemo compliments the Punisher on his determination, but laments that he's still a traitor to Hydra. To highlight his determination, Castle shocks himself with a live wire to incapacitate an intruding Zemo and Ghost, and is about to put them in the ground, when he is interrupted by a persistent Iron Man.

The Punisher pushes himself to the limit and subdues Iron Man with a spray of bullets. Too focused to notice anything else, the huge form of the Manticore tank (a specialized vehicle with flight and submersible capabilities able to take down aircraft, armor, and people with pinpoint precision [Manticore (Vehicle), n.d.]) fills the panel and forcefully subdues the angry vigilante. A very much alive Colonel James Rhodes steps out and has some choice words for a frustrated Castle.

> You've been out here banging up my friends, messing up my suit. I can't have that. That suit is bigger than you. It means a lot of things to a lot of people. And that's not what you've been doing with it [2018h].

Surrounded by heroes and broken by words from a veteran, Frank Castle takes off the War Machine armor and surrenders to the authorities. Perhaps the most insidious line spoken is by the re-apprehended Supreme Commander Rogers, "[Zemo] doesn't think much of you. But I hope you know I do. And there's still room on the team if you want to come back" (2018h). Did the Punisher rid himself of the Hydra influence enough through his actions or did he merely show the world that he was incapable of stopping his violence no matter whose side he was on? In the end, it seems he convinced Bucky and Natasha enough for them to break him out of prison. They will resume the hunt against Hydra, and Frank will continue to seek redemption and take out those in Hydra who deceived him.

The final transformation of Frank Castle spans the issues of *Thanos* #13–18, starting with an abduction of a younger Thanos by a Ghost Rider character, to go millions of years into the future to meet an older Thanos (Cates, 2018a). The story is a tribute to Death, the one mistress that has eluded Thanos for millennia, but the sixteenth issue is devoted to this Cosmic Ghost Rider–Frank Castle. During the last battle for earth, Thanos is fighting the last of the heroes and the Punisher is involved. After a particularly grueling encounter, Castle is hit by falling masonry and is mortally wounded. His dying thoughts centered around one thing, "I would give anything to punish that purple sonofabitch" (Cates, 2018b). The universe, specifically Mephisto, replied, "Anything?" And so, "Frank Castle signed his first demonic deal … and became the Ghost Rider: Spirit of Vengeance" (2018b).

Despite his deal, he wandered an empty Earth for millennia, which caused "Frank Castle rather … aggressively … to lose his mind" (2018b). Finally, the Devourer, Galactus, arrived at Earth, seeking protection and asylum from Thanos. Upon realizing that Earth was destroyed and there was no help, Frank offered him a deal before he left. He bargained for becoming Galactus' "Herald and hook me up with them crazy cosmic powers and all a'that … and together we can go Punish that purple @#$% together" (2018b). Frank offered up Earth as a meal for Galactus to seal the deal, it was deserted anyways so what did it matter. To this end, "Frank Castle made his second deal with the Devil, in as many lifetimes … to become Ghost Rider: Herald of Galactus" (2018b). Together they inspired hope across a destruction ridden galaxy, "that even in the darkest of days … the heartbeat of a hero still beat inside of the chest of a dead man" (2018). Everything seemed to be going their way until their confrontation with Thanos, when Galactus' head was punched off and used as a decoration.

Thanos then offers the Cosmic Ghost Rider a deal, "I cannot kill you. You cannot defeat me. But you come with me, rider, and at my side, I will show you more evil than you can punish in a thousand lifetimes" (2018b). This was a bargain that the Punisher, no matter how twisted and maddened, could not refuse. "With that, Frank Castle made his third and final deal with the devil … [and] became Ghost Rider: Black Right-Hand of the Mad King Thanos" (2018b). In this role Frank Castle would do Thanos' bidding up until Castle's death at the hands of the other herald, the Silver Surfer. Odin transports Castle to Valhalla only to soon send him back to a timeline of his choosing. Odin realizes that Castle does not deserve to be in Valhalla, he's not at rest, and suspect he never will be. He'll spend his eternity fulfilling some vengeful task, and if he doesn't want to be in Valhalla, then Odin can't keep him there, so he sends Castle back with all his powers to a timeline of his choosing (Cates, 2018c). The Cosmic Ghost Rider attempts to right his wrongs and goes to Titan to kill a baby Thanos (2018c). He could not remove an innocent, however, because it went against everything he stood for, so he tried to raise the Mad Titan baby as his own, but that ended up going poorly and he killed a young Thanos before it all got out of control. The entire history of the Marvel Universe is called into question during *Cosmic Ghost Rider Destroys Marvel History*, but we learn a vital fact for this entire Punisher story. The one constant that cannot be changed or modified is the death of Frank Castle's family. With how involved the Punisher and all his transformations are to the Marvel Universe, changing that would cause untold consequences. Even with time travel on his side, Frank Castle himself is punished by Uatu the Watcher (a member of a technologically superior race which observes and records, without interfering, the lives of other races for the purpose of sharing them with each other [Uatu (Earth-616), n.d.]) by having to helplessly watch his family die again and not be able to intervene (Scheer, 2019). With all the power that he has, he is rendered powerless to prevent their murders. If all the previous events of the Cosmic Ghost Rider did not drive him into madness, this one surely did.

These three transformations that Frank Castle willingly accepts— Venom, War Machine armor, and Cosmic Ghost Rider—all arise from his need to be the Punisher. They were done for different purposes: an enhancement on his current abilities, a role that he sought for redemption, and through bargains of desperation. They all are tied together because of the character's need to punish the bad and protect the good. When it is said that the Punisher is a simple character, it is speaking to how predictable he'll be in any given situation. Matthew Rosenberg talks about Frank being a difficult character to write because, "he has a set of rules that most readers understand … challenging those rules and surprising readers is the real trick" (2018b). It's because of his predictability that calls for the necessity of the crazy to engage a reader. However, Rosenberg also states, "at the end of the day, Frank … is just a man with a gun who kills people he thinks deserves it" (2018a). The motive of the character is static, and these three storylines offer up a challenging perspective for readers to engage with his progression.

The aspect of absolute control is very important for Frank Castle, especially in the *What If?* issue. The focus and determination that Baron Zemo points out in the War Machine series is illustrated perfectly here, as the Punisher mentally wrestles with the symbiote in a dream like state, declaring that he'll have no problem killing himself if he can't control the war that he's fighting. Currently, the Venom symbiote is one of the most formidable enemies of Spider-Man. This is not the broken and conflicted Venom that we see in the Lee Price story. Its main drive is to take revenge on Spider-Man, which is why its original host of Eddie Brock was so effective. The Punisher's resolve in controlling Venom speaks to his dedication and devotion to his war on criminals, his reliance on the gear that he uses, and his desire to complete the mission no matter what. Compared to each other, neither of the other soldiers that controlled Venom ever had complete mastery over the symbiote like Frank Castle would.

During the Hydra story we see a Frank Castle who wants to be a part of the war he started so much that he joined up with the bad guys. He tries to shake off the deception and trickery he endured by completing a mission for the good guys. He wants this so badly that he oversteps his bounds and kills a recognized world leader. Now a terrorist, he seeks redemption back home in New York, but that is the place redemption will never come for him. The rest of the heroes who fought against Hydra want to see the Punisher punished. Castle's journey through adversity is met with many problems, and he is always able to solve these with the power of the War Machine armor or his natural ingenuity. It is only when he faces the owner of the armor, James Rhodes, that he realizes this rampage through New York has been more about his own war than the war against crime. For one moment he's able to see beyond his rage and take accountability, even if he doesn't face the consequences.

Finally, the Cosmic Ghost Rider presents us with a version of Frank Castle who stays true to his character's core values. "Punish" is the key word for all the deals that Castle makes with Mephisto, Galactus, and Thanos. For thousands of years he wages wars and punishes those in who his master finds injustice. It is an odd place for Frank Castle to be because he's serving someone other than himself, but as long as he's in a position to punish he's satisfied. It also helps that he is gone completely insane, to the point of breaking the 4th wall in *Thanos Annual Vol. 2 #1* (Cates, 2018d). In all these bargains there's a desperation coming from Castle, the thought that his targets might escape his punishment that they deserve. This scares him and puts him in a position of needing a higher power to intervene and give him powers to complete a mission, even if the cost is unimaginable. This really illustrates Castle's utmost determination and desperation to punish even if it results in desperation, servitude, and madness.

These three journeys that Frank Castle embarks on in different stories helps show that the character is a simple solution to complex problems. His moral code and how he deals with problems is very black and white. There is no gray area with the Punisher. But there are situations that can confound him, fool him, and take advantage of his determination. Anyone who is defined by one event so fervently and pursues a course of action so defiantly will eventually meet an end that is unsatisfactory. They may end up as an irrational, undead herald for a mad titan. Either way, as Rosenberg alluded to, these Punisher stories give readers a way to enjoy a scenario that challenges the boundaries of the Punisher in story lines that normally would not be possible. For that reason, the readers can appreciate the Punisher's absolute drive to punish.

References

Busiek, K. (1992). *What if…Venom had possessed The Punisher vol. 2, #44*. New York: Marvel Comics.
Cates, D. (2018a) *Thanos vol. 2, #13*. New York: Marvel Comics.
Cates, D. (2018b) *Thanos vol. 2, #16*. New York: Marvel Comics.
Cates, D. (2018c) *Cosmic ghost rider vol. 1, #1*. New York: Marvel Comics.
Cates, D. (2018d) *Thanos annual vol. 2, #1*. New York: Marvel Comics.
Cates, D., Ahmed, S., & Taylor, T. (2019). *Free comic book day vol. 2019 Spider-Man/Venom*. New York: Marvel Comics.
Conway, G. (1994, February). War files. *The Punisher anniversary magazine: A Marvel age special, 1*(1), 8–9.
Costa, M. (2017a). *Venom vol. 1, #150*. New York: Marvel Comics.
Costa, M. (2017b). *Venom vol. 3, #1*. New York: Marvel Comics.
Costa, M. (2017c). *Venom vol. 3, #4*. New York: Marvel Comics.
Costa, M. (2017d). *Venom vol. 3, #5*. New York: Marvel Comics.
Costa, M. (2017e). *Venom vol. 3, #6*. New York: Marvel Comics.
Manticore (vehicle). (n.d.). Fandom: Marvel database. https://marvel.fandom.com/wiki/Manticore_(Vehicle)
Novick, G.A. (1994, February). New year's revolution. *The Punisher anniversary magazine: A Marvel age special, 1*(1), 10–14.
Rosenberg, M. (2018a). *Punisher vol. 1, #218*. New York: Marvel Comics.
Rosenberg, M. (2018b). *Punisher vol. 1, #220*. New York: Marvel Comics.
Rosenberg, M. (2018c). *Punisher vol. 1, #221*. New York: Marvel Comics.
Rosenberg, M. (2018d). *Punisher vol. 1, #223*. New York: Marvel Comics.
Rosenberg, M. (2018e). *Punisher vol. 1, #224*. New York: Marvel Comics.
Rosenberg, M. (2018f). *Punisher vol. 1, #225*. New York: Marvel Comics.
Rosenberg, M. (2018g). *Punisher vol. 1, #226*. New York: Marvel Comics.
Rosenberg, M. (2018h). *Punisher vol. 1, #228*. New York: Marvel Comics.
Scheer, P., & Giovanetti, N. (2019). *Cosmic Ghost Rider destroys Marvel history vol. 1, #3*. New York: Marvel Comics.
Spencer, N. (2017a). *Secret empire vol. 1, #5*. New York: Marvel Comics.
Spencer, N. (2017b). *Secret empire omega vol. 1, #1*. New York: Marvel Comics.
Uatu (Earth-616). (n.d.). Fandom: Marvel database. https://marvel.fandom.com/wiki/Uatu_(Earth-616)

Section II
Gender and Feminism

The Punisher as Female
A Thought Experiment
ALICIA M. GOODMAN

> But in this Court, what Diff'rence does appear!
> For every one's both Judge and Jury here;
> Nay, and what's worse, an Executioner.
> —William Congreve, *The Double-Dealer*,
> Epilogue, 1693

> "The man who passes the sentence should swing the sword. If you would take a man's life, you owe it to him to look into his eyes and hear his final words. And if you cannot bear to do that, then perhaps the man does not deserve to die."
> —Eddard "Ned" Stark, *Game of Thrones*, S1 Ep1,
> April 17, 2011

Many of the big-name canon superheroes have an opposite-gender counterpart: Superman has Supergirl, Batman has Batgirl and Batwoman, Iron Man has Iron Woman/Heart, Venom has She-Venom, Captain Marvel has Ms. Marvel, Hulk has She-Hulk, Captain America has American Dream, Aquaman has Aquagirl, and the list continues. However, not every canon character has a gender-equivalent counterpart, such as Marvel's the Punisher. Frank Castle's gender-equivalent is considered to be Cossandra Castle from Kirkman's *Marvel Knights 2099: Punisher* #1, since she is his (and Elektra Natchios's) daughter and has a tragic backstory: has been diagnosed with cancer and is dying. However, Cossandra Castle she is not an equivalent: while she is known for her agility, marksmanship, unarmed combat skills, and weapon mastery, she is not nearly as prolific nor is she the judge-jury-executioner that is the Punisher.

This character appears only one time: in *Marvel Knights 2099*, which is a part of the Earth-2992 storyline (Krikman, 2004), and not to be confused with the Pat Mills and Tony Skinner's early 1990s *Punisher 2099* storyline. In the *Marvel Knights 2099* storyline, Cossandra is given a tragic *current* story, rather than a tragic backstory: her recent diagnosis of a terminal illness is a catalyst for her to retire from her role as the Punisher and pass the mantle to her son, Franklin Natchios. The teen does not want to kill and refuses his dying mother's wish; with Cossandra's death, the Punisher dies as well.

How can Cossandra Castle be considered a female Punisher equivalent if she only appears one time in the comic Marvel universe? Additionally, without a storyline that demonstrates the character in action, how can she be deemed a female Punisher according to the Marvel Database and Wiki? There is no evidence to reveal if she indeed has similar specialized military training and moral compass of her father, Frank Castle. If Cossandra is not a true equal gender-equivalent of the Punisher, what would it take for her to be considered so? This essay seeks to breakdown elements that make up gender-equivalent characters through the lens of visual representation, stage combat experience/theory, psychology of violence, culture, and story to determine why a true female gender-equivalent Punisher does not exist in the contemporary Marvel comic universe, and what it would take for a character to be considered female gender-equivalent Punisher.

Gender

Please note, the author is discussing gender in terms of a binary; however, she recognizes that is problematic since gender is a spectrum. While there are transgender, agender, and genderfluid characters in the Marvel Universe, most are non-human, supporting, and/or underdeveloped characters. For this essay, the author is specifically addressing a gender binary, not because transgender, agender, and genderfluid characters do not apply, but rather because there are no examples of these characters where a fair and well-thought out analysis could occur (whether characters in the Punisher series or the greater Marvel comic universe). Additionally, Marvel does have a lack of a strong superheroine/supervillain, as acknowledged by Marvel Comic's former Editor-in-Chief, Axel Alonso, as there is no immediately recognizable female leading character to the general public (Hudson, 2011); thus, this essay focuses on female-identifying characters.

It is also important to note that the terms "sex" and "gender" are not interchangeable as these have different meanings: "sex" refers to a biological set of organs, and "gender" is a set societal constructs of how a particular gender is expected to behave (Planned Parenthood, n.d.).

Therefore, to be a gender-equivalent counterpart, for the purpose of this particular analysis, a character must identify on the other end of the gender spectrum as the original superhero. They must also be of the "opposite" sex; thus, by positioning the superheroes as opposites, analysis can play with expectations of gender and sex.

Familial Bond

The similarities between male/female iterations of superheroes are necessary for viewers to accept the familial bond that inherently exists when family bamboo grows into a family tree (implying that a singular hero is a bamboo shoot, but once there is an expansion, there is a family tree). To clarify, the phrase "familial bond" can mean, but is not limited to, blood or adopted relationships. Here, familial bond refers to the characters in the comic universe that are linked due to a name. For example, viewers recognize that a super-being with "Super" as a prefix is likely related to Superman (e.g., Supergirl, Superwoman, Superdog, etc.). Having never previously read a Superman comic or watched a Superman television show/film, a consumer of this culture could immediately recognize these other characters as having a relationship with, or are related to, Superman. This literacy of superhero culture turns what is a fictional reality into a "real" one (Weiner, 2009). The same holds true for marital pairs (Mr. and Mrs.) or a gendered pair, usually with the original character bearing the name, and the later female iteration having the honorific "Lady" or Mrs./Ms./Miss added before the name, or "girl" (or "woman") added to the end of the base character's name.

The next element of familial bond for gender-opposite characters, on a more superficial level, is similar visual appearances. The similarities can be repeated symbols (a yellow star emblazoned across the male/female heroes' chest), varying garments with echoed colored schemes (ripped purple shorts versus ripped purple skirt/dress) or even exact replication (red and yellow armor with a power source in the chest). Would Riri Williams (Ironheart) be considered akin to Iron Man if she did not reverse-engineer one of his suits to wear—what if she built a new suit with a different type of power source?

The third familial counterpart element is special abilities. Gender-equivalent counterparts often have extremely similar capabilities or powers, if not the very same abilities. Would viewers accept "May 'Mayday' Parker" Spider-Girl as having the powers of her father if she did not have the Spidey sense? Of course, this would be a hereditary connection. Clones (e.g., Wolverine and X-23) would also fall into this category due to their namesake. Similar abilities also apply when a shared genome is not present. For example, Thor Girl transforms herself into an Asgardian and is able to wield the powers of the hammer as Thor is able to. She fights alongside Thor but is not his wife/girlfriend/daughter/sister/etc. She still shares the familial bond because of her name and abilities.

Beyond birth-inherited and similar abilities, a visual resemblance based on costume, and something in common with a name, there is one more element that is necessary for a gender-equivalent iteration of a character to be considered a true counterpart to a superhero: the way they fight and why. Alternate universe storylines aside, the gender-equivalent counterpart is similar to the original superhero in behavior, more specifically, how and why they fight. A gender-equivalent character who has watered-down skills is not an equal. On the other hand, a gender-equivalent character that possesses skills far beyond the base character, also is not equal. Thus, a Goldilocks Syndrome must be at play: not too much, not too little, the powers must be just right (re: mostly equal). A variance in powers is acceptable, perhaps the base character is stronger, but the gender-equivalent character is faster, but these powers cannot have enough variance that they are totally unlike and without a familial bond to the base character.

As for Cossandra, there is a demonstrated familial bond only in name and visual iconology on her costume. However, the familiar bond in name is masked by Cossandra: in *Marvel Knights 2099: Punisher #1* (Krikman, 2004), Cossandra has adopted by her mother's surname (Natchios) and renounced "Castle" due it its infamous connection to her father, the original Punisher (*ibid.*). Conversely, Cossandra's clothing follows Frank's uniform: black and a giant skull on the chest (of course, the skull on Cossandra's top is placed in such a way that the orbital sockets encompass her breasts, thereby reminding the view that she is indeed a woman). She also wears elbow pads (a deviation) in conjunction with her v-neck tank top, pants, and smart-looking boots appropriate for athletic treks. The comic comments on Cossandra's fighting abilities, but the exact details of how Cossandra carried on her father's mantle is unknown other than Frank and Elektra told Cossandra about "this responsibility" (Krikman, 2004). Thus, there is a missing element to the familial bond aspect between Frank Castle and Cossandra: a demonstration of their powers (fighting and violence) for comparison. To analyze this element, an understanding of fighting styles between males and females is necessary.

Violence Among Males and Females

There are key differences between male and female violence. The first difference is how participants *engage* in violence. There is a common perception of how male and female children in the United States fight, as well as clinical studies analyzing the prevalence of fighting between genders. Rudatsikira, Muula, and Siziya (2014) found that, in the United States, school-aged males are more likely to engage in interpersonal violence (fighting) as compared to females. Additionally, research, especially in crisis intervention, has determined predictors and behavioral differences between genders when it comes to fighting in schools (Crisis Consulting Group, n.d.). For example, think of an afterschool fight at the flagpole/playground/etc., between boys—these fights are surprisingly organized (*ibid.*); the combatants either planned the time and location together, or one informed the other of the details. Either way, the combatants have two options: show up or hide. Hiding can result in postponement, a manhunt leading to a fight, or, on occasion, the opportunity to forget about it and walk away. Showing up, on the other hand, means both combatants fighting, one fighting and one getting hurt, or calling the fight off, much to the chagrin of the large encircled crowd. When thinking about combatants who show up to a fight, what usually ensues is a peacocking of bravado and the inevitable circling of opponents (*ibid.*). During this preshow, there is often dialogue intended to provoke the other—"Come at me, bro!"—into action. This verbal volleying serves a purpose: attempt to deescalate the situation—neither wants to be the first to strike. Verbal volley delays action and this delay may result in a school official breaking up the fight, or friends stepping in to talk the situation down. Combatants' pride gets bruised, but both parties get in a few verbal shots and do not actually have to fight one another. Overall, when males fight, there are several instances for de-escalation built-in to the series of events leading up to the fight and even in the fight itself.

Now, consider a school fight between girls. Wherever the fight is going to happen is not an advertised affair (*ibid.*); there is no option to show up or hide because the fight is brought about seemingly spontaneously (*ibid.*). Fights between girls occur in bathrooms or randomly in the halls; there is no time to prepare or flee. Additionally, given the pouncing nature of the first attack, there is no prefight circling/verbal volley/talk down occurring. Attacks are calculated and quick and there is no opportunity for deescalate (*ibid.*).

So, why is there a difference in fighting styles of males and females? Some scholars suggest that the variation can be traced to a more primitive time where males were providers (Geary, 2019)—they fought/killed when absolutely necessary as they could not risk injury/death since the female(s) and children that depended on him would be unprotected; for males, avoiding fighting was in their best interest—a fight lost equals death, injury, or losing a prominent spot in the tribe. On the other side, females were the caretakers (*ibid.*)—if there was an immediate threat to her or her children's safety, her job was to end the situation by any means to protect her charges; it would not make sense for a female to announce her attack—she could use the element of surprise to her advantage. In summation, males de-escalate and are not quick to resort to action and females pounce at random. This difference of strategy and execution is also seen in males and females in the greater mammalian world (e.g., lions, baboons, wolves, bears and so on). Geary (2019) posits that these gendered differences in violence/fighting exist in both children and adults. Additionally, he states that these behaviors have evolved and still exist in present day "civilized" societies: conflict has been supplanted with competition (physical and mental) and social relationships. It should be notes that social relationships and competition are bound by the society that constructs and reinforces gender expectations.

Cultural Conditioning

Something else to consider when looking at male versus female in terms of fighting is cultural differences. Macro-culturally, dominate fighting modalities can be seen in popular martial arts styles. There are parts of the world where fighting with punches is popular (see boxing in the UK and U.S.). In other parts of the globe, punches are substituted with kicks (see capoeira in Brazil). Still yet there are areas that utilize found-weapons over the body alone, such as in the Philippines, where Filipino stick fighting (also known as Kali stick fighting) is a dangerous martial art, and, finally, parts of the world where all of the above is mixed into a fighting style, like in Israeli krav maga.

From an anatomy and physiology perspective, male and female children are similar in build and strength capabilities, and this physical similarity can be seen in youth martial art weight classes: generally speaking, youth weight classes are divided in at comparable weights, Apart from sex, youth are seen in similar terms of mass, which correlates to strength; it is not until children begin to approach puberty that physical differences become pronounced and strength is demonstrateable different and significant. Like any physical skill, with training, children can become serious fighters that capitalize on their physical strengths.

As children age, the parts of their bodies they utilize in fighting changes. This change in body part preference can be attributed to anatomy/physiology (males tend to have more upper body strength and females tend to have more lower body strength), but also to the culture in which the child is raised in. Culture that influences children includes toys (e.g., guns/swords), media (e.g., cartoons prominently featuring violence/weapons, versus cartoons featuring friendly animals playing), praise/criticism (e.g., "Be a lady!"), and social constructs. By the time children reach tween/preteen age, there is also a significant variance in the types of sports; there is no female full-tackle sport comparable to football in the United States. Even in powderpuff football, tackling is strictly prohibited at the secondary, collegiate, and intramural levels. While full-tackle female football exists, these leagues have developed on the last twenty years and do not have the same popularity or prestige as the full-tackle male-only NFL or AFL.

Holistically, in the contemporary United States, there is a culture of violence (Nogales, 2018), one in which society grooms males *in particular* to be violent, or at the very least, be accustomed to violence—either through participation or observance (American Psychological Association, 2018; Nogales, 2018; World Health Organization, 2009). Females, on the other hand, are raised to be more nurturing. "Girl" toys like babies, dolls, play kitchens, etc., prepare women to be a mother; as girls become women, society expects them to fulfill a nurturing role. These generalized gender roles are based on long-held gendered stereotypes of young people over the decades specific to the United States. (Planned Parenthood, n.d.; Walker, Bialik, & van Kesse, 2018). While this notion feels antiquated, the gender role expectation still exists in the present-day U.S. A 2017 Pew Research Center study determine prevalent attitudes about being the "breadwinner" of the family versus parenting: 76 percent of males face a lot of pressure to support their family financially, compared to 40 percent females, and 77 percent of females feel pressured to be an involved parent, compared to 49 percent of males.

Women are the "Mother" regardless if they have birthed or adopted children (Fineman & Karpin, 1995). Often in the Marvel-related films, women are relegated to the "slash/mother role": girlfriend/mother (Black Widow and the Hulk or Pepper Potts and Tony Stark), friend/mother (Gamora and Star Lord), sister/mother (Negasonic Teenage Warhead and Deadpool), and so on. These female characters, while not being related to the male they accompany, play part of a caretaking mother to a grown man. Black Widow is literally a caretaker to the Hulk, Gamora is like a schoolmarm reprimanding Star Lord for acting like a headstrong martyr, and Negasonic Teenage Warhead is functionally a younger sister to Deadpool: their cat-and-mouse bickering is only surpassed when she reprimands Deadpool's immature behavior. These are just three examples of the slash/mother role, but there are more female characters that fit this idea. Thus, female characters are inseparable from the mother duality they all possess.

Furthermore, the mother duality (slash/mother) can make it difficult for American society to accept female characters that step out of the stereotypical normative, which ties back into the problem of there truly being a female judge, jury, and executioner: this trope removes the slash/mother because a nurturing mother is in direct opposition with cold killing judge, jury, and executioner vigilante antihero. Returning to the Punisher: Cossandra is a hero/mother in *Marvel Knights 2099: Punisher #1* (Krikman, 2004). Her entire story involves her teaching her son about becoming the Punisher in order to pass along the Punisher legacy. In a way, the fact that Cossandra is Frank's daughter supersedes the actions she herself has done over her lifetime. In fact, the focus of this story line is not so much Cossandra's life as the Punisher, but rather, the focus is on Franklin's struggle with becoming the Punisher in his own right; Cossandra's death is the turning point in Franklin's story, not the conclusion of her own. Thus, Cossandra's legacy is not that she is one iteration of the Punisher; her legacy is being the daughter of the previous Punisher and the mother to the next one.

Weapons of Choice

In a previous section, this essay considered the differences between fighting and violence in male and female children and alluded to a historic precedent for the psychological reasoning for the differences to exist. One might question the relevance of youth differences and psychological reasoning in relation to an adult who is highly trained military fighter. In terms of fighting, adult males in the United States typically default to fists for punching. Interestingly, kicking in a fight is seen as "fighting dirty." Albeit, no respect is to be gained from winning a fight that was fought "dirty," there is also no respect for the person who loses a fight—"dirty" or otherwise. Generally, males will aim for the face in the nose/temple/cheek regions and the stomach/solar plexus. Females, on the other hand, generally tend to opt for hair pulls, eyes/orbital sockets scratches, stomping toes, and convenient grabbing points that could lead to damage, e.g., necklaces, earrings, hair accessories, etc. Now, there are exceptions to these gendered fighting choices; again, these generalizations are based on long-held gendered stereotypes of young people over the decades specific to the United States. Nonetheless, the variances between attack points of choice can be tracked back to anatomy and physiology—punching the face or solar plexus is not enough to cause extreme injury, but rather, both cause sharp pain, and have the ability to "knock the wind out" of the victim, thus rendering them temporary disabled, which could allow the attacker to make a getaway—or offer a "break" in the action which would allow a person (or character) to converse with their victim. Raking nails across an orbital socket, choking with a necklace, ripping out earring, and stomping on toes can lead to serious maiming or injury. However, hair pulling is a bit different; a hair pull is a compliance technique used to maintain a physical advantage over a victim and is usually done in conjunction with another attack. In visual media, when fighting with other adult females, adult females are often depicted attacking physical features that are celebrated as highly feminine—namely hair and face—and often equated with a female's worth: society's perception of her facial beauty. On the other hand, in visual media, when fighting with other adult males, adult males are rarely depicted attacking physical features that are celebrated as highly masculine—namely, groin or hair. To review, generally speaking, males use force via fists to temporarily disable opponents, whereas females directly attack vulnerable body parts with an intent to damage their opponent.

Turning to the Punisher, Frank Castle, when using his hands, follows this typical gender-dominate attack point expectation. Usually, when his fight scenes are depicted, the fight is interspersed with conversation—a "bad guy" pleading/reasoning/threatening the Punisher, or the titular character verbally condemning the "baddie." This is fairly standard in comics: if the (anti)hero kills the villain too quick, there is no chance for affirmation, justification, penance, or redemption. Thus, a female Punisher, too, must demonstrate physical attacks that allow her to de-escalate the violence long enough pass judgment (conversation) before execution of the victim. Should a female Punisher attack in a way that would not allow for this interspersed conversational trial, then she is not truly a gender-equivalent Punisher character. Therefore, Cossandra Castle fails at being a gender-equivalent Punisher because she is not shown to engage in hand-to-hand combat—in fact, in *Marvel Knights 2099: Punisher #1*, she flees both instances where hand-to-hand combat was about to commence—*without* a fight.

Of course, violence is not limited to attackers' bodies as weapon. The United States has a culture of violence and, more specifically, gun violence. Men are more likely to use guns for violence than women. As of April 2017, only 30 percent of Americans over the age of 18 own a gun (Parker). The study goes on to highlight how men are twice as likely as women to own guns, and more likely to shoot guns. Statistically speaking, in this way, Frank Castle very much fits the demographics of a typical American gun owner: he is an adult white male, who is Christian (Catholic) and is without a complete college education as he did not finish seminary; however, Frank Castle does possess an extraordinary amount of military training and education (military training was not a demographic considered in the education area of the Pew study).

The Punisher clearly fits into the culture of violence fought with weapons. For Castle, his weapon(s) of choice is usually a gun, or multiple guns, both automatic and/or semi-automatic rifles and handguns. According to the Marvel Wiki, Castle is also proficient in the use of:

> fragmentation and tear gas grenades, other explosives, and combat knives. A personal favorite is his ballistic knife, which can launch its blade with lethal force. He commonly uses M16 .223 caliber automatic rifles, Sterling Mark 6 9mm, semi-automatic rifles, 9mm Browning Llama automatic pistols, .45 caliber automatic frame rechambered for 9mm. ammunition, .223 caliber Derringers, and Gerber Mark II combat knives.

Frank Castle's style of fighting must be attributed to his training as a U.S. Marine Green Beret and former Special Forces instructor. Castle's extensive training according to Marvel's Wiki, is as follows:

> United States Marine Corps Basic Training, Infantry School, Reconnaissance, Force Reconnaissance, and Sniper Schools, U.S. Army Airborne School, and U.S. Navy Underwater Demolition Team training (which qualified him as a Navy Seal [Sea, Air and Land]).

All of this training has resulted in a well-rounded killing machine. Marvel describes Castle as being proficient in:

> basic infantry skills; special operations, which includes the use and maintenance of specialized firearms and explosive ordnance; infiltration into heavily-guarded enemy territories and structures for the purpose of assassination; captures; military intelligence; … various forms of camouflage and stealth; …pack[ing] and maintain[ing] his own parachute rigs, … professionally control his landings, in daylight and at night; extended underwater operations, including demolitions; … many types of explosives, ranging from simple dynamite to plastique to improvised explosives; … hand-to-hand combat; …killing … without weapons; extremely deadly in knife training, preferring the knife he learned to fight with in the USMC: the ka-bar; … preternaturally-precise marksman; thoroughly trained and experienced in unconventional ("guerrilla") warfare; [and] … is an armorer, a gunsmith, and an expert in field medicine.

This is an extensive list showing what Punisher is capable of doing. To summate, the Punisher is accomplished in guerrilla tactics, a variety of weapons, hand-to-hand combat, day and night parachuting, underwater operations, explosives, field medicine, and more. A gender-equivalent female Punisher must be equally as specialized in the above tactics; Cassondra Castle does not have a demonstrated résumé with these skills.

The Aftermath of Violence

Going beyond the actual fight into the aftermath, there is also a major difference in the stereotypes and perceptions of how males and females react to violence both committed and observed. How does this notion of familial bond translate to the Punisher and a gender-equivalent female Punisher? Cossandra Castle does not react to violence because she runs from violence in *Marvel Knights 2099: Punisher #1*. Perhaps a look to a character that is also referred to as Lady Punisher would be more fitting than Cossandra Castle: Rachel Cole-Alves.

Rachel Cole-Alves appears in *The Punisher* series and *Punisher: War Zone*. Nineteen out of her 21 appearances in comics are in *The Punisher* (both *Punisher Vol. 9 #1–6, #8–16,* and *Vol. 10 #11–12*), and *Punisher: War Zone Vol. 3 #33, #4,* and *#5* (Rucka, 2013), which is excellent visibility for the character in the terms of a repeating female character. Rachel Cole-Alves has a tragic backstory: her family was murdered at her wedding due to gang violence. In seeking revenge for her lost friends and family (the NYPD was not making progress on her case), she ends up teaming up with the Punisher as they share a common enemy. Like Frank Castle, she has a military background: she is a Marine Sergeant but does not have the special training or the brute strength of Frank Castle.

However, the character is still relegated to female tropes—she actively risks danger in order to have a friend obtain a photograph depicting her deceased husband and herself. Rachel is further removed from being a gender-equivalent Punisher when, unfortunately, near the end of her tenure of fighting side-by-side with Frank Castle, Rachel accepts responsibility for the death of an innocent person (Walter Bolt), which causes her to become "deeply affected and twisted" whence she realizes the volume of her slaughter by fighting alongside Punisher.

This type of emotional vulnerability is not something that is indicative of Punisher and an emotional breakdown renders her character of truly being an equal of the Punisher. When does Frank Castle have a mental breakdown due to guilt after killing a criminal? The answer is *never*; Castle falls more into the toxic masculinity notion of not showing emotions. From smelling salts to fainting couches, a mental breakdown is more in line with a stereotypical "delicate" female psyche and concept of hysteria. Once again, Rachel Cole-Alves fails to be a gender-equivalent Punisher because she is burdened by her moral guilt. This "delicate" female psyche is seen in yet another female character called Lady Punisher: Lynn Michaels.

Presented in *Punisher War Journal #75*, Lynn Michaels met Frank Castle as she was attempting to exact revenge on her attempted rapist. After working side-by-side for a time, Lynn is portrayed as petty and emotional when she discovers Frank does not have romantic feelings for her after reading his War Journal (*Punisher War Journal #75*). Her failure to induce his romantic interest leads her to seemingly have a break down. Due to this realization of her solitude, Lynn decides to disappear from Punisher's life.

Additionally, as a police officer (NYPD), she does not have the specialized training or skills that Frank has, thus rendering her unequal to him as a gender-equivalent character.

Yet another example in the Punisher universe is in 1994's *Punisher 2099* ("Son of the Punisher" Vol. 1 No. 21). This story is a part of the Earth 928 timeline/universe and follows Jake Gallows, a human cyborg who, after his mother, brother, and sister-in-law were murdered by a gang, discovered the original Punisher's war journal and a command from Frank Castle for the possessor of the journal to carry on the Punisher Mantle (there is no blood relationship between Jake Gallows and Cossandra or Frank Castle). In this issue, the Punisher, Jake Gallows, is fighting Vendetta, an angry female hero with similar justice goals as the titular character. Vendetta challenges Punisher, stating that she feels she could do his job better than him to which he offers her the chance to prove herself. Punisher exposes the even darker side of his endgame—it is not just shootouts with criminals, but, moreover, it is keeping prisoners (as he cannot kill someone under the age of 21) until a time when they can be killed. Vendetta is perturbed by this additional component to the Punisher's "work." Jake Gallows insists that Vendetta executes a prisoner he is keeping, as it is the prisoner's 21st birthday and, thus, it is to for his execution. Vendetta cannot bring herself to push the button for the vaporizing chair. Her inability to push that button reveals a wavering mental state and her moral compass renders her an unequal gender-equivalent of the Punisher.

What Is Needed?

Even the Punisher himself does not see a female as capable of being his equal. In *Punisher 2099*, "Return of Vendetta" (Vol 1. No. 20, 1994), when confronted with the idea of a female Punisher whose goals and targets align with his, Jake dismisses her as "a sick harpy" and "some nut who's probably been dumped by her boyfriend and is on a revenge kick."

So, what would it take for the Punisher to have a truly equal gender-opposite? A gender-equivalent female Punisher character would have to, to truly be judge, jury, and executioner, possess the following qualities:

1. Appear in multiple comics,
2. Possess a strong familial bond,
3. Obtain years of extensive specialized tactical and military training,
4. Have a tragic backstory of the loss of her husband and children,
5. No hesitation or regrets before, during, or after execution, and
6. Exist as a Punisher—not as a Punisher/mother.

The first criterion would be fairly easy to achieve. The second criterion, in the grand scheme of things, is also fairly easy to accomplish. If the gender-equivalent female Punisher (hereinafter referred to as "Punishette" or "Fran" in homage to comic universe naming tropes) is wearing all black with the iconic head of death emblazoned across the chest, a visual familial bond is met. Punishette should wear a practical tactical pants and a tee shirt, rather than a skin-tight catsuit. After all, if Fran is to have a familial bond with Frank, she also needs to have a militaristic discipline of being prepared and practical. Frank Castle is known to work out and eat a good diet to maintain his physique. His body is depicted as bulging with muscles in comic, film, and Netflix iterations. Fran should also have a similar dedication to bulking up—she should look more like a female body builder rather than a swimsuit model or adult actress.

The third requirement is a trickier qualification for our Punishette. In the United States, it was only in 2015 (Myers, 2017) that the first female officer, and in 2018 that the first female enlisted soldier (Barnett, 2018) graduated from the prestigious U.S. Army Ranger School; as of April 2020, 50 women total have graduated Ranger School, compared to over 3,500 men. Furthermore, is was only recently, in 2019 that the first female completed Navy SEAL officer assessment and selection (Seck, 2019); as of December 2019, she remains the only female SEAL (National Post, 2019). Lastly, as of July 2020, there is yet to be a female Army Green Beret; however, a woman is currently in the final stages of the Green Beret training and is expected to graduate later this year (Gibbons-Neff, 2020).

According to Global Firepower, an organization dedicated to ranking countries' military power using 50 separate factors that control for variables so that large and small (in terms of size, population, defense budget, technology availability, etc.) can be compared, the United States is ranked the most powerful military and best in the world (Global Firepower, 2020). Yet, there is a paucity of women who are completing highly specialized military training. This could be partially attributed to a ban of women in specialized combat and special operations job that was only lifted by the Pentagon in 2016 (Gibbons-Neff, 2020).

At this time, it seems that the training Frank Castle received during his tenure in the army as a Green Beret, and in the navy as a Navy SEAL, for at least the near future, realistically would elude the gender-equivalent Punishette. For starters though, our Punishette could be an Army Ranger, which is a start to equaling the Punisher's training.

For the fourth qualification, Punishette's tragic backstory will come across as extra tragic: her child has been murdered. American society often unfairly puts all expectations of child rearing and protection on the mother. A mother who "allows" something to happen to her child is a monster, whether guilty or not, in the eyes of the societal jury. This could be an issue with adapting the character of the Punisher to a female opposite. The loss of a husband can be seen as a husband's duty to sacrifice himself for the sake of his family. While sad, the death of Mr. Punishette is expected, not tragic.

In the original Punisher series, the mother character is Castle's wife, Maria, who is *actually* a mother. Sadly, Maria and their children, Lisa and Frank Jr., are murdered. Their deaths give birth to the antihero that is the Punisher; he does not have the caretaker that many other superheroes do. Even at their worst rage (Hulk), hotheadedness (Star Lord), or buffoonery (Deadpool), superheroes have their moral girlfriend-sister-friend/mother to reel them in. Frank Castle is missing his moral compass; Maria is not there to help him control and redirect his anger. If she were to be there, she would quell the monster that rages within. What does this mean for a female Punisher, as, she, a woman, is typically relegated to the slash/mother role.

As the antihero vigilante, can Fran still be this trope? Is it possible to separate out a female character from the slash/mother? If she is to be equal with the male Punisher, then no. She cannot have the sense of balance or moral compass, as he does. However, this can be problematic in the perceptions of contemporary Usonian society: a woman who is judge, jury, and executioner is nearly unheard of, and women without a nurturing mother aspect can be considered shrill, broken, or less-than. Moreover, these designations are typically reserved for the completely villainous evil women. With current gender role expectation in the U.S., this notion is incompatible with the Punisher as a character because Punisher still has redeeming qualities. Readers, and characters within his stories, while disagreeing with his methods, understand where he comes from. If the character had no redeeming qualities, he would not be as popular as he is today in American popular culture. For the time being, the Punisher stands on his own. Until a time comes where women are viewed as without the dual role of the girlfriend-sister-friend/mother, female versions of the Punisher will continue to fall short of being a gender-equivalent iteration of the character. Cossandra Castle, while not an gender-equivalent female version of the Punisher; she is, however, a step in the right direction to female representation in comics. In time, as societal gender roles evolve, a Punishette will be written that will truly harbor the qualities of the Punisher and break gender stereotypes and allow comic fans to discover powerful female characters that share familial bonds with characters they know, embody characteristics they love, and represent gender equality in representation.

References

Barnett, R. (2018, November 2). *1st female enlisted soldier to be an Army Ranger shares her story: "Failure's not an option."* Army Times. https://www.armytimes.com/news/your-army/2018/11/04/1st-female-enlisted-soldier-to-be-an-army-ranger-shares-her-story-failures-not-an-option/.

Benioff, D. & Weiss, D.B. (Writers), & Van Patten, T. (Director). (2011, April 17). Winter is coming (Season 1, Episode 1) [Television series episode]. In D. Benioff, & D.B. Weiss (Producers), *Game of thrones*. United States: HBO.

Bowman, T. (2002, December 15). U.S. Army Green Berets accused from within of lowering standards [Radio broadcast]. In *NPR Morning Edition*. Washington, D.C.: National Public Radio.

Congreve, W. (1706). *The double-dealer*. (2nd ed.). London: William Congreve.

Crisis Consulting Group. (n.d.). *Fighting in schools—boys vs. girls*. https://www.crisisconsultantgroup.com/school-violence-prevention/fighting-in-schools/.

Edmondson, N. (2014, October). *Punisher vol. 10*, #11. New York: Marvel Comics.

Edmondson, N. (2014, November). *Punisher vol. 10*, #12. New York: Marvel Comics.

Faram, M.D. (2018, February 16). *Two women could enter Navy special operations training this year*. Navy times. https://www.navytimes.com/news/your-navy/2018/02/16/two-women-could-enter-navy-special-operations-training-this-year/.

Fineman, M.A., & Karpin, I. (1995). *Mothers in law: Feminist theory and the legal regulation of motherhood (Culture & gender)*. New York: Columbia University Press.

Geary, D. (2019, August 29). *Do women fight? Female-female competition in an evolutionary context*. Psychology today. https://www.psychologytoday.com/us/blog/male-female/201908/do-women-fight.

Global Firepower. (2020). *2020 military strength ranking*. https://www.globalfirepower.com/countries-listing.asp.

Grant, S., & Texeira, M. (1995). *Punisher war journal vol. 1*, #75. New York: Marvel Comics.

Hudson, L. (2011, December 8). Marvel editors discuss women in comics and the lack of female-led titles. [Interview]. *Comics alliance*. https://comicsalliance.com/marvel-women-comics-editors/.

Krikman, R. (2004). *Marvel knights 2099: Punisher #1*. New York: Marvel Comics.

Marvel. (2018a). *Punisher*. http://marvel.com/characters/43/punisher.

Marvel. (2018b). *Punisher (Frank Castle)*. Marvel Wiki. http://marvel.com/universe/Punisher_(Frank_Castle).

Marvel. (2018c). *Rachel Cole (Earth-616)*. Marvel Wiki. http://marvel.wikia.com/wiki/Rachel_Cole_(Earth-616).

Mills, P., & Skinner, T. (1994, August). *Punisher 2099 vol. 1*, #19. New York: Marvel Comics.

Mills, P., & Skinner, T. (1994, September). *Punisher 2099 vol. 1*, #20. New York: Marvel Comics.

Mills, P., & Skinner, T. (1994, October). *Punisher 2099 vol. 1*, #21. New York: Marvel Comics.

Mills, P., & Skinner, T. (1995). *Punisher 2099 vol. 1*, #25. New York: Marvel Comics.

Myers, M. (2017, January 18). *This woman will be the first to join the Army's elite 75th Ranger Regiment*. Army times. https://www.armytimes.com/news/your-army/2017/01/18/this-woman-will-be-the-first-to-join-the-army-s-elite-75th-ranger-regiment/.

National Post. (2019, December 18). *For first time, a woman has completed the demanding U.S. Navy SEAL officer test*. https://nationalpost.com/news/for-first-time-a-woman-has-successfully-finished-demanding-u-s-navy-seal-officer-screening-program.

Nogales, A. (2018, January 31). *We live in a culture of violence: Violence is a social and political problem, as well as a personal one*. Psychology today. https://www.psychologytoday.com/us/blog/family-secrets/201801/we-live-in-culture-violence.

Parker, K., Horowitz, J., Igielnik, R., Oliphant, B., & Brown, A. (2017). *America's complex relationship with guns*. Washington, D.C.: Pew Research Center.

Pew Research Center. (2017). *On gender differences, no consensus on nature vs. nurture*. Pew Research Center Social & Demographic Trends. https://www.pewsocialtrends.org/2017/12/05/on-gender-differences-no-consensus-on-nature-vs-nurture/.

Planned Parenthood. (n.d.). *Sex and gender identity.* https://www.plannedparenthood.org/learn/gender-identity/sex-gender-identity.
Planned Parenthood. (n.d.). *What are gender roles and stereotypes?* https://www.plannedparenthood.org/learn/gender-identity/sex-gender-identity/what-are-gender-roles-and-stereotypes.
Rucka, G. (2011a, August). *Punisher vol. 9,* #1. New York: Marvel Comics.
Rucka, G. (2011b, August). *Punisher vol. 9,* #2. New York: Marvel Comics.
Rucka, G. (2011, September). *Punisher vol. 9,* #3. New York: Marvel Comics.
Rucka, G. (2011, October). *Punisher vol. 9,* #4. New York: Marvel Comics.
Rucka, G. (2011, November). *Punisher vol. 9,* #5. New York: Marvel Comics.
Rucka, G. (2011, December). *Punisher vol. 9,* #6. New York: Marvel Comics.
Rucka, G. (2012, February). *Punisher vol. 9,* #8. New York: Marvel Comics.
Rucka, G. (2012, March). *Punisher vol. 9,* #9. New York: Marvel Comics.
Rucka, G. (2012, April). *Punisher vol. 9,* #10. New York: Marvel Comics.
Rucka, G. (2012, May). *Punisher vol. 9,* #11. New York: Marvel Comics.
Rucka, G. (2012, June). *Punisher vol. 9,* #12. New York: Marvel Comics.
Rucka, G. (2012, July). *Punisher vol. 9,* #13. New York: Marvel Comics.
Rucka, G. (2012, August). *Punisher vol. 9,* #14. New York: Marvel Comics.
Rucka, G. (2012a, September). *Punisher vol. 9,* #15. New York: Marvel Comics.
Rucka, G. (2012b, September). *Punisher vol. 9,* #16. New York: Marvel Comics.
Rucka, G. (2013a, January). *Punisher: War zone vol. 3,* #3. New York: Marvel Comics.
Rucka, G. (2013b, January). *Punisher: War zone vol. 3,* #4. New York: Marvel Comics.
Rucka, G. (2013, February). *Punisher: War zone vol. 3,* #5. New York: Marvel Comics.
Rudatsikira, E., Muula, A., & Siziya, S. (2008). Variables associated with physical fighting among U.S. high-school students. *Clinical Practice and Epidemiology in Mental Health,* 4(16). https://cpementalhealth.biomedcentral.com/articles/10.1186/1745–0179-4-16.
Seck, H.H. (2019, December 11). *The first woman has made it through SEAL officer screening.* Military. https://www.military.com/daily-news/2019/12/11/first-woman-has-made-it-through-seal-officer-screening.html.
Walker, K., Bialik, K., & van Kessel, P. (2018, July 24*). Strong men, caring women: How Americans describe what society values (and doesn't) in gender.* Pew Research Center social demographic trends. https://www.pewsocialtrends.org/interactives/strong-men-caring-women/.
Weiner, R. (2009). Sequential art and reality: Yes, Virginia, there is a Spider-Man. *International Journal of Comic Art,* 11(1), 457–477.
World Health Organization, & Liverpool JMU Centre for Public Health. (2010). *Violence prevention: The evidence.* Geneva: WHO.

Frank Castle, Fanfiction and the Female Gaze

ELIZABETH JENDRZEY *and*
MEREDITH PASAHOW

The Marvel Cinematic Universe has celebrated over ten years of exceedingly successful films, spanning more than twenty films and, in 2015, moving into television with the introduction of their Netflix series, *Daredevil*. With the move to both big and small screens, Marvel comic characters have been made even more accessible to the public, rather than remaining primarily in the comic book world. One of the dozens of Marvel characters to be introduced, or rather reintroduced, to the public was Frank Castle, the Punisher.

The Punisher of the comics is a complex and violent man, one with a strict black-and-white moral code that often brings him into conflict with more wholesome heroes, such as Captain America or Spider-Man. Frank Castle was brought into the Marvel Cinematic Universe by way of the second season of their *Daredevil* series, pitting Frank against the show's protagonist, Matt Murdock. This meant that a fresh new audience was able to get to know Frank and, if the sheer number of fanworks are anything to go by, fall in love with him anew. Any new audience also brings with it a swell of new authors; that is to say, fanfiction authors and other creators of fan-based works. However, the Frank Castle of fanfiction is not quite the same as the one presented in the pages of a comic book or the screen of a television. He is the one written by the fans, for the fans, in a way that mainstream media is not likely to approach.

Fanfiction in its current form is often noted as taking shape in the 1960s with the distribution of fanzines. However, it is simply the latest development in a long history of transformative literature (Jendrzey, 2017). In online fanfiction, fans take a source media, called canon, and write their own story featuring those characters or that world. They may choose to ignore or deliberately change various aspects of canon to suit their purposes, resulting in alternate universes, or AUs. Most fanfiction incorporates some level of divergence from the canon, technically forming an AU, but the label is generally reserved for those stories that deviate significantly, such as stories that incorporate metaphysically predetermined soulmates, which has dozens of iterations and variants and hundreds of stories that play off of them. Or one could indulge in a story in which all characters spend the majority of their time in a coffee shop, like the aptly named series "Frank Castle Just Wants to Sell Coffee, Dammit!" (blue_girl, 2016). These changes to canon often reflect avenues of thought that fans wish the creators would pursue but cannot or will not. Other changes are not something the fans actually wish for in canon, but a thought exercise about "what if?" This is because, at its core, fanfiction is a form of reader response.

Reader response theory focuses on just that, the response of the readers to a given text. With fanfiction (and also fan films), the fans respond by creating additional texts, expanding the world of the story as it might appeal to themselves and other fans. This is in line with the ideas Barthes (1977) laid out in "The Death of the Author," with fans viewing ultimate authorial intent as a limiting factor to their understanding of a work. Instead, they draw from their own contextualizations to create meaning, which often creates variations from the narrative they are given. While there has been concern in the past about issues of copyright infringement, fans do not see fanfiction as a threat to the canon text. They see it as a participation with canon, a way to connect more fully with the text. This desire for a better connection is in a way a love letter to canon. Fans like the canon content, so they create more, similar content that they can share with other fans who can't get enough just from canon. In order to create new content, some kind of revision must occur or risk those very issues of copyright infringement. It is this culture of celebrated changes that keeps fanfiction a thriving community.

This revisionist approach to fiction is often a function of the composition of the fanfiction community. Fanfiction authors are more likely to be members of the LGBTQ community, women, or members of other marginalized classes; a survey of roughly 10,000 users of fanfiction site Archive of Our Own showed only 4 percent of users were men and 29 percent identified as something other than straight (centrumlumina, 2013). As a result, they are less likely to see satisfying portrayals of themselves in mainstream fiction. Fanfiction allows them to find or create these satisfying portrayals without relying on professionally produced media. Sometimes this manifests in "racebending" or "genderbending" fanfiction, which alters the race or gender of a character to increase representation of different social groups (*Bending Narratives*, 2016). Most often, it is simply using the existing characters and universe to tell stories more likely to hold the interest of each respective community.

Because the fanfiction community contains a minority of heterosexual men (centrumlumina, 2013), the collective desires tend to veer away from those traditionally "male" desires to reflect "female" preferences, despite presence of non-binary individuals. This manifests in two main ways concerning fanfiction. The first is in the content of the stories. As Flynn (2011) discusses in her essay on women and composition, men are more likely to write about actions while women are more likely to write about relationships. This is heavily reflected in fanfiction, as most stories feature romantic relationships, even when based on a canon that does not contain any. Even those stories that do not have a romantic focus will often heavily feature a platonic or familial relationship. Though most of these stories do have plots propelled by actions, it is the relationships and their development over time that hold the interest of the readers.

Female preferences also manifest in the tone of the stories, especially in regards to male-driven media. Feminist theorists talk about the male gaze, but the female gaze is more difficult to describe. Laura Mulvey (1989) presented one potential definition, focused on women as viewed by women, in which the female audience is stuck between embracing the passively feminine or the intrusively masculine alongside their given heroine. While generally true at her time or writing, this version of the female gaze is still in relation to male-targeted media. As she points out in a prior essay, "According to the principles of the ruling ideology and the physical structures that back it up, the male figure cannot bear the burden of sexual objectification" (Mulvey, 1989, p. 20). However, today's online bloggers can give plenty of examples in which the male becomes the object for female viewing. One notable case in point is a pair of magazine covers featuring Hugh Jackman following the 2013 premiere of his movie *The Wolverine*. The male-marketed *Muscle & Fitness* shows him flexing shirtless and staring down the camera as if ready for a fight; the female-marketed *Good Housekeeping* has Jackman smiling softly in a sweater. As Tumblr user jadelyn (2013) points out, each magazine knows what their audience wants to see and is appealing to their desires.

This attention to audience desires carries into writing as well. Comics, especially *Punisher* titles, are generally written by men, for men. Across three articles discussing which *Punisher* comics are must-reads (Buxton, 2016; Buxton 2019; Francisco, 2017), a total of twenty-five authors are mentioned. Garth Ennis comes in first as the most mentioned *Punisher* writer in each of the three articles. Of the twenty-five total authors, the only woman mentioned is Becky Cloonan. Of course there have been many more authors over the forty-five years that *Punisher* comics have been around, but it is interesting to note that the names that come up again and again as the "best" writers of the series are all male (Galati, 2019; Harley, 2018; Markus, 2019; Schedeen, 2016; Serafino, 2011; Thomason, 2013). This is in contrast to the world of fanfiction, in which 80 percent of those involved identify as women (centrumlumina, 2013). The gender divide has a clear correlation with the temperament of the characters as written; where the men in comic books (more often written by men) are often assertive, aggressive, or angry, the same men in fanfiction (more often written by women) are often kinder, more compromising characters.

Fanfiction authors are not the only ones who draw from other sources to create content. The creative team behind Frank's Netflix storyline drew from various comics for ideas. Even Jon Bernthal, who plays Frank, did his research by selecting a few highly regarded texts for reading to help with his understanding of Frank Castle (Fitzpatrick, 2015). Allusions to the comics can be seen throughout the shows, from the blatant, such as the inclusion of Frank's battle van, to the subtle, such as the men hanging from meat hooks in *Daredevil*'s "Dogs to a Gunfight" (Ramirez & Petrie, 2016), which is likely a nod to Frank's fight in a meatpacking plant seen in *Punisher MAX: Frank* (Aaron, 2011b). Though a majority of Punisher fanfiction is based on the television shows, this chain of creative sources means that it would be neglectful to ignore the impact of the comics.

Whether in the comics or in the Netflix *Daredevil* and *Punisher* series, Frank's backstory has remained roughly the same: a war vet who voluntarily did several tours before finally returning home to his wife Maria and their two children. His family was killed in front of him in Central Park, which lead Frank to put his violent tendencies to "good" use by becoming the vigilante the Punisher. The Punisher is feared by most everyone in New York City, although many of New York's superheroes, such as Spider-Man or Daredevil, disagree with his methods. Frank believes in killing bad people who do bad things rather than relying on law enforcement to jail them only to have them walk free after their sentence is complete. Frank's world view is very absolute: a person is either a good guy or a bad guy; things are white or black; there is no room for grey for Frank Castle. According to one fan-made wiki, Frank has killed approximately 370 named characters, making his true body count (including unnamed peons, etc.) truly astronomical ("Frank Castle [Earth-616]," 2018).

Despite the body count as evidence of Frank's certainty in his moral code, he is actually less sure of himself, especially at the beginning of his crusade in the comics, before he officially becomes the Punisher. In *Punisher MAX: Frank*, the reader sees his time in the military, as well as the period immediately following his return home. He struggles with whether and how to accept the violent side of himself, which results in a fair amount of indecision as he tries to sort out his new moral code (Aaron, 2011b). Though he worries about whether this level of violence was in him all along, he does not dwell on the thought for long. Instead, he puts the worry out of mind and continues on his newfound mission, with his body as the greatest weapon he could have (Aaron, 2011a). The way he treats his body simply as a tool shows just how far Frank's dehumanization of himself goes (Aaron, 2011a), which in turn allows him to dissociate from the guilt and worry he lived with after the death of his family. This distance from humanity is what allows him to continue acting as an impartial judge, jury, and executioner, producing large numbers of casualties across the pages of the Marvel universe.

Still, in terms of mass casualties, it is hard to hold a candle to the various films made about the Punisher. Created before Frank Castle made it to Netflix, the plots of these films revolve around Frank doling out as much pain and violence as possible to whomever is his enemy at that time. These movies are gratuitous, filled with blood and bullets, and the body counts are huge. They do, however, also show a somewhat softer side to Frank, if any side of Frank can truly be called soft. For instance, in Lexi Alexander's 2008 film, *Punisher: War Zone*, Frank is shown taking care of and sharing his safehouse with a young girl and her mother.

This film is an interesting dichotomy; it shows Frank both at his most violent and at his softest. This could be because of the combination of female and male influence on the film; while Anderson directed it and Gale Anne Hurd produced it, the script was written by Nick Santora, Art Marcum, and Matt Holloway. In the film, we see Frank punching a man so viciously that his head explodes in a spray of blood. The movie is filled with scenes like these, of Frank turning the villains into little more than a smear on the wall through the use of guns, knives, and his own fists. However, in the same film, we see him taking the wife and young daughter of a dead FBI agent under his care. He kills and maims in order to keep them safe, out of respect for the agent that was killed (Hurd & Alexander, 2008).

Although we do see Frank's softer side here, in the way he protects the woman and her daughter, bringing them to various safehouses and working to keep them alive, these actions are almost completely overshadowed by the almost comic amount of violence in the movie. The scenes with the girl and her mother are few and far between, whereas the scenes of blood and gore take up the majority of the film (Hurd & Alexander, 2008). Yet it is these smaller scenes, the ones where Frank shares an army MRE meal with a little girl, that female fans want to see more of.

We also see this in the Netflix series. As Jon Bernthal says, "[Frank] was a grieving father and husband who was reeling from this unbelievably traumatic event" (Birnbarum, 2017). In the series, both *Daredevil* and

The Punisher, we are shown Frank's pain and grief. He returns to his family home and to the scene of their deaths time and time again, looking at pictures of them and forcing himself to remember that tragedy. While in the comics, the source of Frank's violence is more ambiguous—various characters debate whether Frank was the way he is before the war, because of the war, because of losing his family, etc.—the show makes it fairly clear that Frank is a vigilante due to what happened to his family. We see Frank protect the people he loves, we see him go out of his way to *not* do harm to those who do not deserve it. In one episode of *Daredevil*, he rescues a dog that was abused by mafia members.

And yet these are only glimpses, glimmers of compassion in a character that is, at his core, exceptionally brutal. The world of Frank Castle, whether it be in the comics, the older films, or the new series, is one of pain and blood and broken bones. This is where the Netflix series stays closest to its source material. Everywhere Frank goes, even when he is helping people by taking out those that are hurting them, he leaves a wake of destruction and dismembered bodies.

These are views of the Punisher as written largely by and for men. In a further six must-read articles, all authored by men, Garth Ennis remains the favorite, while Becky Cloonan is mentioned only once. Even Bernthal, who sees him as a grieving father, says of his portrayal, "I'm not interested in making him likable. I'm not interested in making him relatable[…]. He's a guy who's living in darkness. He's not trying to win people over" (Birnbaum, 2017). However, as previously mentioned, fanfiction is written primarily for the female gaze. This can easily be seen in a statistical look at the character tag for Frank Castle on Archive of Our Own, a leading fanfiction website. Exactly six months after the premiere of Netflix's *The Punisher*,[1] there were 2,500 works claiming Frank as a character of some note. Of those, only 343 bore the warning tag for graphic depictions of violence; in contrast, 511 reported fluff as a genre descriptor for their writing, referring to writing which is happy, sweet, and affectionate ("Fluff," n.d.). This is not by any means a definitive representation of content as these tags are generated by the authors of each work, any of whom may either mistag or opt not to tag something, but they are sufficient for creating an idea of the landscape in which fanfiction exists. This does not mean that the canon characterization of Frank is ignored. Rather, his traits are reframed in the context of what the female audience is more likely to desire.

The expression of Frank's violence is an example of that reframing. In canon, violence is generally a tool, used in service of his mission. In fanfiction, violence is more often a reaction, enacted against immediate threats to that which Frank holds dear. This is possible because, whereas both canon and fanfiction Frank have lost everything, fanfiction authors generally give something back to him. This is usually in the form of a romantic partner (80 percent of Frank Castle fanfiction places him in a romantic relationship), but it may also be friendships with those he encounters. Regardless of the form, there are two main candidates that fanfiction authors provide as a partner for Frank.

The overwhelming choice of partner for Frank is Karen Page. Just under half of all Frank Castle fanfiction positions him in a romantic relationship with Karen, while approximately 12 percent make note of their platonic connection, though there is a generous amount of overlapping stories that tag both. This presence is due to the nature of their connection in the Netflix series. Throughout the second season of *Daredevil*, Karen is Frank's staunchest believer in who he is as a person; in *The Punisher*, Frank drops everything to come to Karen's aid when she is in trouble (LaManna & Jobst, 2017). Fanfiction gleans romantic pairings from the barest hint of a glance between characters, so despite the lack of confirmed romance between the two (or perhaps because of it), this is considered a popular pairing with a solid foundation.

Some fan authors see Karen as Frank's second shot at domesticity, albeit a very different domestic life than with Maria. Where Maria represented the white picket fence ideal, a relationship with Karen is more likely to involve breaking into her apartment to perform first aid in the bathroom (nighimpossible, 2016). In fanfiction, Karen often finds herself confessing to her sins, such as her murder of James Wesley in the first season of *Daredevil*, as a way to connect with Frank and show that there is not such a moral difference between them (nighimpossible, 2016; etirabys, 2016); in their work "Heaven Sent the Saints Down (Hell Sent Them Up)," Ambrosia (2016) says "She's never told anyone. Not Foggy, or Matt…. But with Frank, it's somehow different. Like she's staring into a mirror, or an imperfect reflection that somehow still manages to resonate with something deep inside her that she never plans to let out." She provides a home base, an emotional touchstone for Frank that he thought lost for good after the death of his family, allowing him to open up and share stories about his past, like "how Lisa loved stealing Frank Jr.'s trucks and hoarding them under her bed when she got real pissed off at him" (nighimpossible, 2016). In pairing him with Karen, someone with broken pieces to fit his own, fanfiction authors are halfway taming the Punisher, allowing the man and the monster under the bed to exist in separate but coinciding spheres.

The other common partner for Frank in fanfiction is Matt Murdock. This is a pairing that preceded and was strengthened by Frank's Netflix debut (at 17.6 percent of fanfiction), as the opposing moral codes of the two characters often conflict. What comes across as an interesting character foil in canon can create a range of effects in a romantic relationship, from bickering about their different ideals like "an old married couple," as Peter Parker told Foggy (BeanieBaby, 2018), to a more vicious bone of contention, with Matt claiming, "I hate what he does but—he's good. *For* me" (vibishan, 2016). The appeal of this clash lies not only in the drama it can create between the characters, but in the similarity to the rom-com trope of lovers who don't get along at first.

Not all works featuring this pairing hinge on this difference of opinion; with two vigilantes in the relationship, there is a solid presence of hurt/comfort fanfiction as well. A survey of top fanfiction[2] in the Frank Castle tag shows a tendency for writers to hurt Matt and have Frank care for him in the aftermath, from a broken leg (Beguile, 2018), to a sonic grenade that renders Matt deaf (marchingjaybird, 2011), to the fallout of an explosion which nearly kills Matt (allofuswithwings, 2016). The prevalence of this dynamic may be due to a number of factors, such as Matt's closeness to enemies in hand-to-hand combat versus Frank's distance when using his guns, or Matt's solo mentality versus Frank's military training to work with a team and never leave a man behind. Regardless of the cause, the result is a Frank Castle who spends a decent amount of time watching out for Matt Murdock. Given the popularity of these works, one can assume that this caring side is more appealing to the overwhelmingly non-male audience of fanfiction than it is to the primarily male implied audience of comics.

Frank's moral code also changes slightly when written into fanfiction. As he stated in the *Daredevil* episode "New York's Finest" (Verheiden & Jobst, 2016), a reiteration of his comics code for the fanfiction-prone population, Frank wants to permanently eliminate the evil in the world. However, this often combines with his previously mentioned soldier's mentality of not leaving a man behind to manifest in the opposite of eliminating evil: protecting that which is good. More specifically, and likely due to the loss of his family, Frank protects that which is his. Frank has shown a tendency several times in canon to protect Karen, and his desire to look after Matt in fanfiction has already been discussed, but fanfiction places his circle of safety much wider, even more so than his soft spot for children as seen in *Punisher: War Zone.*

One example is Claire Temple, often considered the Night Nurse (though this has not been confirmed by canon) of the Netflix branch of Marvel. As the accidental medical professional for vigilantes, fans feel it is especially important that she be kept safe. In one story, "3rd Shift in Hell's Kitchen," this results in Frank showing up at her apartment to replace the locks and install a second security door (monroesherlock, 2016). Another story, smilebackwards's (2016) "Disarm," shows that Frank's desire to protect what is his is not entirely a function of his loss; in a world where Frank never lost his family but still sought the legal services of Nelson &

Murdock, he ends up replacing their window that had been shot out by a gang because "these are people Maria cares about." Other stories focus on a desire for Frank to protect the innocent in general. In prettybirdy979's (2016) work "Learn to Live with the Unimaginable" which features Matt and Elektra Natchios de-aged into childhood, Frank is adamant that he will not put children in danger when hunting down a means of reversal, despite their repeated (and truthful) assertions that they've trained for fighting. Overall, Frank's moral code in fanfiction plays as much to this protective side as it does to the desire for vengeance and justice, often in new and different ways not found in canon sources.

There are other trends in fanfiction that serve to smooth the rough edges of the Punisher. One of these is Frank's love of dogs; a background part of the second season of *Daredevil* that went neglected in the first season of *The Punisher*, many fanfiction authors make it a point to include this detail, with 5 percent of stories mentioning dogs in the tags or summary and a greater number still incorporating it into the text of the story. This is not a casual love of dogs as seen in the canon series. In the third part of BeanieBaby's (2018) series "Peter Parker's Home for the Wayward Villain," a Frank groggy from blood loss tells Peter Parker that he shouldn't speak poorly about dogs because the dog wouldn't do the same to him. In "Heaven Sent the Saints Down (Hell Sent Them Up)," he is given the epithet "Patron Saint of Revenge, Violence, and Vengeance. And dogs. And coffee" (Ambrosia, 2016). This caring towards man's best friend further humanizes and softens Frank, giving him another similarity to readers and making him more appealing to the general female public.

Though the topic of how Frank Castle is viewed in the female gaze has been addressed, there is still the question of why. Why are fans writing fanfiction that generally changes aspects of Frank as seen in canon? Recall the two Hugh Jackman covers: one of an aggressively shirtless fighter, the other of a sweater-wearing romantic. For the most part, canon Frank is squarely in the camp of the aggressively shirtless, as are many comic book heroes, which runs the risk of alienating half of the potential audience. What has happened is that the fandom and those who create fanworks zero in on the *potential* for something other than violence. They see Frank rescuing a dog and say, for instance, "Why not let Frank play ball in the park with that dog?" They see the possibility of romance, or compassion, or anything that isn't dark and bloody in Frank, and yet they do not see these things fulfilled.

Nonetheless, fanfiction authors are not retaliating with another extreme; they are retaining his mission and method of accomplishment, his faults and rough edges, but they are also finding little bits and pieces of kindness, of compassion, and expanding them to create entire universes. They push their work into these small pockets of kindness that Frank displays and take root there. It is because they are given scraps of what they think Frank could be, what the canon itself suggests he could be, that they create these universes. They are trying to find a balance between the two extremes when they feel they are not given one. Their desires are sparked by the idea that Frank could play with a dog, or have a romantic relationship, but these desires are not fulfilled to their greatest extent in canon, leaving fan authors with the need to fill the remaining void themselves. Frankly, as long as the mainstream media fails to appeal to the female gaze, fanfiction authors will continue to write the Punisher they want to see in the world.

Notes

1. All statistics mentioned in this essay are based off the state of the Frank Castle tag of Archive of Our Own on this date, May 17, 2018.
2. For this essay, "top fanfiction" was determined by sorting the Frank Castle tag on Archive of Our Own by number of hits (indicative of traffic), number of kudos, and number of bookmarks (both indicative of reader enjoyment). Ignoring multi-fandom short story collections, the top twenty story postings for each indicator were taken as a representative sample.

References

Aaron, J. (2011a). *Punisher MAX: Bullseye*. New York: Marvel.
Aaron, J. (2011b). *Punisher MAX: Frank*. New York: Marvel.
Alexander, L. (Director). (2008). *Punisher: War zone* [Film]. Santa Monica, CA: Lionsgate.
allofuswithwings. (2016, June 9). *Protect what I found*. Archive of our own. https://archiveofourown.org/works/7033309.
Ambrosia. (2016, May 31). *Heaven sent the saints down (Hell sent them up)*. Archive of our own. https://archiveofourown.org/works/6299413.
Barthes, R. (1977). *Image-music-text* (S. Heath, Trans.). New York: Hill and Wang.
BeanieBaby. (2018, June 20). *All the colors in between*. Archive of our own. https://archiveofourown.org/works/6301660.
Beguile. (2018, June 14). *It takes a village*. Archive of our own. https://archiveofourown.org/works/6961093.
Bending narratives: Racebending, genderbending and remix geektvism. (2016). https://bendingnarratives.wordpress.com/.
Birnbaum, D. (2017, November 24). *Remote controlled: 'The Punisher' star Jon Bernthal on why the role scared him*. Variety. https://variety.com/2017/tv/news/the-punisher-jon-bernthal-podcast-remote-controlled-1202621804/.
blue_girl. (2016, April 17). *Frank Castle just wants to sell coffee, dammit!* Archive of our own. https://archiveofourown.org/series/446875.
Buxton, M. (2016, April 10). *Hit list: The Punisher's greatest writers*. CBR. https://www.cbr.com/hit-list-the-punishers-greatest-writers/.
Buxton, M. (2019, January 22). *Marvel's Punisher comics reading order: Does Jon Bernthal as the Punisher on Netflix have you hungry for more Frank Castle action? These are the comics you should read next*. Den of Geek. https://www.denofgeek.com/us/books/the-punisher/253900/marvels-punisher-comics-reading-order/.
centrumlumina. (2013, October 2). *AO3 census: About you*. Tumblr. http://centrumlumina.tumblr.com/post/62895609672/ao3-census-about-you.

etirabys. (2016, April 14). *Better natures.* Archive of our own. https://archiveofourown.org/works/6471604.
Fitzpatrick, K. (2015, July 1). *Here are the 'Punisher' comics Jon Bernthal is reading for 'Daredevil' season 2.* Screen crush. http://screencrush.com/daredevil-punisher-jon-bernthal-comics/.
Fluff. (n.d.). Fanlore. https://fanlore.org/wiki/Fluff.
Flynn, E.A. (2011). Composing as a woman. In V. Villanueva & K.L. Arola (Eds.), *Cross-talk in comp theory: A reader* (3rd ed.) (pp. 581–595). Urbana, IL: National Council of Teachers of English.
Francisco, E. (2017, November 9). *The 7 best 'Punisher' comics to read before Netflix binging the show.* Inverse. https://www.inverse.com/article/38269-7-best-punisher-comics-marvel-netflix-spoilers.
Frank Castle (Earth-616). (2018, June 21). Marvel Database. http://marvel.wikia.com/wiki/Frank_Castle_(Earth-616).
Galati, J. (2019, January 17). *A bullet for every occasion: The best Punisher graphic novels.* Comic Book Herald. https://www.comicbookherald.com/a-bullet-for-every-occasion-the-best-punisher-graphic-novels/.
Harley, J. (2018, September 18). *10 Punisher graphic novels you must read before you die.* WhatCulture. http://whatculture.com/comics/10-punisher-graphic-novels-you-must-read-before-you-die?page=10.
jadelyn. (2013, August 10). *Enterprisingly: This is the same man.* Tumblr. http://jadelyn.tumblr.com/post/57900205049/enterprisingly-this-is-the-same-man-this.
Jendrzey, E. (2017). Fan fiction as a digital descendant of transformative literature. *The Phoenix Papers,* 3(1), 10–17. http://fansconf.a-kon.com/dRuZ33A/wp-content/uploads/2017/08/03-Fan-Fiction-as-a-Digital-Descendant-of-Transformative-Literature.pdf.
LaManna, A. (Writer) & Jobst, M. (Director). (2017). Front toward enemy [Streaming series episode]. In M. Ambrose (Producer), *The Punisher.* Los Gatos, CA: Netflix.
marchingjaybird. (2011, July 23). *All in the dark.* Archive of our own. https://archiveofourown.org/works/227410.
Markus, T.C. (2019, January 28). *The 5 Punisher comics you need to read.* Marvel. https://www.marvel.com/articles/digital-series/the-5-punisher-comics-you-need-to-read.
monroesherlock. (2016, March 26). *3rd shift in Hell's Kitchen.* Archive of our own. https://archiveofourown.org/works/6359053.
Mulvey, L. (1989). *Visual and other pleasures.* Bloomington: Indiana University Press.
nighimpossible. (2016, March 26). *Ain't nothing but a monster.* Archive of our own. https://archiveofourown.org/works/6359393.
prettybirdy979. (2016, April 21). *Learn to live with the unimaginable.* Archive of our own. https://archiveofourown.org/works/6614641.
Ramirez, M., & Petrie, D. (Writers) & Abraham, P. (Director). (2016). Dogs to a gunfight [Streaming series episode]. In D. Buckley (Producer), *Daredevil.* Los Gatos, CA: Netflix.
Schedeen, J. (2016, March 15). *9 Punisher comics to read before watching Daredevil: Season 2.* IGN. https://www.ign.com/articles/2016/03/15/9-punisher-comics-to-read-before-watching-daredevil-season-2.
Serafino, J. (2011, August 2). *The top 10 Punisher stories of all time.* Complex. https://www.complex.com/pop-culture/2011/08/the-top-10-punisher-stories/.
smilebackwards. (2016, April 9). *Disarm.* Archive of our own. https://archiveofourown.org/works/6502163.
Thomason, N. (2013, May 18). *The Punisher: 7 essential stories you must read.* WhatCulture. https://whatculture.com/comics/the-punisher-7-essential-stories-you-must-read.
Verheiden, M. (Writer) & Jobst, M. (Director). (2016). New York's finest [Streaming series episode]. In D. Buckley (Producer), *Daredevil.* Los Gatos, CA: Netflix.
vibishan. (2016, April 12). *The ultimate double dare.* Archive of our own. https://archiveofourown.org/works/6536596.

Takes One to Kill One
Punisher MAX's *War on Hegemonic Masculinity*

Kelly Kanayama

With his penchant for murder, the stark white skull on his chest, and his staggeringly exhaustive arsenal, the Punisher could easily be read as a basic symbol of destructive hegemonic masculinity. Yet it is one of the bloodiest and most brutal installations in the franchise that sought to critically engage with the Punisher's troubled relationship to these structures of masculinity in the context of then-contemporary America. The 65-issue comic book series *Punisher MAX*, published from 2003 to 2008, deals with an older Punisher's violent exploits against the backdrop of post-9/11 America. Written by veteran comics author Garth Ennis, the series pits Frank Castle against such enemies as sadistic Mafiosi, human traffickers, and the U.S. military.

This last point was not exactly new territory for Ennis, who had already written a comic where the Punisher breaks into the White House to confront the President (Ennis & Dillon, 2001). By 2003, however, a series with a protagonist who exacted bloody reprisal on American military operatives presented a much more loaded message—especially since both said protagonist and the corpses in his wake were emblematic of the hegemonic masculinity that had come to dominate sociopolitical discourse in the aftermath of 9/11. Hegemonic masculinity is defined by sociologist Raewyn Connell (2005) as:

> the configuration of gender practice which embodies the currently accepted answer to the problem of the legitimacy of patriarchy, which guarantees (or is taken to guarantee) the dominant position of men and the subordination of women [p. 77].

How can the Punisher, a character known for his homicidal acts in the name of vigilante justice, possibly undercut such an image? The answer is deceptively simple: by turning hegemonic masculine violence upon itself. As Ennis states, *Punisher MAX*, and indeed most of his body of work, aims to convey that "there's a price for certain kinds of behaviour and that eventually you're going to have to pay it—particularly if you go around treating life as a John Wayne movie" (personal communication, March 9, 2017).

Punisher MAX takes pains to establish early on that the Punisher is not free from the constraints of hegemonic masculinity. Its opening story arc, *Born*, depicts Frank Castle communing with a mysterious voice during his last tour of duty in the Vietnam War. Notably, the voice's lines appear as white text in black narration boxes—the same format as the Punisher's inner monologue in the rest of the series, suggesting that he has absorbed the essence and/or ethos of whatever entity produces this voice into his own psyche. The voice continually urges him to give in to his murderous impulses, culminating in what appears to be a life-or-death bargain in the midst of a potentially fatal battle:

> I can give it to you, FRANK—
> There'll be a price, but nothing's free—
> Say no, and you're one more K.I.A. on a hill that no one cared about to start with.
> Say yes—And I'll give you what you've wanted all these years.
> [...]
> A war that lasts forever, a war that never ends, *but you have to say the word,* FRANK [Ennis & Robertson, 2003].

Frank accepts with a "*Yes*" hissed through gritted teeth, which in the moment allows him to singlehandedly slaughter twenty-four enemy fighters despite sustaining seven gunshot wounds (Ennis & Robertson, 2003), but in the long term destroys his only source of emotional connection. When he returns from Vietnam, the mystery voice reminds him of their bargain, hinting, "You remember I mentioned there'd be a price...?" (Ennis & Robertson, 2003) over a full-page image of a skull outline drawn around Frank's wife and children. For Frank, the pursuit of "a war that never ends" means forsaking the bonds that tether him to his humanity.

The historical setting of these events plays a significant role with regard to the masculinity that the Punisher embodies in *Punisher MAX*. During the Vietnam War, increasing anti-war sentiment threw into question models of hegemonic masculinity and their reliance on militaristic aggression, leaving behind "the potential for an ethically reconstituted masculinity" (Boose, 1993, p. 71). In practice, this involved tearing down extant masculinities more than rebuilding new ones; popular narratives about the Vietnam War, such as the movies *Apocalypse Now* (1979) or *Full Metal Jacket* (1987), tended to center on men losing their senses of self, their faith in America, and often their sanity as they attempted to navigate an incomprehensible theater of death (Kord & Krimmer, 2011). Notably, such narratives rarely offered an alternative or any real chance at rehabilitation, instead leaving their main characters to bleed out in a jungle or be burdened with terrible psychological and physical damage for the rest of their lives. It is this brand of masculinity that Frank carries with him in *Punisher MAX*: destructive, hopeless, and, most importantly, laden with a brokenness that stems from a conscious, deliberate choice.

By contrast, post–9/11 America was preoccupied with a classic model of hegemonic masculinity built on male authority and female submission. Pre-9/11 America was still very much beholden to hegemonic masculinity—as a brief example, women's average earnings in 2000 were 73.7 percent of men's average earnings (Status of Women in the States, 2015), a noticeably wider gender pay gap than today, where women in America earn on average 80 percent of men's earnings (U.S. Census Bureau, 2018). However, the country's attempts to recover from the World Trade Center attacks pushed this construction of gender to the forefront of public consciousness, in what Kord and Krimmer (2011) describe as the "remasculinization" of America (p. 2), borrowing Jeffords' (1989) term from *The Remasculization of America: Gender and the Vietnam War*.

Three days after the attacks, *Time* featured an angry op-ed by editor Lance Morrow (2001) that called for "the nourishment of rage" and opened with the following:

> For once, let's have no "grief counselors" standing by with banal consolations, as if the purpose, in the midst of all this, were merely to make everyone feel better as quickly as possible. We shouldn't feel better.
>
> For once, let's have no fatuous rhetoric about "healing." Healing is inappropriate now, and dangerous. There will be time later for the tears of sorrow.

To drive the point home, the piece also called for America to "relearn why human nature has equipped us all with a weapon (abhorred in decent peacetime societies) called hatred" [Morrow, 2001].

Morrow dismisses grief counseling as "banal" and suggests that even considering emotional recovery is "fatuous," "inappropriate," and "dangerous," with sarcastic quotation marks around "grief counselors" and "healing" for good measure. The implication is that trying to cope with collective national emotion would be downright un–American. Instead, the country must embrace its most aggressive impulses, which is usually considered harmful on a personal level but becomes praiseworthy at an international one. Good Americans, in other words, must eschew the weak language of feelings for the stereotypical masculinity of angry retaliation.

In the years that followed, these ideologies were conveyed more subtly, but their core sentiment remained the same: America was strong, manly, and ready to fight. President George W. Bush's second State of the Union address (2002), for instance, dictated an action-over-emotion credo for the nation: "For too long our culture has said, 'If it feels good, do it.' Now America is embracing a new ethic and a new creed: 'Let's roll.'" In the same address, he criticized "our enemies" for mistakenly believing that "America was weak and materialistic, that we would splinter in fear and selfishness" (Bush, 2002). Again, being perceived as displaying stereotypically masculine traits (strength and courage) takes priority. Even the occasional foray into human interest anecdotes is male-focused:

> Every day a retired firefighter returns to Ground Zero, to feel closer to his two sons who died there. At a memorial in New York, a little boy left his football with a note for his lost father: Dear Daddy, please take this to heaven. I don't want to play football until I can play with you again some day [Bush, 2002].

Not only is everyone in this vignette male, their characters are fleshed out by their traditionally masculine activities—firefighting, contact sports—and their father-son relationships; the tragedy here lies in the severance of male legacies. There are no daughters who died while working in the Twin Towers, no mothers who gave their lives in the line of duty as rescue workers or medical responders, no little girls leaving dolls for their lost parents.

By itself, however, foregrounding maleness is not enough to maintain hegemonic masculinity; female agency must also be subsumed into male desires and worldviews. As a result, America's recovered machismo was accompanied by a backlash against femininity. In Susan Faludi's (2007) words, "women's independence had become implicated in our nation's failure to protect itself," and the nation's reaction was a "discounting of female opinions, a demeaning of the female voice, and a general shrinkage of the female profile" (p. 21). Some mass media outlets began urging women to return to traditional gender roles, i.e., to accept male dominance in both public and private spheres, so that America could regain its strength. From a magazine writer suggesting that the *Band of Brothers*-style ethos the country needed could not survive in "a female-centered *Sex and the City* culture" (Faludi, 2007, p. 24), to a *New York Times* columnist decrying "feminists" who "wanted to rescue males from masculinity" and "put boys in touch with their feelings" (Tierney, 2001), to *Newsweek* comparing Susan Sontag's relatively mild critique of political rhetoric around 9/11 ("Who doubts that America is strong? But that's not all America has to be" [Sontag, 2001]) with blaming sexual assault victims and male bodies in women's clothing—"the same people always urging us not to blame the victim in rape cases are now saying Uncle Sam wore a short skirt and asked for it" (Alter, 2001)—the message was clear: granting voice and influence to the feminine had been a mistake, one that America was trying to correct by adhering to a hegemonically masculine self-image.

In *Punisher MAX*, these impulses manifest as men exploiting female bodies to further the aggressive masculine hegemony associated with post–9/11 America, which the title character must then, well, punish. At times this link to American militarism is very apparent, as with Rawlins, a CIA operative who becomes one of the series' recurring antagonists. To illustrate exactly what aspects of said American militarism he stands for, his first *Punisher MAX* appearance takes place after he has finished mustering a Saudi Arabian terrorist cell to fly a plane into a Russian military installation in order to justify continued U.S. intervention in the Middle East (Ennis & Braithwaite, 2004), or, more broadly, to spread violence, fear, aggression, and death as a representative of America. That is, Rawlins takes up the "weapon ... called hatred," to use the verbiage of Morrow's (2001) *Time* article and wields it deftly on the nation's behalf.

Rawlins' ability to promulgate this hegemonic masculinity is bolstered by his willingness to treat women as expendable objects, particularly his former wife, ex-CIA agent and eventual Punisher ally/lover Kathryn O'Brien. During a stakeout, O'Brien reveals that on what should have been their honeymoon, Rawlins pushed her out of a helicopter over Afghanistan to protect a hidden cargo of heroin, which results in her being captured and sexually assaulted by "the mujahs" (Ennis & Fernandez, 2005, #22). Later, when she and the Punisher torture him for information, Rawlins makes light of her past ordeal, deriding the idea that "the bukkake queen of Kabul [is] gonna make me talk" (Ennis & Fernandez, 2005, #23). The term "bukkake" is Japanese in origin and refers to a sexual act and/or type of pornography wherein multiple men ejaculate on one person. Describing O'Brien's assault in such terms equates it, at least from Rawlins' point of view, with the commodified sexuality of pornography, where participants knowingly present their bodies as part of a product for mass consumption. Eliding the important distinction between rape and voluntary participation in the commodification of one's own body, as Rawlins does here, points toward a misogynistic worldview where female sexual autonomy—or more broadly, female agency concerning the body—does not matter or perhaps does not even exist, and, by extension, where women are reduced to the status of objects with no real agency regarding the bodies they inhabit.

Additionally, by pushing O'Brien from the helicopter, Rawlins further objectifies her body by setting off a chain of events that devalue her professional, political, and any other statuses that she has gained through her own actions, and emphasize the femaleness of her body above all else. When she is captured, the sociopolitical power that her CIA credentials provide is dwarfed by her feminine status as object and victim. The fact that it is the "mujahs" who attack her, i.e., religious extremist leaders whose regime rests at least partially on keeping girls and women subordinate to male authority, underscores this gendered victimization. Additionally, Rawlins' actions offer something of an updated parallel to the Punisher's choice in Vietnam between human connection and endless fighting, albeit with a different focus; unlike the Punisher, who chose war for its own sake, Rawlins sacrifices his wife for self-preservation and financial gain. It is perhaps fitting, therefore, that the Punisher murders Rawlins in an airport bathroom, a place where people are reduced to the most basic bodily functions within a larger locus of post–September-11-era anxieties regarding American national identity, security, and strength: the anxieties for which the "Let's roll" ethos was crafted. Having the Punisher kill Rawlins in such a setting implicitly positions these ideals as part of his demise and the Punisher as destroyer of the embodiments of said ideals.

However, the battle against America's early 2000s hegemonic masculinity involves more than simply surpassing an opponent's capacity for violence. The Punisher also stops institutions that thrive on hegemonically masculine social structures from objectifying female bodies. In the story arc *Mother Russia*, he saves the life of a young Russian girl, Galina, whose scientist father injects her with a flesh-eating virus and its antidote, which the U.S. military wants to extract from her blood and synthesize into biological weapons. When the Punisher infiltrates the base where Galina is held, he discovers that she has been greatly mistreated during her confinement and that she was forced into becoming part of her father's research, or, in her words:

> My daddy was mean to me. He stuck a thing in my arm and it really, really hurt. Then these people took him away and they brought me here, and *they* were mean to me too. They stuck things in my arms and they took my *blood* ... and they kept doing it, they said they had to do *tests*, and I didn't want to [...] [Ennis & Braithwaite, 2004, #15].

To her father and the men sending the Punisher into Russia, Galina is merely a body to be invaded, as demonstrated by the repeated mention of scientists "sticking things into her arms," appropriated ("they took my blood"), and distributed as a commodity. This is underscored when an American soldier, after attempting to murder Galina via lethal injection, informs the Punisher that his orders in case of obstruction were to "kill the kid and bring her blood out" (Ennis & Braithwaite, 2005, #17).

The Punisher stands in direct opposition to this attitude toward Galina. In addition to beating the soldier who tries to kill her, he refuses to let any military personnel perform tests on or draw blood from her on the voyage back to America, which leads to the virus dying inside her body before it can be extracted and thus prevents her from being treated as an object for the purposes of global conflict. He also continually refers to

Galina by name both in conversation with her and when speaking to others about her, in contrast to the U.S. military officers who refer to her as "the sample" (Ennis & Braithwaite, 2005, #15). While it is his propensity for violence that enables his actions, his ultimate aim, and the goal toward which he directs the remnants of his humanity, is to prevent a hegemonically masculine institution from dehumanizing and commodifying Galina's body. To accomplish this, he leverages his connection to violent hegemonic masculinity by shooting, fighting, and murdering his way through an entire military base.

These multiple axes of hegemonic masculinity—war, militarism, subjugation and objectification of women—converge most prominently in the story arc *The Slavers*, which pits the Punisher against an Eastern European sex trafficking ring. Its leaders, Tiberiu and Cristu Bulat, are a Romanian father and son team who start out as the heads of an anti-Muslim militia outfit in Serbia before turning their aptitude for carnage into a human trafficking business venture. Their vocational shift occurs at some point during their last four invasions when Cristu, the son, realizes there is "[m]ore profit in slavery than in massacre" (Ennis & Fernandez, 2005). In practice, this means rounding up girls and younger women and relocating their new sex trafficking enterprise to the States, where the Punisher deals with them in spectacularly gory fashion.

The father-son relationship helming the operation reflects a superficially mutable yet ideologically unchanged legacy of hegemonic masculinity. While on the surface its methods move away from death and militarism to commodification and profit, its core ethos remains the same: the bodies of the sociopolitical "Other," or, in other words, those deemed "lesser" according to hegemonic masculine hierarchy, are expendable tools to better the status and power of those individuals privileged by that structure. A panel juxtaposing the mass shooting of men and boys, led by Tiberiu, with an image of Cristu and several soldiers menacing traumatized women and girls, several of whom are covering their eyes, ears, and mouth in a symbolic but futile effort to close themselves off from the violence occurring around them (Ennis & Fernandez, 2005), presents war and trafficking as two parts of the same dehumanizing diptych.

It is also notable that the Bulats head up a militia outfit dedicated to killing Muslims in Europe, leaving behind a body count that can be read as an extrapolation of the Islamophobic rhetoric that sprang up in the U.S. and other Western countries during the War on Terror; America's post–9/11 words are given gory shape in the charnel houses Cristu and Tiberiu leave in their wake. This connection is reinforced when Jen, a social worker whom the Punisher enlists in his fight against the traffickers, reveals America's complicity in facilitating sex trafficking as a whole, especially among the military. Unlike drugs, which are one-time use products, people "can be sold and resold, used indefinitely" (Ennis & Fernandez, 2005), creating what is in essence an engine of potentially infinite commodification. As a result, "criminal syndicates are switching over from narcotics to the trafficking of women," and "girls [...] are trafficked through Saudi to Iraq, set up as whores for American and British soldiers" (Ennis & Fernandez, 2005).

Jen's statements are rooted firmly in horrifying fact: according to the U.S. Department of State's June 2004 Trafficking of Persons Report, "80 percent of the victims trafficked across international borders are female and 70 percent of those females are trafficked for sexual exploitation" (2004, p. 23). In other words, 56 percent of *all* human trafficking at the time was dedicated to sexually enslaving women and girls. American armed forces also have a long history with the sex trafficking industry, since for decades prostitutes working near overseas military bases have been victims of international trafficking (Hughes, Chon, & Ellerman, 2007), and there are multiple instances of U.S. servicemen and private military contractor employees purchasing girls and women from known slavery ring operators in Bosnia and elsewhere (Maffai, 2009).

The relationship between sex trafficking and the American military also calls into question the Punisher's connection to these mechanisms of exploitation, given his service in Vietnam. In the popular Western imagination, the Vietnam War is practically synonymous with exploited female bodies, courtesy of movies such as *Full Metal Jacket* (1987), featuring a Vietnamese prostitute who repeats the now-infamous lines, "Me fucky sucky.... Me love you long time," and images like the "Napalm Girl" photo (1972), which depicts a sobbing, naked girl running away from a napalm attack. Additionally, Poulin (2003) argues that contemporary Southeast Asia's massive sex tourism trade, which caters to Westerners and depends heavily on trafficked women and underage girls, arose from U.S. troops' demand for and frequent use of prostitutes during the Vietnam War. While sex work is not exploitative per se, its association in this instance with the colonial implications of America's presence in Vietnam, as well as its laying the foundation for a trafficking-reliant sex trade across an entire world region, means that it feeds into a drive to globalize hegemonic masculinity.

Of course, the Punisher does not participate in these exploitations while serving in Vietnam, as the recent prequel comic *Punisher MAX: The Platoon* (2017–2018) makes clear. When most of his fellow soldiers visit Saigon's red light district to sleep with numerous prostitutes, he opts to sit outside a cafe and converse with his sergeant instead (Ennis & Parlov, 2017). He is, however, responsible for arranging their leave in Saigon and, therefore, facilitating his subordinates' participation in this enterprise; he also criticizes their activities by referring to the prostitutes as "the dirtiest I've ever seen" (Ennis & Parlov, 2017), placing blame and judgment on the women they purchased. Considering, furthermore, that Vietnam is where he makes the choice that leads him to become the Punisher—namely never-ending war over the emotional bonds that domestic family life entails—his battle against Cristu and Tiberiu Bulat's trafficking enterprise not only condemns contemporary hegemonic masculinity's oppression of girls and women, but begins to look like (perhaps unintentional) atonement for the effects of his earlier complicity in the same.

Being the Punisher, or rather being a man who has chosen a life built on war, means that said atonement consists of paying back sex slavers' hegemonic masculinity in kind, as in the cases of Galina and Rawlins. Since their business rests on treating female bodies as objects to be brutalized for profit, it is no coincidence that the executions of Cristu and Tiberiu are the series' most violent; the Punisher burns Tiberiu alive on camera after disemboweling Cristu in the woods and stringing his intestines across the branches of several trees. Their bodies are reduced, penetrated, and redistributed, in a microcosm of what they have inflicted upon numerous girls and women. Hegemonically masculine bloodshed may beget further hegemonically masculine bloodshed, but here, at least, that means it destroys itself.

By using this approach to critique contemporary hegemonic masculinity, *Punisher MAX* puts forth a grim view of America's sociopolitical climate: one where the best immediate fix for the exploitation enabled by unchecked hegemonic masculinity is a sort of self-destruction, or, to rephrase an old saying, it takes one to kill one. While such self-destruction may seem to provide satisfying closure in individual story arcs, its continued foregrounding throughout the series portrays the worldviews and ideologies associated with hegemonic masculinity as ultimately futile. In the Punisher's and Garth Ennis's post–9/11 America, masculinity must acknowledge its own brokenness and attempt to redress the wrongs perpetrated by other, unreconstructed masculinities in order to deserve survival.

References

Alter, J. (2001, October). Blame America at your peril. *Newsweek*, 41.
Boose, L.E. (1993). Techno-muscularity and the "boy eternal." In M. Cooke & A. Woollacott (Eds.), *Gendering war talk* (pp. 67–106). Princeton: Princeton University Press.
Bush, G.W. (2002, January 29). *President delivers State of the Union address*. https://georgewbush-whitehouse.archives.gov/news/releases/2002/01/20020129-11.html.
Coe, K., Domke, D., Bagley, M.M., Cunningham, S. & Van Leuven, N. (2007). Masculinity as political strategy: George W. Bush, the "War on Terrorism," and an echoing press. *Journal of Women, Politics and Policy, 29*, 31–55.
Connell, R. (2005). *Masculinities: Second edition*. Cambridge: Polity Press.

Ennis, G., & Braithwaite, D. (2004, November). *Punisher MAX*, #14. New York: Marvel Comics.
Ennis, G., & Braithwaite, D. (2004, December). *Punisher MAX*, #15. New York: Marvel Comics.
Ennis, G., & Braithwaite, D. (2005, January). *Punisher MAX*, #16. New York: Marvel Comics.
Ennis, G., & Braithwaite, D. (2005, February). *Punisher MAX*, #17. New York: Marvel Comics.
Ennis, G., & Dillon, S. (2001). *Punisher vol. 6*, #5. New York: Marvel Comics.
Ennis, G., & Fernandez, L. (2005, June). *Punisher MAX*, #22. New York: Marvel Comics.
Ennis, G., & Fernandez, L. (2005, July). *Punisher MAX*, #23. New York: Marvel Comics.
Ennis, G., & Fernandez, L. (2005, November). *Punisher MAX*, #27. New York: Marvel Comics.
Ennis, G., & Parlov, G. (2017). *Punisher MAX: The platoon*, #4. New York: Marvel Comics.
Ennis, G., & Robertson, D. (2003, October). *Born* #3. New York: Marvel Comics.
Ennis, G., & Robertson, D. (2003, November). *Born* #4. New York: Marvel Comics.
Faludi, S. (2007). *The terror dream: Fear and fantasies in post-9/11 America*. New York: Metropolitan Books.
Hughes, D.M., Chon, K.Y., & Ellerman, D.P. (2007). Modern-day comfort women: The U.S. military, transnational crime, and the trafficking of women. *Violence Against Women, 13*, 901–922.
Jeffords, S. (1989). *The remasculization of America: Gender and the Vietnam War*. Bloomington: Indiana University Press.
Kord, S., & Krimmer, E. (2011). *Contemporary Hollywood masculinities: Gender, genre and politics*. New York: Palgrave Macmillan.
Kubrick, S. (Director, Producer). (1987). *Full Metal Jacket* [Film]. United States: Warner Bros.
Maffai, M. (2009). Accountability for private military and security company employees that engage in sex trafficking and related abuses while under contract with the United States overseas. *Wisconsin International Law Journal, 26*, 1095–1139.
Morrow, L. (2001, September). The case for rage and retribution. *Time, 158*, n.p.
Poulin, R. (2003). Globalization and the sex trade: Trafficking and the commodification of women and children. *Canadian Women Studies, 22*, 38–47.
Sontag, S. (2001, September 24). Tuesday, and after. *The New Yorker*. https://www.newyorker.com/magazine/2001/09/24/tuesday-and-after-talk-of-the-town.
Status of Women in the States. (2015). *Earnings and the gender wage gap*. https://statusofwomendata.org/earnings-and-the-gender-wage-gap/.
Tierney, J. (2001, December). The big city; G.I. stands tall again (12 inches). *The New York Times*.
U.S. Census Bureau. (2018, September 12). *Income and poverty in the United States: 2017*. https://www.census.gov/library/publications/2018/demo/p60-263.html.
U.S. Department of State. (2004, June). *Trafficking in persons report*. https://www.state.gov/documents/organization/34158.pdf.

Section III
Veteran Studies

Recalling Vietnam in Marvel Cinematic Universe's Punisher Storylines

MIKE LEMON

Time proves a complicated concept within Marvel's shared comic book and adapted cinematic universes. For all the company's time-traveling adventures, most superheroes, villains, and citizens perceive their relationship to time as being (mostly) linear. The company relies on a historical temporality, or the progression of events to shape past, present, and future (Serra, 2016). According to Serra (2016), Marvel's use of historical temporality ensures that "Characters and readers, because of the linearity of these adventures, have to forcibly bear in mind a past that becomes richer month after month" (pp. 648–649). However, the emphasis on causal events can prove difficult for readers: an almost eight-decade publication history across multiple storylines and universes may dissuade new readers. To invite new and long-time readers, Marvel compresses historical time in their shared universe, floating closer towards a contemporary temporal context. In the recent "soft" reboot, "Legacy," Zdarsky and Cheung's *Marvel Two-in-One* (2018) depicts Reed Richards and Ben Grimm pranking Victor Von Doom while the three are in college. A throwaway panel to the prank—altering Doom's name on an award—reveals the three characters attended college together in 1998 (Zdarsky and Cheung, 2018, p. 19). This situates the main, 616, Universe into a post–9/11 sociopolitical context, although not all characters remained "fixed" in time. Some characters, most famously Captain America, become fixed to their original historical context, which allows them to omit decades-long gap between World War II and the character's presence in current storylines. Other characters receive soft reboots to their origin stories. These soft reboots distance characters from their origins' historical context but retain their inherent qualities.

Frank Castle, the Punisher, paradoxically remains positioned between the two. His official universe origin story remains rooted to the Vietnam War. O'Nale (2010) reminds readers that the Punisher's "alter ego, Frank Castle, was a Marine and Vietnam veteran" (p. 489). Ennis and Dillon's early twenty-first century *Punisher* series notably kept Frank a Vietnam veteran, despite the floating timeline. Nevertheless, recent comic series and cinematic adaptations have distanced Frank from the mid–twentieth century. Rosenberg and Vilanova's *Punisher: War Machine* (2018) open their series by evoking Frank's military service before detailing his character's origin story. Witnessing his family's death during a botched mob hit, Frank Castle becomes the Punisher (Rosenberg and Vilanova, 2018, p. 1). The opening tag retains the Punisher's inherent characteristics and trauma but separates him from Vietnam. The subtle shift suggests that authors and illustrators do not have to link Frank to Vietnam but can move his military service to any appropriately contemporary military operation. Obscuring the Punisher's initial links to Vietnam extends to recent cinematic adaptions, which follows the comic book's shifting historical temporality.

In adapting the character for the Marvel Cinematic Universe (MCU), Frank Castle's appearances in Season 2 of *Daredevil* and his own series follows a similar pattern by updating the character's history. Frank (Jon Berthnal) is now a veteran of the War on Terror. Such a move positions him as a post–9/11 character, which fits within the printed universe's latest chronological reboot. Nevertheless, there exists references to the Punisher's canonical roots, in that Frank and other characters interact with Vietnam veterans. Such references reflect C. Silvino (1995), who argues the Marvel Universe functions as a postmodern, transmedia text, granting fans autonomy to construct the narrative across multiple series (p. 44). While C. Silvino's claim arises from the comic book universe, it easily translates to the MCU and its Netflix series that occur within this larger, shared universe. This essay contends that interactions or references to Vietnam are intentional: in *Daredevil* and *The Punisher*, scenes and storylines with veterans from various international conflicts maintain the character's paradoxical connection to the Vietnam war. While the adaptation's temporal shifts allow the series to explore contemporary issues like PTSD, the MCU series does so by simultaneously recalling his connection to the Vietnam War and separating the character from that historical position.

When the character first appears in the MCU, *Daredevil*'s Season 2 showrunners, Doug Petrie and Marco Ramirez, emphasize his recognizable qualities—brutal vigilantism and efficient military training—before revealing his face, name, and trauma. In the second season's premiere "Bang" (Petrie, Ramirez, and Abraham, 2016), his attacks on several New York gangs and Daredevil intensify the series' vigilante violence. The episode opens with Daredevil (Charlie Cox) stopping armed robbers, but he does so with his fists and billy club. While Daredevil relies on violence to fight crime, his level of aggression does not rise to Frank's. The Punisher's opening attack on the Irish gang is an extended, one-sided gun battle, in which the vigilante does not appear. Instead, this and subsequent scenes highlight his violent war on crime as "massive gang-on-gang overkill" (Petrie, Ramirez, and Abraham, 2016). This casual comment from police office—and reluctant ally to Matt Murdock/Daredevil—Brett Mahoney (Royce Johnson) signals a common misconception. Many characters link the carnage to an army, comments that imply his military training. When the character finally reveals himself to camera, his face remains largely obscured. Director Phil Abraham uses backlighting and darkened environments to shadow his face, until the character shoots Daredevil (Petrie, Ramirez, and Abraham, 2016). In this premiere episode, the character receives neither a name nor a face. Moreover, the showrunners have not explored his trauma, relying instead on viewers' background knowledge on the Punisher.

Episode 3 begins the series' exploration into Frank's history, and a Vietnam veteran serves as the unknowing expository catalyst. "New York's Finest" (Verheiden and Jobst, 2016) opens with Daredevil chained to a chimney, as the newly nicknamed "Punisher" drinks coffee and prepares military grade weapons. As the two argue the Punisher's ethics, a belligerent tenant, Jerry (Ray Iannicelli), goes to investigate the noise. In confronting the man, the Punisher is at once charming and foreboding. He reveals his name—Frank—and strikes up a conversation with the old man. But when Daredevil makes some noise, the scene cuts to Frank holding a loaded pistol behind the door. The camera pans to frame the tenant's head between Frank and the gun, visually suggesting that Frank will shoot the older man. Fortunately for the tenant, Frank guides the conversation to military service:

FRANK: Yeah. You serve?
JERRY: 'Nam, 3rd Marine Division.
FRANK: Fighting 3rd, huh?
JERRY: Goddamn right. You?
FRANK: Yeah, yeah. Iraq. Afghanistan.
JERRY: Welcome home [Verheiden and Jobst, 2016].

Military comradery defuses the tense situation and allows the Punisher to reveal details about his past. Frank discloses his name and his military service in the Middle East and Afghanistan. Doing so to a Vietnam veteran recalls the character's official comics origins. Ennis, Parlov, and Bellaire's *Punisher: The Platoon* (2018), a limited series, has Frank serving with the Echo Battalion, part of the 3rd Marine Division. In this scene, *Punisher: The Platoon*, and other origins stories, Frank participates in what

Silvino calls the Marvel Universe's "sprawling and ever shifting narrative tapestry whose composite threads endlessly cross, re-cross and double back upon each other in a process of continuous relativization and revision" (p. 43). These "texts" exist across time and multiple media. Moreover, they relate to and complicate each other in fascinating ways. This scene in *Daredevil* seemingly functions as an Easter egg for comic book fans. It pay homage to Frank's Vietnam origins, while also updating the character's military service to more recent international conflicts. This scene constitutes a soft reboot for the character; it also separates Frank from his printed origins, in more ways than a pointed gun to the tenant's head.

While the hidden gun proves the most ominous detachment between these characters, director Jobst (2016) uses camera angles to suggest temporal distance for Frank, Jerry, and the Vietnam War. From their first visual interaction, camera angles imply Frank's domineering size. When Jobst shoots the scene from Frank's perspective, he angles the camera down. Viewers observe Jerry from Frank's perspective: they too look down upon Jerry, suggesting his age and diminutive state. The opposite occurs when Jerry speaks to Frank: Jobst (2016) angles the camera up. This frames the Punisher's beaten, but youthful face. These camera angles argue the time lapse between the mid-century Vietnam War, and the series' contemporary time setting. Frank is a recent vet: Jerry has aged. Another scene in the episode further suggest Jerry's disempowered position. As an angry biker gang descend on the apartment building, the tenant comes to investigate. The camera position has Daredevil in the foreground, Jerry in the middle, and the gang rushing from the background. Even though the Vietnam veteran appears tall in the initial action, screaming, "What the hell's going on?," he is quickly swallowed up by the approaching gang (Verheiden and Jobst, 2016). When Daredevil arrives, Jerry is bent over, surrendering his earlier bravado. In the presence of younger men, the older veteran physically and figuratively diminishes.

Jerry's murder in "A Cold Day in Hell's Kitchen" (Petrie, Ramirez, and Hoar, 2016) further reinforce Vietnam's irrelevance within the Punisher's MCU origins. Tied up and surrounded by Hand ninjas, Jerry demonstrates his bravado as he shouts, "I was a POW in Laos. This is a cakewalk" (Petrie, Ramirez, and Hoar, 2016). Camera angle and scale again prove important. The scene is mostly shot from medium distance, with the camera angle looking slightly upward. The angle suggests that viewers are watching from the position of crouching hostages. Jerry is at once present and vulnerable. His show of courage cannot save him from being shot. Jerry's death and his interactions in Episode 2 propose that while Jerry plays an important role for the Punisher's exposition, his age and temporal separation from active duty precludes him from the series' action.

These references extend to the MCU series *The Punisher*, continuing the dismissal of the Vietnam War for Frank and other veterans' origins. Showrunner Steven Lightfoot includes a supposed Vietnam veteran, O'Connor (Delaney Williams), early in the series. His first appearance in "3 AM" (Lightfoot and Shankland, 2017) does not reveal O'Connor's alleged service in Vietnam. This comes in Episode 6, "The Judas Goat," where the older man relates how he received a Silver Star: "April 1968. About 20 miles west of Tam Ky. I killed 13 of those gooks with their own grenades. 'For gallantry in action.'" (Boylan and Webb, 2017). In "3 AM" (Lightfoot and Shankland, 2017), viewers learn about his characteristics and ideological views. O'Connor participates in a therapy group run by Frank's friend, Curtis Hoyle (Jason Moore). A long shot shows that he is the oldest participant in the group, the rest mostly comprised of Iraq and Afghanistan veterans. While a few veterans have military or patriotic clothing, O'Connor wears an NRA hat. This suggests his sociopolitical conservatism. His dialogue further separates him as a belligerent presence in the group. He rails, "The real persecuted minority in this country today is the Christian American patriot" (Lightfoot and Shankland, 2017). Director Shankland (2017) pairs this dialogue with an extreme close-up of O'Connor's face, and then cuts to Hoyle for reaction.

As a black veteran, Hoyle seems unshaken by O'Connor's tirade, suggesting that he has heard it before. His expression also demonstrates his leadership within the group. Other black group members, however, are quick to call the older man out for his extreme views. Nevertheless, O'Connor continues, "We've got to do something about the liberal, do-gooding assholes who are running this country into the ground. The ones that want to take our rights and our guns" (Lightfoot and Shankland, 2017). Again, Shankland (2017) uses an extreme close-up for this dialogue, although something ominous occurs in the background. O'Connor shifts his head slightly as he speaks, revealing in the blurred background another veteran—another white man in a hat—nodding his head in agreement. This unnamed extra implies at least one audience member who agrees with O'Connor's ideological views. The substantial use of extreme close-up shots when O'Connor speaks sets him apart from the group (Lightfoot and Shankland, 2017); coupled with his supposed Vietnam status, O'Connor and his dialogue embody the white patriot movement. Subsequent cuts, shot scales, and dialogue suggest that a few members agree with his ideology.

Even though Frank has no personal interactions with O'Connor, he is present at this meeting, and his hidden movement suggests his apparent acceptance and eventual rejection of O'Connor's diatribe. A cross-cut edit towards the beginning of the scene reveals that Frank is outside the room, listening into the conversation. The director does not include any edited cuts to Frank's reaction to O'Connor's initial thoughts on the white Christian patriot, though his friendship with Hoyle suggests a rejection of the older man's prejudiced views. When Lewis Wilson (Daniel Webber), a recently returned veteran, admits feeling lost after returning home, O'Connor replies:

> They're scared, man. Because they aren't stupid. They spent fifteen years training an army and then abandoned it on the streets. *A time is gonna come when we have to defend ourselves and, and put things back to how they were. You love this country, you better be ready,* 'cause the next war's gonna be here [Lightfoot and Shankland, 2017, emphasis added].

The director again uses extreme close-up for most of O'Connor's speech (Lightfoot and Shankland, 2017). However, for the italicized dialogue, the scene cuts to Frank outside the room. He moves towards the door, implying either his interest or agreement with O'Connor's opinion. Given the character's violent disposal of those how murdered his family, Frank's movement could denote him agreeing. A subsequent cut, however, signals his separation from O'Connor's ideology. Wilson agrees with O'Connor, saying "sic semper tyrannis" (Lightfoot and Shankland, 2017). When questioned by Hoyle whether he believes the government to be hostile, Wilson pauses and looks around for resolution, before replying, "All I know is that we risked our lives and we did terrible things and it meant nothing when we got home" (Lightfoot and Shankland, 2017). The scene cuts to Frank; in profile, he bows his head. Whatever agreement may have existed between the Punisher and O'Connor's world views is gone. Hearing these statements reiterated by an Iraq veteran gives Frank pause. He recognizes a kinship with this younger soldier that he does not with the bellicose older man. The separation between the Punisher and the Vietnam War persists.

Frank and O'Connor may not interact during the *Punisher*, but the probable Vietnam veteran proves integral to the Wilson's character arc. In addition to flashbacks, Wilson has difficulty sleeping: he almost shoots his father in the episode "Kandahar" (Lightfoot and Goddard, 2017). In another meeting where Wilson shares his feelings of betrayal, O'Connor approaches him. The older man hands him a pamphlet entitled "Guns: Our Fundamental American Right." He tells Wilson, "Read this kid. You're right to feel betrayed. And there's plenty men who feel just the same. This touchy-feely bullshit ain't gonna solve nothing" (Lightfoot and Goddard, 2017). This scene begins in a medium shot, showing both men as level. After the close-up on the pamphlet, the scene cuts to medium close-up, O'Connor slightly behind Wilson. Camera angle suggests a mutual power level, but O'Connor's position behind the younger man implies his persuasive characteristics. This scene may not explicitly recall Vietnam, but O'Connor still acts within his supposed veteran status. This assumed brotherhood implicitly convinces Wilson to advocate for gun rights with O'Connor. It also suggests Wilson's rejection of Hoyle's support, which subsequent episodes confirm.

Even though Wilson has participated in Hoyle's support group, an interaction in "Resupply" (Scardapane and Skogland, 2017) emphasizes the disconnect between these two men. The writer and director include another reference to Vietnam that reinforces the ideological separation. In this episode, Wilson digs a foxhole in his backyard. Hoyle checks on Wilson and offers advice from his father who served in Vietnam. Even though both men are veterans of the War on Terror, Hoyle recognizes that his father's experience might prove useful for Wilson. Recommending a sump for water collection, he says, "You see, my pops, he served in Nam. In Nam, you're talking, you're talking jungle. *The ground's soft, but the rain…*" (Scardapane and Skogland, 2017, emphasis added). When Hoyle begins this dialogue, the camera remains level to Hoyle, looking over the foxhole's surface. Wilson is not present. But as Hoyle says the emphasized dialogue, the director cuts the scene to focus on Wilson, with a medium scale shot and the camera angle looking down from Hoyle's perspective. Nondiegetic music fades in and obscures Hoyle's dialogue. The scene then cuts to Wilson's perspective, with the camera angled towards Hoyle, but Wilson is not looking at him. Viewers can hear snippets of dialogue, but a combination of nondiegetic music and diegetic sound—clinking dog tags—signal that the young man is not listening. Camera perspective several times, but the conclusion remains the same. The younger veteran rejects Hoyle's advice, because it does not fit his emerging ideological radicalism. This reference to the Vietnam War becomes nuanced for Wilson's story. It further distances the story from Vietnam, yet Wilson remains aligned with O'Connor, whose alleged Vietnam service influences his gun right activism.

When Wilson discovers O'Connor's feigned veteran status, the revelation proves fatal to the older man. It also begins the show's most explicit declaration that the MCU's Punisher and his story line do not directly connect to the Vietnam War. The disclosure comes from Hoyle in "The Judas Goat" (Boylan and Webb, 2017). After Wilson and O'Connor's gun rights activism has the younger man thrown in jail, Hoyle posts Wilson's bail. He then tells Wilson, "He never served in Vietnam. He didn't sign up till '77 and never saw a combat. He's a fraud and a liar, Lewis. He didn't serve, not like you. And he's not worth your respect" (Boylan and Webb, 2017). Director Webb (2017) cuts between medium shots of the two veterans to reflect their perspectives. Hoyle's comments and facial expression signal his disgust with O'Connor, and also his concern for Wilson. Wilson, however, does not speak.

He demonstrates the same pause as in "3 AM" (Lightfoot & Shankland, 2017), but not the same search for resolution. Anger and betrayal simmer below Wilson's calm demeanor. In disclosing this information, Hoyle attempts to persuade the younger veteran to seek counseling, but this does not occur. Instead, Wilson confronts O'Connor about his duplicity. At first, he attempts to discredit his military records, claiming "Where'd you get my records from? The Internet? You know, the Jews run the Internet" (Boylan and Webb, 2017). But when Wilson asks for the name of the air base outside of Tam Ky—where O'Connor alleges to have served—the older man cannot answer. The scene involves an extended pause: the camera is positioned behind Wilson's shoulder, indicating that audience members should witness O'Connor's duplicity along with the troubled Iraq veteran. When O'Connor does not reply, the camera shifts to a medium close-up of Wilson. He appears visibly disappointed and angry, as he accepts the truth.

Wilson and O'Connor's final interaction ends with the older man's death and provides further evidence that the MCU's Punisher is not a Vietnam story. Having been caught in his duplicity, O'Connor attempts to rectify the situation. The following exchange signals the turn:

> O'CONNOR: How the hell am I supposed to remember that? I'm an old man. Look if, if you don't like my stories—
> WILSON: No, they're not just stories! *You can't just do that* [Boylan and Webb, 2017, emphasis added].

The camera angle remains consistent for this conversation. The camera is positioned behind Wilson. Wilson's body posture indicates disappointment in O'Connor. The older man's dialogue recalls the temporal separation between the Vietnam War and the contemporaneously set series. In this, O'Connor mirrors Jerry, the tenant from *Daredevil*. Both are old men past their prime. Unlike Jerry though, O'Connor cannot claim Vietnam veteran status; while he has served, he was neither stationed nor saw combat in the war. This fact makes O'Connor's use of "stories" particularly offensive to Wilson, because the older man reduces combat to narrative. Wilson erupts at stories; even though the camera remains behind him, the younger veteran's body language matches his dialogue. With the italicized dialogue, the camera shifts the camera to Wilson. The shot is medium close-up, showing the young veteran from the chest up. Wilson moves his arm across his body, signaling his dismissal of O'Connor. The phrase "You can't just do that" has layered meanings (Boylan and Webb, 2017). First, it condemns O'Connor's assumption of combat veteran status. He cannot claim Silver Star, awarded for combat gallantry, because he did not see combat. This recalls Hoyle's line of questioning earlier in the episode: "Is that why you served? For gratitude" (Boylan and Webb, 2017)? Second, O'Connor's reduction of combat to stories de-emphasizes other veterans' accomplishments and trauma. Wilson, Frank, and other veterans within the series struggle with PTSD. For O'Connor to presume combat status becomes a mockery to Wilson. The gap between them becomes most obvious as they fight. O'Connor escalates the attack, but Wilson's combat experience and youth prove too much for the older man. On its surface, this scene signals Wilson's turn towards domestic terrorism and away from Hoyle's support group. It also indicates that Wilson's path will mirror darkly Frank's, in terms of service in the War on Terror at the expense of supposed Vietnam roots. Wilson's murdering of O'Connor proves the series' most explicit detachment from the Vietnam War.

In adapting the Punisher for the Marvel Cinematic Universe, *Daredevil*'s Season 2 and *The Punisher*'s Season 1 showrunners, directors, and writers are intentional in their references towards the Vietnam War. Through their use of story, frame composition, dialogue, and more, these series demonstrate the Punisher's tenuous relationship to the mid-twentieth century conflict. The series adhere to the MCU's contemporary temporal setting and participate in the Marvel Universe's postmodern narrative tapestry. On their surfaces, these interactions serve as Easter eggs for Frank's comic book origins. However, referring to these moments and characters as Easter eggs would diminish their importance within the series, reducing them to one narrative function. References to Vietnam in *Daredevil* allow for expository moments, and also signal the MCU's contemporary temporal shift. *The Punisher*'s references to Vietnam are more complicated. O'Connor's ideological rhetoric and fraudulent service become important for Wilson's descent into domestic terrorism. His murder at the younger veteran's hands brutally separates the series' narrative from its Vietnam roots. Moreover, Hoyle's reference to Vietnam becomes muted as unnecessary; while not as explicit, it indicates the MCU's shift. With these varying references to the Vietnam War and its veterans, the Punisher maintains his origin's inherent characterizations and trauma, simultaneously participating in the cinematic adaptions' revised timeline and winking at his comic book counterpart's paradoxical reliance on a mid-twentieth century conflict.

References

Boylan, C. (Writer), & Webb, J. (Director). (2017). The Judas goat [Streaming series episode]. In M. Ambrose (Producer), *The Punisher*. Scott's Valley, CA: Netflix.

Ennis, G., Parlov, G., & Bellaire, J. (2018). *The Punisher: The platoon*. New York: Marvel Comics.

Lightfoot, S. (Writer), & Goddard, A. (Director). (2017). Kandahar [Streaming series episode]. In M. Ambrose (Producer), *The Punisher*. Scott's Valley, CA: Netflix.

Lightfoot, S. (Writer), & Shankland, T. (Director). (2017). 3AM [Streaming series episode]. In M. Ambrose (Producer), *The Punisher*. Scott's Valley, CA: Netflix.

O'Nale, R. (2010). The Punisher. In M. Booker (Ed.), *Encyclopedia of comic books and graphic novels* (pp. 489–491). Santa Barbara, CA: Greenwood.

Petrie, D., & Ramirez, M. (Writers), & Abraham, P. (Director). (2016). Bang [Streaming series episode]. In D. Buckley (Producer), *Daredevil*. Scott's Valley, CA: Netflix.

Petrie, D. & Ramirez, M. (Writers), & Hoar, P. (Director). (2016). Cold day in Hell's Kitchen [Streaming series episode]. In D. Buckley (Producer), *Daredevil*. Scott's Valley, CA: Netflix.

Rosenberg, M., & Vilanova, G. (2018). *The Punisher: War machine vol. 1*. New York: Marvel Comics.

Scardapane, D. (Writer), & Skogland, K. (Director). (2016). Resupply [Streaming series episode]. In M. Ambrose (Producer), *The Punisher*. Scott's Valley, CA: Netflix.

Serra, M. (2016). Historical and mythical time in the Marvel and DC series. *The Journal of Popular Culture, 49*(3), 646–659.

Silvino, C. (1995). Narrative, the Marvel Universe, and the reader. *Studies in Popular Culture, 17*(2), 39–50.

Verheiden, M. (Writer), & Jobst, M. (Director). (2016). New York's finest [Streaming series episode]. In D. Buckley (Producer), *Daredevil*. Scott's Valley, CA: Netflix.

Zdarsky, C., & Cheung, J. (2018). *Marvel 2-in-one, # 2*. New York: Marvel Comics.

Fighting a Lonely War
Frank Castle and the Domestication of Vietnam

KATHLEEN MCCLANCY

Throughout his history, depictions of Frank Castle, also known as the Punisher, have oscillated between dedicated yet cold-blooded killer and enraged avenger, between disordered and organized, between callous and merciful, even as his character has straddled the line between hero and villain. The explanation for both his dedication and his pathology, however, remains the same: the murder of his family by mafia gunmen. Yet equally important to his characterization is his status as a veteran of the Vietnam War. This essay examines the ways in which the shifts in Castle's initial characterization reflect the shifts in early cultural perceptions of Vietnam veterans even as sourcing Castle's original trauma in the murder of his wife and two children erases the real legacies of American military involvement in Indochina. In the war's aftermath, the depiction of returning soldiers has transformed along with public opinion about the war itself. In American culture, Vietnam veterans are sometimes heroes while at other times psychotics; sometimes wounded by war while at other times wounded only by their return home; sometimes stone cold killers, while at other times SuperVets. Frank Castle's various incarnations have reflected this greater cultural iconography; the character thus becomes emblematic of the tradition of Vietnam veteran characters whose superficial hauntings by dead wives hide the deeper damage done by their service in Vietnam, even as their traumatic experiences in Indochina provide the explanation for their near-superpowers of destruction. This essay considers the history of the Punisher in the context of the cultural representations of the Vietnam veteran from the war years to the early to mid–1980s.

The character of the Punisher first appeared in 1974. For the first decade of his existence, he was limited to guest appearances in other Marvel comics, most commonly the various *Spider-Man* series, in which he usually occupied an antagonistic role to the title superhero before the inevitable team-up. He did not receive his own title until 1986's *The Punisher: Circle of Blood* mini-series, the success of which paved the way for an ongoing *Punisher* solo title in 1987 (Worcester, 2016, p. 37). Over the years, the character has seen multiple manifestations depending on the creative team writing him, from an angel to a zombie. Ostensibly, Castle's psychotic determination to assassinate all criminals stems from the murder of his wife and family, and his history as a soldier in Vietnam is incidental—while he learned the murderous skills he uses in his war on crime in Indochina, he was not turned into a murderer until the death of his family. As Marc DiPaolo puts it, Castle "has been portrayed as a normal, law-abiding citizen who returned from an honorable tour of duty in Vietnam," only to see his family murdered and to transform "into the Punisher, a merciless, one-man army" (2011, p. 116). Nevertheless, while DiPaolo's reading certainly echoes the surface presentation of the character, as much as the comics try to lay the blame for the Punisher's insanity on the murders of his family, their stories continually contradict this reasoning, compulsively returning to Vietnam. Cord Scott points out how the character's veteran status as well as his ambiguous morality reflects the confusion of the time of his origin, and Kent Worcester argues that the Punisher is part of a larger surge in revenge fiction which itself was born in part out of the aftermath of the Vietnam War (Scott, 2012, p. 123; Worcester, 2016, p. 36). In the end, throughout all his various manifestations, Castle's characterization has been grounded in his veteran status: his war on crime is presented as a continuation of his earlier war. While this essay focuses particularly on Castle's appearances before the publication of his solo title, these early depictions of the Punisher set the template for the later ones. The Punisher's origin in Vietnam may be hidden, superficially replaced with family tragedy, but it remains the subtext, and as different as Castle's manifestations may be, they all echo the various stereotypical representations of the iconic Vietnam veteran.

As multiple critics have noted over the years, the first fictional portraits of returning Vietnam veterans in American culture were in general far from positive, and the original Vietnam veteran icon was usually deeply psychologically disturbed, "a crazed psychopath who threatened at every moment to bring the war home with him" (M. Clark, 1986, pp. 49–50). This psychotic Vietnam veteran stereotype begins to emerge in the earliest days of the war, and Jerry Lembcke dates the crazed veteran image from *Motor Psycho* in 1965, but it would become ubiquitous after the Tet Offensive in 1968 and the revelations of the My Lai massacre in 1969 (1998, p. 158). Veterans on the page and on the screen in this period were, at best, miserable and completely disconnected from society; at worst, they rampaged across the American landscape, raping and murdering everything in their path.

This image was, of course, far from the heroic screen representations of the veteran of World War II, who by the time of the Vietnam war had become indelibly embodied in the persona of John Wayne. But even in 1965, the Vietnam War seemed a very different war from World War II to American audiences, and by 1968, when Walter Cronkite called the war a "stalemate" on the *CBS Evening News*, it was obvious that Americans were not in Iwo Jima anymore. Large segments of the population were joining in increasingly visible protests against the war, and the American government seemed to have difficulty explaining the reasons for the war to the public in terms even approaching the moral unquestionability of World War II. The Tet Offensive of early 1968 gave the lie to military claims of swift and inevitable victory over a demoralized enemy. As the war continued, rumors and then proven reports of atrocities committed by American soldiers, particularly the 1969 reports of the My Lai massacre, horrified the populace. The image of the soldier in Vietnam, and then of the returning veteran, were shaped by American ambivalence towards the war itself (Dean Jr., 1992, p. 61).

Popular culture reflected these anxieties about returning veterans, and in particular the anxieties about what these veterans would do once they had left the war behind them and returned home. Julian Smith eloquently outlines the problem:

> Though the films are rarely specific about the exact relationship between Vietnam and violent veterans, three general categories can be dimly perceived: the Vietnamese experience has turned healthy young men into sick killers; it has pushed latently violent men over the line or has transformed blatant maniacs into honored representatives of our culture; most commonly, it has embittered men (be they normal or neurotic) while teaching them skills that can be put to dangerous use [1975, pp. 155–156].

Since as far back as Odysseus' return from the Trojan War, societies have struggled with how to reincorporate soldiers upon their return: how to tame the violence that warfare instills before that violence can be turned against society itself. This problem was complicated after Vietnam by the association of that war with *immoral* violence: with the rape and murder of Vietnamese civilians, with the "fragging," or murder by fragmentation grenade, of superior officers, and even with the larger military policies of carpet bombing and napalm and defoliant use, none of which seemed to further American goals. In addition, the Vietnam War could not be celebrated in the aftermath, as certainly by 1975 it proved to be a defeat for the United States; the violence of the soldier, already only tenuously justified to many Americans by the war aim of preventing a communist government in Indochina, in the end did not even accomplish that limited goal, much less succeed in installing a permanent democratic, capitalist regime. Vietnam veterans were thus depicted as excessively violent in part because the war itself seemed pointless (Auster & Quart, 1988, p. xiv). As Rick Berg writes: "Always a killer, the vet is seen as one who is infected spiritually and mentally—never politically—by the senseless genocide in Vietnam, the continuing murder of women and children. In a war of containment, he has failed and is contaminated. He is now part of the problem, a carrier who must be sterilized" (1986, p. 116).

In his first iteration, Frank Castle embodies this icon of the psychotic Vietnam veteran. When the Punisher first materialized in comics, he was far from the heroic figure he would later become. In fact, he was a villain, not a hero, and he tries to kill Spider-Man repeatedly during his first appearance, having mistaken the web-slinger for a murderer. The very first image of the Punisher shows him destroying an effigy of Spider-Man with a sniper rifle (Conway, Andru, Giacoia, Hunt, & Costanza, 1974a, p. 2). Furthermore, the Punisher by definition breaks the cardinal rule of superheroes. He does not arrest, wound, or contain villains; he kills them, often quite violently. The Punisher has to be the super-villain to Spider-Man's hero because he is in fact what he mistakenly accuses Spidey of being: a murderer. This early version of the Punisher is given no background that might explain his determination to kill, rather than capture, criminals. Like the other psychotic veteran villains that proliferated at the end of the war— Smith mentions catching three different instances of these interchangeable bad guys on television over the course of a few days in 1974 (1975, p. 210)— the Punisher's extreme response to crime seems entirely unmotivated by any mitigating cause besides his wartime service. In fact, for his first four appearances, he does not even have a name, much less a secret identity or back story. The only facet of his character that is made clear is his veteran status when he tells Spider-Man he spent three years in the Marines (Conway et al., 1974a, p. 18). As a result, on some level his actions seem to stem directly from this veteran status. When Spider-Man asks the Punisher to explain his determination to eradicate criminals everywhere, the Punisher evasively answers:

> It's not something I *like* doing.... It's simply something that has to be *done*.... And I've got nothing to *lose* by risking what's left of my *life* wiping out *your* kind of parasite. You're all *alike* ... using whatever means to get control of the public ... drugs, gambling, *loan-shark* operations ... some of it *legitimate*, but all of it *evil*. Sometimes I wonder if that evil's rubbed off on *me* ... but I know that doesn't *matter*. All that matters is the *job* [Conway et al., 1974a, p. 11].

Like a soldier who does not question orders, the Punisher is on a mission to wipe out crime, but this mission seems not to be one he has chosen; it is simply something that has to be *done*. But because all we know about the Punisher is his Vietnam veteran status, his mission seems like an American extension of the Vietnam War. The Punisher has nothing left to lose, one can only assume, because he has already lost it all in Vietnam, and the evil that has rubbed off on him is both the evil of the criminals he assassinates and the evil of the war he fought, a war he brought back to the U.S.

Once Spider-Man has convinced the Punisher of his innocence, he again looks for some kind of understanding of his new nemesis, asking why the Punisher is fighting "over *here*"; the U.S., after all, is supposedly not a war zone (Conway et al., 1974a, p. 20). But to the Punisher, it is. He embodies the threat that returning Vietnam veterans presented to American society: that he would bring back the violence he learned in Vietnam and turn that violence on the American public. He responds by signaling his disaffection with Vietnam, saying, "Maybe when I'm *dead* it'll *mean* something," and telling us that he remains at war, even if not in Indochina: "Right now I'm just a *warrior* ... fighting a lonely *war*" (Conway et al., 1974a, p. 20). Ross Andru and Frank Giacoia's artwork here reminds us that the Punisher is a villain—his eyebrows in particular are terrifying, and the depth of his widow's peak is proof of his warped nature—and his uncontrollable violence is more than demonstrated when he punches a hole in a brick wall in his fury at the Jackal. The Punisher's brow is permanently creased in a scowl, and his hairline gives the impression of horns, further demonizing him; the lines in his face suggest an intensity bordering on psychosis.

Throughout the rest of the decade, the Punisher continued to make cameo appearances in various Marvel titles, but despite his popularity he still did not receive his own title; his violence made him too volatile a character, and his determination to kill rather than incarcerate criminals was entirely at odds with the prevailing moral code of superheroes. In fact, in most of these comics the title hero ends up protecting various criminals from the Punisher's murderous impulses, and from time to time, Castle finds himself under arrest. When the Punisher inevitably escapes prison after one of those arrests in 1982's *Daredevil* #182, he has become even more psychotic. Attacking a truck transporting drugs, Castle shoots and kills multiple drug dealers, including one who drops his gun and begs for mercy; Castle responds: "This is *war*. I don't take prisoners" (Miller, Janson, & Rosen, 1982, p. 20). When on the next page Castle discovers that this drug dealer was little more than a child, he is not beset by guilt over his actions; instead, he becomes even more determined: "The enemy enlists *children*. The war has gotten dirtier. I'm needed more than ever" (Miller et al., 1982, p. 21). There is no soul-searching here, or grief, or any question that perhaps his level of violence is leading him to burn villages in order to save them; there is only the conviction that any level of violence, any amount of killing, is justified in pursuit of this just cause. As the stereotypical insult would suggest, this version of the Punisher is a remorseless baby-killer, and his violence threatens every aspect of American society. When the Punisher returns after another brief stint in prison in the pages of *Peter Parker, the Spectacular Spider-Man* #82 in 1983, his definition of his enemies has become exceedingly broad. No longer simply in pursuit of drug dealers or of murderers, he now opens fire on litterers and cabbies who run red lights (Mantlo, Milgrom, Mooney, Sharen, & Albers, 1983a, p. 5). His violence has become utterly uncontrollable and makes him a threat to America itself—Castle is the archetypal psychotic Vietnam veteran, seeing enemies everywhere, and prone to unpredictable and uncontainable violence.

By the early 1970s, this psychotic Vietnam veteran image came to be used by advocates for veterans themselves. In particular, a group of psychologists including Robert Jay Lifton, Chaim Shatan, and Sarah Haley began to campaign for the recognition of what would eventually be known as Post-Traumatic Stress Disorder (PTSD). As Eric T. Dean, Jr., argues, the push for recognition of PTSD cemented the image of the psychologically damaged Vietnam veteran (1992, p. 68). However, this version of the Vietnam veteran was no longer depicted as predominantly threatening, but as suffering: this veteran might still be crazy, but was the object of sympathy rather than fear. Furthermore, over time, the ostensible cause of these veterans' trauma came to shift, and by the late 1970s, as Lembcke argues, Vietnam veterans were described as being victimized not by the war but by the homefront, in particular by their own government (1998, p. 100). According to this narrative, the U.S. government's policy of "self-imposed restraint" was ultimately responsible for the loss of the war to the Vietnamese (Gibson, 1994, p. 28). This shift undercuts the original danger of the Vietnam veteran; far from being *too* violent in war, these soldiers were apparently *not violent enough*. Furthermore, the government is not the only entity to blame for the iconic Vietnam veteran's victimization; the veteran is also traumatized by the welcome (or lack thereof) he received upon his return home. In popular memory, Vietnam veterans were treated abominably upon their return from the war; ignored at best, spit upon at worst, these demobilized soldiers were blamed for both for the immorality of the war and for its eventual loss. While both Lembcke and Dean have outlined how this story of the exceptionally poor treatment of Vietnam veterans is largely a myth, the myth remains the standard cultural memory of their experience. As Christian Appy writes: "By the 1980s, mainstream culture and politics promoted the idea that the deepest shame related to the Vietnam War was not the war itself, but America's failure to embrace its military veterans" (2015, p. 241). Furthermore, both Lembcke and Susan Jeffords note that this "homefront" that has traumatized the Vietnam veteran is particularly characterized as feminine (Lembcke, 2010, p. 63; Jeffords, 1989, p. 146). Vietnam veterans were prevented from winning the war not just by an unsupportive government but by an unsupportive and effeminized public epitomized by the female antiwar protester.

Just as the psychotic Vietnam veteran became the wounded Vietnam veteran when his trauma was located at home, the Punisher's rage would be explained in 1975's *Marvel Preview* #2, the character's fifth appearance. This issue provided the character with a name as well as a trauma, but this trauma unexpectedly came not on the battlefield but on the home front. Frank Castle, it seems, watched his wife and children be brutally murdered when the four of them stumbled upon a mob execution while on a picnic (Conway & Dezuniga, 1975). Before this moment, Castle was an outrageously proficient soldier, winning "the Medal of Honor, the Bronze Star, the Silver Star, and the Purple Heart—four times," and was almost awarded the Presidential Medal of Freedom. When his family was slaughtered while he was on leave, Castle went AWOL, leaving the war in Vietnam for his personal war against the Mafia. As the Punisher himself recognizes: "After a thing like that, I suppose a man *does* go—mad." The reader now understands Castle's violence as a symptom of his PTSD; he has become the wounded Vietnam veteran, who is not responsible for his actions but rather has been driven mad by his suffering. And in keeping with the shift in blame for trauma from the war to the homefront, the traumatic incident that made Frank Castle into the Punisher has been shifted from his Vietnam experiences, as implied by his early *Spider-Man* appearances, to his domestic loss. Castle has been driven mad, not because of any wartime atrocity, but specifically because of the destruction of his family. This transfer of the Vietnam veteran's trauma from Indochina to America reinforces the impression that the war was really fought at home, and the emphasis on Castle's family makes it clear that that war was a domestic one, both in the general and the specific senses of the world.

Ultimately, Castle himself seems to blame not Vietnam for his wounding, or the mafia hitmen who murdered his family, but the American government itself. After his brief rampage against jay-walkers and cab-drivers, Castle is again arrested, but this time, his trial (or, to be precise, his pre-arraignment hearing) plays out on the page. In *Peter Parker, the Spectacular Spider-Man* #83, Castle's defense attorney argues that Castle is obviously insane, and the judge agrees, ordering him to a maximum security mental institution. This decision, ironically, sends Castle over the edge; he interrupts the hearing by attacking bailiffs, protesting his sanity: "No. I'm not crazy. It's the state that lets criminals go free while putting people like me in prison! It's the *state* that's insane!" (Mantlo, LaRocque, Mooney, Roussos, & Rosen, 1983b). Castle then breaks down completely, kneeling and weeping in the center of the courtroom. The sequence ends in a thin, borderless horizontal panel running the width of the page; Castle, guards, his defense attorney, and a photographer are drawn in silhouette as Castle is escorted from the courtroom, his attorney telling the photographer: "Please—no pictures." Castle's emotional pain is obvious, but it stems not from the murder of his family, but from the insanity of the criminal justice system: Castle has been victimized by the state. The Punisher who once seemed so cold, so unstoppable, that he could even turn a prison into a playground for violence, has been reduced to weeping in the middle of a crowded courtroom.

By the mid–1980s, the image of the Vietnam veteran took on another facet. The completion of the Vietnam Veterans Memorial in Washington, D.C., led to a discourse of "healing" surrounding Vietnam veterans, suggesting that the lingering wounds inflicted on them by larger American society's poor treatment were finally cured. At the same time, President Reagan actively worked to revise the country's memory of the Vietnam War, describing it as a noble cause, and in the process allowing Vietnam veterans to access a discourse of heroism unmediated by concerns about the war's morality. Mike S. Dubose has argued that heroes "were particularly vital" in the 1980s in part because of Reagan's campaign to restore America's faith in itself (2007, p. 915). Thus it is only natural that the Vietnam veteran would become the iconic hero of the Reagan era. Whereas once a lazy writer might describe a character's past in Vietnam as a shorthand to indicate psychosis, now such a past immediately suggested skills that the soft 1970s had forgotten, and characters from John Rambo to the A-Team were not heroes in spite of their Vietnam service but *because* of it. Far from threatening, the "dangerous skills" these veterans learned in country have transformed them, if not quite into superheroes, then into SuperVets. As Albert Auster and Leonard Quart note, these SuperVets are still defined as inherently different from non–Vietnam veterans, and as a result are positioned as outside of American society; however, that difference is seen as transcendent rather than dehumanizing (1988, pp. 71–72). Furthermore, like earlier iterations of the Vietnam veteran, the SuperVet is still traumatized, but this trauma has not left him wounded or weakened. Instead, it is specifically the SuperVet's traumatic experiences that have hardened him into an unstoppable force of violence. Thus the SuperVet's violence hearkens back to that of the psychotic Vietnam veteran figure, but while the psychotic veteran turns that violence against society, recreating the chaos of Vietnam in America, the SuperVet does the opposite, using that violence to purge America of the chaos associated with Vietnam. In fact, in SuperVet narratives, the Vietnam Era itself is rewritten, and the war at home is itself recharacterized as not an internal division, but as a threat by the outside forces of criminals and drug dealers on the American family. Vietnam veterans have been driven crazy not by warfare, and not by the controversy over warfare, but by specific incidents that happened to their specific families because of a government unable to preserve order (Gibson, 1994, p. 34). Unlike the soldiers in Vietnam tasked with fighting a controversial war against a sympathetic enemy, SuperVets battle unambiguously evil criminals who use terrorism to solidify their empires. Furthermore, unlike the Vietnam veterans who were constrained by U.S. government policy and prevented from winning the Vietnam War, SuperVets refuse to be controlled by policy or regulation; SuperVets are always loose cannons who don't play by the rules.

Frank Castle obviously fits this description: his entire persona is founded on his refusal to play by the rules of society, and unlike the feminized government, Castle never negotiates. Furthermore, both Worcester and DiPaolo note that Castle's ability not only to brazenly murder thousands of criminals but even to survive without superpowers in the Marvel Universe suggests he has become something more than human (Worcester, 2016, p. 39; DiPaolo, 2011, p. 126). Finally, Castle's enemies throughout his early appearances are the iconic villains of SuperVet narratives. Castle is constantly fighting paramilitary drug dealers, like the Tarantula, a South American guerrilla revolutionary turned narco-terrorist, in *Amazing Spider-Man* #135 (Conway, Andru, Giacoia, Lessmann, & Simek, 1974b, pp. 11–12). He is surrounded by other Vietnam veterans, like the Hitman, who saved Castle's life in Vietnam before being discharged as mentally unfit (Wein, Andru, Mooney, Wein, & Rosen, 1977, p. 7). And through it all, as Worcester points out, Castle seems only occasionally motivated by his family's murder (2016, p. 39). That murder becomes a pretext, a cover for the real trauma that drove Castle insane, but which can no longer be acknowledged. SuperVets are far too masculine to be scarred by combat. Instead, they have been wounded by their families themselves. The death of those families simultaneously proves the dangers of a domesticated masculinity and removes the SuperVet from contamination by the feminine. Jeffords explains this iteration of the veteran figure in the seminal book on masculinity and Vietnam, *The Remasculinization of America*: "Vietnam veterans are portrayed in contemporary American culture as emblems of an unjustly discriminated masculinity. Through this image of the veteran, American manhood is revived, regenerated principally by a rejection of the feminine and sexuality; reborn and purified, the veteran takes his place as an experienced leader and spokesperson for a conjointly revived morality and social politics that will regenerate America itself" (1989, p. 116). Even in the issue that first revealed Castle's origin, his family's picnic-gone-wrong takes up three pages of thirty-two; the other twenty-nine seem significantly more concerned with re-appropriating the history of Vietnam.

Worcester is correct when he describes the Punisher as "an intrinsically political character"; the character's grounding as a veteran of a particularly controversial war permanently positions him as a reflection of larger political debates (2012, p. 330). Oddly, that political nature seems to have carried over even as the character's origins have been redefined. Since Greg Rucka took over the character in 2011, Frank Castle's backstory has been retconned,[1] and the canonical Castle is no longer specifically a Vietnam veteran, but now served in an unspecified, but recent (and desert), war (Rucka, Checchetto, Hollingsworth, & Caramagna, 2011). To be fair, given the shifting timeline of the greater Marvel Universe, it is surprising that Castle's Vietnam origin remained as long as it did, and Rucka has explained that the change stemmed from the need to keep Frank from aging in real time (Richards, 2011). Still, it is intriguing that that loss of Castle's Vietnam origin should have had very little effect on his characterization. In fact, even the television version of Castle seems defined as a Vietnam veteran, regardless of his actual service in Iraq and Afghanistan, and the recent Netflix incarnation of the character sees him embroiled in a plot straight out of Vietnam: an assignment to an off-the-books black-op kill squad modeled on Vietnam's Phoenix Program, a drug-running ring organized by his Colonel and reminiscent of Air America, all organized by a rogue CIA agent who is protected by the U.S. government bureaucracy even as he orders the assassination of Castle's family. It seems today's wars are seen through the lens of Vietnam just as today's veterans are seen through the lens of the Vietnam veteran. The Vietnam War has replaced World War II as the paradigm for warfare in popular culture. James Clark has noted the popularity of the Punisher character with real life service members; at the same time, Alan Yu notes the prominence of the Punisher in *American Sniper* (2014), and suggests that the lauding of a psychopathic mass murderer by soldiers might be cause for concern (J. Clark, 2016; Yu, 2015). American culture seems stuck in a pattern, cycling through the various versions of the Vietnam veteran and applying that iconography to new conflicts, in the process obscuring the specifics of those new conflicts, making war seem inevitable. The Punisher, with his never-ending war on crime, thus embodies not only the legacies of Vietnam, but the permanence of wartime in the War on Terror.

Note

1. "Retcon" is short for "retroactive continuity"—the common practice in comic series of changing a characters' backstory to suit more recent publications. Seen Andrew J. Friedenthal's *Retcon game: Retroactive continuity and the hyperlinking of America* for further explanation.

References

Appy, C.G. (2015). *American reckoning: The Vietnam War and our national identity.* New York: Viking.

Auster, A., & Quart, L. (1988). *How the war was remembered: Hollywood & Vietnam*. New York: Praeger.
Berg, R. (1986). Losing Vietnam: Covering the war in an age of technology. *Cultural Critique*, (3), 92–125.
Clark, J. (2016, March 17). Bone deep: The relationship between the Punisher and the military. Task & Purpose. https://taskandpurpose.com/bone-deep-relationship-punisher-military.
Clark, M. (1986). Remembering Vietnam. *Cultural Critique*, (3), 46–78.
Conway, G., Andru, R., Giacoia, F., Hunt, D., & Costanza, J. (1974). *The amazing Spider-Man*, #129. New York: Marvel Comics.
Conway, G., Andru, R., Giacoia, F., Lessmann, L., & Simek, A. (1974). *The amazing Spider-Man*, #135. New York: Marvel Comics.
Conway, G., & Dezuniga, T. (1975). *Marvel preview*, #2. New York: Marvel Comics.
Dean, E.T., Jr. (1992). The myth of the troubled and scorned Vietnam veteran. *Journal of American Studies*, 26(1), 59–74.
DiPaolo, M. (2011). *War, politics, and superheroes: Ethics and propaganda in comics and film*. Jefferson, NC: McFarland.
Dubose, M.S. (2007). Holding out for a hero: Reaganism, comic book vigilantes, and Captain America. *The Journal of Popular Culture*, 40(6), 915–935.
Gibson, J.W. (1994). *Warrior dreams: Paramilitary culture in post–Vietnam America*. New York: Hill and Wang.
Grant, S., Zeck, M., Beatty, J., & Bruzenak, K. (1986). *The Punisher: Circle of blood*, #1. New York: Marvel Comics.
Jeffords, S. (1989). *The remasculinization of America: Gender and the Vietnam War*. Bloomington: Indiana University Press.
Lembcke, J. (1998). *The spitting image: Myth, memory, and the legacy of Vietnam*. New York: New York University Press.
Lembcke, J. (2010). *Hanoi Jane: War, sex & fantasies of betrayal*. Amherst: University of Massachusetts Press.
Mantlo, B., LaRocque, G., Mooney, J., Roussos, G., & Rosen, J. (1983). *Peter Parker, the spectacular Spider-Man*, #83. New York: Marvel Comics.
Mantlo, B., Milgrom, A., Mooney, J., Sharen, B., & Albers, D. (1983). *Peter Parker, the spectacular Spider-Man*, #82. New York: Marvel Comics.
Miller, F., Janson, K., & Rosen, J. (1982). *Daredevil*, #182. New York: Marvel Comics.
Richards, D. (2011, November 17). Rucka storms the Castle in "Punisher." CBR. https://www.cbr.com/rucka-storms-the-castle-in-punisher/.
Rucka, G., Checchetto, M., Hollingsworth, M., & Caramagna, J. (2011). *The Punisher*, #4. New York: Marvel Comics.
Scott, C.A. (2012). Anti-heroes: Spider-Man and the Punisher. In R.M. Peaslee & R.G. Weiner (Eds.), *Web-spinning heroics: Critical essays on the history and meaning of Spider-Man* (pp. 120–127). Jefferson, NC: McFarland.
Smith, J. (1975). *Looking away: Hollywood and Vietnam*. New York: Charles Scribner's Sons.
Wein, L., Andru, R., Mooney, J., Wein, G., & Rosen, J. (1977). *The amazing Spider-Man*, #175. New York: Marvel Comics.
Worcester, K. (2012). The Punisher and the politics of retributive justice. *Law Text Culture*, 16(1), 329–352.
Worcester, K. (2016). The Punisher: Marvel Universe icon and murderous antihero. In F. Peters & R. Stewart (Eds.), *Antihero* (pp. 34–45). Bristol, UK: Intellect.
Yu, A. (2015, January 31). Chris Kyle loves the Punisher: Why American Sniper is a terrifying superhero movie. Medium. https://medium.com/@alan_yu039/chris-kyle-loves-the-punisher-why-american-sniper-is-a-terrifying-superhero-movie-455ec4744847#.kcyccarsu

Frank Castle's Other War

Meaning, Memory and the Vietnam War

STEPHEN CONNOR

In February 1974, the Punisher declared a one-man war in the pages of Marvel Comics' *The Amazing Spider-Man*.[1] Determined to eradicate the scourge of crime, the former marine vowed to "kill ... those who deserve killing." But this war was not his first. Before the vigilante launched his assault on the concrete jungles of the United States, he had battled under the triple canopy of Vietnam. Considering the decades long evolution of Frank Castle's other war offers insights into ways in which the Punisher's connection to Southeast Asia reflected contemporary sense-making about that war and other American interventions that followed. To that end, this essay focuses primarily on story arcs specifically set in-country to consider how Punisher publications reinforced and challenged the meaning and memory of the war in Vietnam.[2]

Prior to the publication of *The Punisher* #1 in 1986, only passing reference was made to Frank Castle's other war. In the character's first appearance in 1974, he informed Spider-Man that he had "spent three years in the Marines" (Conway, G., & Andru, R., 1974 February. *The Amazing Spider-Man* #129). While writer Gerry Conway did imply extensive war service, no specific reference to the conflict was made. In April 1975, Conway again referenced Punisher's military past, further fleshing out the character's martial pedigree in *Marvel Preview* #2. Somewhat outlandishly, Castle had been "twice promoted in the field" and the recipient of the "Medal of Honor, Bronze Star, Silver Star and Purple Heart—four times!" (Conway, G., & DeZuniga, T. 1975 August. *Marvel Preview* #2). Yet even here, Vietnam itself remained only implied with the story neither set in or really about the war but rather post–Vietnam America. Specifically detailing Castle's Vietnam service took place at the height of the character's popularity in the late 1980s and early 1990s coinciding with a renewed focus, particularly in popular culture, on the war. In this context creators placed him *in* Vietnam and his experiences there became an essential element in the on-going development of the character.

Understandably, given the range of creators connected to the character, contractions in the Castle's Vietnam record required "ret-conning."[3] According to current Marvel Comics canon, Frank Castiglione enlisted as a private in the Marine Corps following a crisis of faith. After abandoning seminary, the young marine was stationed first in the United States before deploying to Vietnam for the first time. Two subsequent tours followed. Prevented from returning to the war yet again, Castiglione re-enlisted under an assumed name: Frank Castle. Whatever his affection for his young family, re-enlistment and a return to Vietnam proved more appealing. His martial prowess and experience evident, Castle received advanced training and re-deployed not as an ordinary grunt, but elite Green Beret advisor to irregular Degar (Montagnard) fighters. Over the course of this fourth deployment, Castle operated with a range of allies throughout Vietnam and even returned on a covert mission to the United States. Seemingly in constant combat, Castle battled enemies both Vietnamese and American. Indeed, it was during this fourth tour that creator's retroactively placed Castle's tipping point in the transformation from marine to Punisher. Duly promoted and recognized for his service, he returned to the U.S. and his family's murder in Central Park (Youngquist, 2012).

Part I: Wounded Warrior, 1974–1977

Clearly the Vietnam experience formed part of the context in which Gerry Conway, Ross Andru and John Romita, Sr., created the Punisher. Quite simply, any highly trained ex-military character would certainly have served in Vietnam, whatever the publisher's or public's perceptions of the war. More importantly however is the deeper cultural milieu from which the character emerged. As others have noted, the Punisher represented an agent of retributive justice shaped by a broader social anxiety, a *Death Wish* "backlash culture of the 1970s and 1980s … an implicit rebuke to counterculture fantasies concerning peace, love and brotherhood" (Worcester, 2012).[4] In effect, the character was firmly rooted in the immediate post-war context and shaped by what the war *meant*, at that time.

It is important to note that the Punisher was created after the United States withdrew from Vietnam. While the war still raged in late 1973 despite a ceasefire, Americans no longer viewed nightly news broadcasts recounting the day's casualties. For most Americans, and certainly at Marvel Comics, the war was over.[5] Predictably, the first wave of Punisher stories focused little attention on the aftermath of the war, and even less on the war itself (Wright, 2001). Indeed, it was not until April 1975, ironically the same month as the fall of Saigon, that Vietnam came up at all (Conway, G., & DeZuniga, T. [1975 August]. *Marvel Preview* #2). In "Death Sentence," Castle prevented the murder of an unnamed politician only to discover that the would-be assassin was Mike Hauley, a Vietnam veteran and former comrade. When questioned on his transition from marine to assassin, Hauley bluntly stated: "I'm just like a lot of guys. You get back home— nobody wants to even look at you.... That's what happens 'cause of a war like that. And it makes you sort of bitter ... heck I jumped at it.... Make money—pay back the bums who sent me to Nam!" (Conway, G., & DeZuniga, T. [1975 August]. *Marvel Preview* #2). The would-be killer was then doubled-crossed and murdered by his unknown employers. An enraged Punisher followed a trail of murdered Vietnam veterans turned assassins to foil an "International Industrial Alliance" plot to overthrow the U.S. government. In the end, destroying the conspiracy not only punished the exploiters of the wounded warriors but reinforced Castle's sense of purpose in fighting his new war, a clear purpose he claimed he did not have in Vietnam.

In late 1977, Punisher re-surfaced, again in the pages of the popular *The Amazing Spider-Man*. Over two issues, writer Len Wein recycled the wounded warrior trope. In "The Hitman's Back in Town" and "Big Apple Battleground," Castle and Spider-Man teamed up to rescue J.J. Jameson from the clutches of the People's Liberation Front. Jameson's kidnapper, code-named the Hitman, was revealed as Lieutenant Burt Kenyon who had rescued Castle from certain death in Vietnam (Wein, L., & Andru, R. [1977 November], *The Amazing Spider-Man* #174 and Wein, L., & Andru, R. [1977 December], *The Amazing Spider-Man* #175). The story concluded with the Punisher choosing to save the endangered Spider-Man rather than Kenyon, watching him plunge stoically to his death from atop the Statue of Liberty. The war however served more than just as a means to link protagonist to antagonist. In this story, Vietnam explicitly mattered. As Castle recalled, the war damaged Kenyon even as he served, as "declared mentally unfit" he was unceremoniously "discharged from the service!" (Wein, L., & Andru, R. [1977 December], *The Amazing Spider-Man* #175).

While certainly not as sophisticated nor academic as some reflections on the war at the time perhaps best represented by Robert Jay Lifton's pioneering *Home from the War*, Wein's story reflected the popular re-telling of it as a "grim exercise in futility" (Lawrence, 2008).[6]

Indeed, Punisher's early narratives in which wounded warriors brought the war home had much in common with other popular culture representations of the veteran such as Martin Scorsese's Travis Bickle and

Don Pendleton's Mack Bolan (Kraft, 1985). In such cases, violent performance proved an instinctive, even inevitable response to post-war dislocation, disillusionment and catalytic traumatic crisis (Worcester, 2012).[7] As letter writers noted in the 1976 *Marvel Super Action* #1, Castle represented a case study of post–Vietnam syndrome, equally "a victim, twisted and corrupted by a war [Vietnam] ... programmed ... by years of war-zone action and ... corrupted by military madness" (Goodwin, A., & DeZuniga, T., [1976 January], *Marvel Super Action* #1).

Part II: This Time We Win, 1986–1994

The collapse of South Vietnam did not end the conflict, whether in the American national psyche or attendant political discourse. Indeed, beginning in the early 1980s, President Ronald Reagan demanded a re-interpretation of the war not as a disastrous mistake but rather "a noble cause" undone by enemy propaganda abroad and a stab in the back at home (Reagan, 1980). For Reagan (and seemingly many Americans), the time had come for both the public and government to shake off Vietnam Syndrome, and the United States to reassert itself domestically and internationally. Renewed interest in the war also blossomed elsewhere. In November 1982, a largely privately funded Vietnam Veterans Memorial opened in Washington, D.C., while a deluge of films, TV series and books, both popular and academic, re-interpreted and in some cases re-imagined the war. While perspectives were certainly legion, all shared a cardinal question: What did the war mean, at least for Americans?

American comic books too followed the growing "Vietnam boom."[8] Such post–1975 Vietnam comics intended to provide a specific re-telling of the war that offered contemporary significance to the American reader (Klein, 1990).[9] For Marvel Comics this meant a complete about face from their position during the intervention and immediate aftermath (Dagilis, 1990).[10] In 1986, Marvel launched *The 'Nam* written by Vietnam veteran Doug Murray. Murray, supported editorially by another veteran Larry Hama, intended the comic to give the war meaning and relevance to both postwar readers and former combatants alike (Sandy, 2016).[11] As he put it, the book was "designed as a way to present a representative history," a re-telling of "what happened to people in that war," or at least at least the grunt's eye view of it (Dagilis, 1990, Murray & Golden, 1986 December).[12]

Concurrent with publication of *The 'Nam*, Marvel also re-introduced the Punisher beginning with the 1986 mini-series conceived by Steven Grant and Mike Zeck. Over five issues, Frank Castle dispatched a range of villains and criminals and the success of the run led Marvel to launch two ongoing series in 1988, *The Punisher* and *The Punisher War Journal*. Initially tapping into a fearful zeitgeist, over seven years a combined 187 issues were published. Throughout the height of the character's popularity, references and flashbacks to Vietnam were made across the entire line (Youngquist, 2012). However, the most significant consideration of Castle's war in Southeast Asia appeared in a series set outside the Marvel universe of superheroes.

By the early 1990s, popular culture interest in the Vietnam war had significantly waned. For Marvel, Murray's departure after issue #51 in late 1991 prompted a series of creative changes. By the time of cancellation in 1993, the book had strayed far from its original intention of producing "realistic" war stories (Scott, 2014). Throughout the 1990s, Marvel introduced a number of stylistic and creative initiatives in an effort to revive the flagging title beginning with issue #52, the first under new writer Roger Salick. In these two issues, Frank Castle (Castiglione) took center stage (Salick, R., & Harris, M. [1991 January–February], *The 'Nam* #52–53). At one level, introducing Castle was certainly an effort to leverage the character's popularity in the hope of rescuing *The 'Nam* (Dixon, C., & Vansant, W. [1991 March], *The 'Nam* #54).[13] Yet at another level, specifically situating him *in* Vietnam allowed creators to develop reinterpretations of the war in which Castle's exploits offered a model of how the conflict *should* have been fought.

Between early 1991 and 1994, Marvel published seven issues of *The 'Nam* featuring the future Punisher. The first effort, "The Long Sticks" written by Salick, pitted Castle against a Vietnamese insurgent in a battle of wits, will, and weapons (Salick, R., & Harris, M. [1991 January–February], *The 'Nam* #52–53). The Vietnamese sniper, troublingly dubbed "The Monkey," presented an enemy based on familiar racialized tropes (Dower, 1986).[14] This vision, resting largely on a set of recognizable depictions of the "Oriental" as an inscrutable, yet physically weak "mastermind" undone by the brains and brawn of the hero, fit snugly into long-standing American fears and representations of the "Orient" and the "Yellow Peril" (Dower, 1986).[15] Over the course of the two issues, Castle single-handedly defeated both the villain and his henchmen, employing a range of creatively violent tactics. In the end, Castle not only killed the Monkey but effectively consumed him, appropriating his "Mark of the Executioner," the (in)famous white skull insignia (Salick, R., & Harris, M. [1991 January–February], *The 'Nam* #52–53). In important ways, Castle's exploits mirrored the most significant and mistaken success metric of the conflict itself; body count could win the war.

The following year, prolific writer Chuck Dixon produced a three issue "The Punisher Invades *The 'Nam*" arc (Dixon, C., & Kobasic, K. [1992 April–June], *The 'Nam* #67–69). Set prior to the events in the Salick run,

Dixon depicted the early days of Castle's tour of duty in Vietnam. Despite being a "new guy" in-country, his natural martial abilities, selflessness and quick-wittedness empowered him to dispatch hordes of Vietnamese enemies with his rifle, knife and bare hands. Over the course of the story, readers witnessed Castle's metamorphosis from inexperienced young marine to bare-chested, bandana-wearing avenger reminiscent of John Rambo, to a sleeveless, two-gun wielding, cigar-chomping Nick Fury doppelganger (Dixon, C., & Kobasic, K. [1992 June], *The 'Nam* #69). This story, unlike Salick's, did provide a more nuanced depiction of the Vietnamese. Indeed, in issue #67, Dixon described them as dedicated, effective, and capable, if brutal and often fool-hardy (Dixon, C., & Kobasic, K. [1992 April], *The 'Nam* #67). "Their history book" he reminded readers "was just one long war" and while not an enemy to be feared, Castle "respected them," even as he killed them in droves. Whatever their merits, the Vietnamese could (and would) be defeated in the field. However, Dixon's story was not really about the Vietnamese enemy at all. Rather, the true enemy proved American, in this case, a far-reaching and shadowy "military mafia." Operating a range of criminal enterprises stretching from remote firebases to Saigon, these villains not only squandered the lives of American combatants and undercut the war effort but also the supposed nobility of the cause. In effect, Castle was the American fighting-man writ large who did not lose the war at the front, but was stabbed in the back. The Vietnamese did not defeat America, but rather, Americans defeated themselves. By the end of the story, Castle had only succeeded in destroying the lowest level of the conspiracy. In doing so, he discovered "his purpose in life, his purpose in the 'Nam…. He was here to punish." He returned again to Vietnam to do just that. Punishment on the home front would come later.

In 1994, after the series' cancellation, Marvel published Don Lomax's *The 'Nam: Final Invasion* (Lomax, D., & Saichann, A. [1994], *Punisher Invades the 'Nam: Final Invasion*. New York, NY: Marvel Comics). In many ways Lomax, himself a Vietnam veteran, retread much of the same ground as Salick and Dixon. Importantly however, the context in the which he published had changed profoundly. Not only had the Cold War ended but the United States seemed to have triumphed. Indeed, as President George Bush claimed: "…by God, we've kicked the Vietnam syndrome once and for all" (Bush, 1991). In "Final Invasion," shadowy forces prevented Castle from returning to Vietnam once again. Unable to cope with his American exile and a public that refused to support the war, he changed his name and re-enlisted, returning to the warzone as an elite Green Beret. Aided by his trusty sidekick un-ironically nicknamed "Junior," Castle prosecuted the war as it should have been fought, by any means necessary. For Lomax, akin to Dixon, the real enemy was neither the National Liberation Front ("Viet

Cong") nor their North Vietnamese allies but an American military-run drug cartel. However just as Castle was poised to eradicate this evil, he was forced to choose between punishment and loyalty. In a rather bizarre twist to the story, Lomax lead the protagonist on a mission to rescue downed U.S. airmen from a private prison camp, the "Hell Hole" run by rogue Chinese mad scientist "Dr. Death" and his Cuban henchmen. Again sporting bare chest and bandana, Castle predictably destroyed the villain and his hi-tech laboratory. He then turned his sights on his original target, the traitorous American "Colonel No-Name," assassinating him in the same manner he had dispatched so many Vietnamese enemies. The story concluded with Castle visiting the Vietnam Memorial Wall in the aftermath of his family's murder. Handing his Congressional Medal of Honor to a disabled veteran, he disappeared into the crowd, in effect bringing closure to one soldier's war while he embarked on his new one. For Lomax, by the end of the conflict in Vietnam, Castle was primed for war, this time on the streets of the United States rather than the jungles of Southeast Asia.

"Final Invasion" marked an important end point for Marvel Comics only significant foray into Vietnam story-telling. Over the course of *The 'Nam*'s publication, the meaning and interpretation of the war had evolved. By the Lomax run, the book had very little connection to its roots as "grunt's eye view" of the war as Murray originally intended. Further, gradually the nature of the enemy shifted until the real "bad guys" were in fact criminals rather than enemy combatants. While Castle never shied away from killing his Vietnamese enemies, and he did so in droves, they were not punished. Rather retributive justice was reserved for those whose activities undercut the nobility of the war and the honor of its participants. In effect, Castle's war in Vietnam became a crime-fighting campaign, a dry-run for the character's later exploits.

Critically, in the Vietnam stories published at the height of the character's popularity, the war itself was not perceived as a crime, nor were the actions taken in prosecuting it. Rather crime existed *within* the conflict, to the eventual detriment of the war effort. Clearly the meaning of the war had shifted. Taken together, Castle narratives in *The 'Nam* reflected a revisionist version of the conflict as a necessary war "to stop the rampaging hordes of Communism" (Lomax, D., & Saichann, A. [1994], *Punisher Invades the 'Nam: Final Invasion*. New York, NY: Marvel Comics). In this telling, intervention of behalf of the beleaguered Republic of Vietnam represented a noble and just cause undone by sinister forces at home and abroad. In effect the United States military was hamstrung from the outset by a government, as Reagan claimed, "afraid to let them win" (Reagan, 1980). On the home front too, a vocal minority actively supported the enemy's cause while gradual war-weariness undercut the resolve of the silent majority. Seemingly,

Vietnam was not lost on the battlefield but rather betrayed on the home front. Similarly, concurrent with a range of pop culture fantasies in which Vietnam was re-fought to a better outcome, Castle's war served as a blueprint to victory. In effect, the character's predilection for retribution and willingness to "get the job done and ask questions later" fused with the perception that one dedicated man could make a difference. Such imaginings in turn provided the foundation for an ahistorical "what if" scenario in which the war was, in fact, winnable (Lomax, D., & Saichann, A. [1994], *Punisher Invades the 'Nam: Final Invasion*. New York, NY: Marvel Comics, Wright, 2001). In the alternate world of Marvel Comics at least, the Punisher in Vietnam "could make us [Americans] feel better about the war" as the United States "could've won the war if we had had more soldiers like Frank Castle" (Lomax, D., & Saichann, A. [1994], *Punisher Invades the 'Nam: Final Invasion*. New York, NY: Marvel Comics).

The Punisher was created and written with the knowledge that one could understand and to an extent empathize with his motives; if not his methods (Goodwin, A., & & DeZuniga, T. [1976 January], *Marvel Super Action* #1). While Punisher stories explored the application of violence they also provided critical assessments of the broader contexts and circumstances that spawned him. Indeed, the contested and evolving meaning of his violence has been a constant, fundamental aspect of the character from 1970s to present. In stories published about the American war in Vietnam at the height of the character's popularity, creator's displayed little uncomfortableness, ambiguity or even irony surrounding Castle's violence. Justice was delivered not in the form of retribution on an enemy but rather restoratively, if belatedly, for the generation of who served there. Yet neither was he simply an apolitical moral crusader. Rather Castle prosecuted the war as revisionists insisted the U.S. should have. If reservations existed about the Punisher's war on criminals, they did not in regards to his war against the Vietnamese. In short, Frank Castle's other war represented a prime example of how the United States *should* fight its wars. As President Ronald Reagan put it: "The true lesson of the Vietnam War is: certainty of purpose and ruthlessness of execution win wars" (Reagan, 1978).

Part III: *War Crime and Punishment, 2003–2018*

Concurrent with the rise of U.S. hegemony at the end of the Cold War, interest in Castle's brand of vigilantism waned. By 1995, Marvel had cancelled both Punisher titles. However, by the end of the century, creators had begun to resurrect Frank Castle. Certainly, there was a need to update the character as both his age and the decline of popular culture interest in

Vietnam made his origin story increasingly untenable. However, at least in comic books (and the Netflix series) the character's military pedigree was retained. He remained a war-fighter, just in other wars. Yet particularly after 9/11 and the series of American interventions eerily reminiscent of Southeast Asia, space remained for alternate and alternative re-telling of Castle's Indochina adventures (Scott, 2014). Where other creators largely drifted away from his Vietnam past, Garth Ennis returned him there twice.

Published throughout the latter half of 2003, *Born* encompassed a four issue story arc in which Castle, now a captain, lead marines at the remote and poignantly named Firebase Valley Forge (Ennis, G., & Robertson, D. [2003 August–November], *Born* #1–4). Set late in the war, he was aware that the base would soon be abandoned and that no marine in his command wished to be the last American killed in Vietnam. Yet in the face of chronic apathy, failing morale and widespread addiction, Ennis' clear metaphor for the war itself, Castle remained "in love with war" (Ennis, G., & Parlov, G. [2013 February–April], *Fury: My War Gone By* #7–9). Unwilling to surrender to the inevitable end of American intervention, he continued to take the fight to the enemy, ruthlessly killing them, whether Vietnamese or American.

In *Born*, Castle was alternately driven by forces both beyond him and within himself. On the wrong side of history, Castle was "running out of war" as the firebase, akin to South Vietnam itself, finally fell despite his best efforts. For Ennis, Vietnam was a "tragic misstep into darkness," and defeat the inevitable outcome of a misguided, even immoral intervention (Ennis, G., & Robertson, D. [2003 August–November], *Born* #1–4). Yet the story also presented a re-telling of the war that did not seriously consider motivation nor the war experiences of most American participants. Taken together the series pointed where Castle was *going* rather than deeply considering where he *was*. In ways akin to Jason Aaron's *The Other Side*, the arc proved less a war comic and more "a psychological horror story" of a kind Ennis has long embraced (Kodosky, 2011, Aaron, J. [2007], *The Other Side*. New York: Vertigo).

In 2017, Ennis returned Castle to the warzone in a sequel, *Punisher: The Platoon*. The six-issue series focused on his first tour in Vietnam and further developed long-held tropes and interpretations of the war. Told through a series of flashbacks, author Michael Goodwin interviewed surviving members of Castle's first command. Over the six issues, the story again traced the familiar ground of his evolution from inexperienced junior officer to battle-hardened defender who valued the lives of his men "above all else, including protocol." Deployed again at a strategically useless firebase, Castle gradually won the respect and trust of his "neglected, tired, and disillusioned" marines, convincing them to fight for each if not a remote national cause. Simultaneously, Ennis also told the story from the other side, focused on Colonel Letrong Giap and Ly Quang, a woman sniper obsessed with revenge. Akin to Castle's own transformation to the Punisher, the "hardcore little gook chick" sought vengeance for the butchering of her family at the hands of American war criminals (Ennis, G., & Parlov, G. [2017 December–2018 April], *Punisher: The Platoon* #1–6).

Punisher: The Platoon presented a thoughtful consideration of the motivation of participants, whether American or Vietnamese and on the nature of the war itself, aspects largely undeveloped in *Born*. In his interpretation, Ennis portrayed Castle as a savior of men who sacrificed his own future so others might enjoy theirs. In effect, he represented what was best about Americans in times of war. Yet in the context of Vietnam, this best was not good enough. For Ennis, this war "was where the American story in the twentieth century went wrong. Horrifically, tragically wrong. Which is why it's such a good starting point for Frank Castle" (Ennis, G., & Parlov, G. [2017 December–2018 April], *Punisher: The Platoon* #1–6). Like creators before him, Ennis considered the Vietnam war as the explanatory springboard to his war on crime. But it is also true that he reflected deeply on the meaning and memory of the war on its own terms, rather than a simply as a precursor. Taken together, both *Born* and *The Platoon* present a challenging counter-narrative to the revisionist interpretation of the war. For Ennis, Vietnam was an unjust war rife with villains from firebase profiteers to the military-industrial complex that sent them there in the first place. Certainly, criminality was presented but did not undercut a noble cause. Rather criminality rested at the very heart of the conflict.

Conclusion

Placing Frank Castle in Vietnam was an obvious means to establish the backstory of a highly trained combatant and killer, particularly in the mid-1970s. But as we have seen, what the war meant to him and indeed to creators and readers continued to evolve. Indeed, by the late 1980s as the character's popularity exploded, the Punisher's war was no longer confined to destroying the criminal underworld. As editor Tim Tuohy declared in 1994: "Whether or not we like to admit it in today's world of blind political correctness, we like the Punisher. The thought of a crime free society deeply appeals to us. The Punisher's methods may give you pause, but the end result is intriguing. What if the same theme that drives the regular Punisher books … was applied to the Vietnam war" (Lomax, D., & Saichann, A. [1994], *Punisher Invades the 'Nam: Final Invasion*. New York: Marvel Comics).

Such sentiment reveals a deeply rooted false equivalency between war-fighting and the Punisher's form of vigilantism. Quite simply, portraying Castle's path to retributive justice as a straight one from Vietnam to Central Park ignores the war's uniqueness, its meaning and memory whether then or now. In the end, Frank Castle has never been an apolitical automaton. In the case of the Vietnam war he acted as a willing executor of U.S. foreign policy. However macabre, excessive yet effective his actions, he carried them out in the service of his country's cause. Castle remained morally untainted from Vietnam, even if America itself had not. There has yet to be a convincing explanation for why Castle *chose* to fight in Vietnam beyond a crisis of faith and his personal, terrible love of war. In the end, he chose war, whether against the Vietnamese or criminals. But Vietnam was not just *any* war.

From his inception, creators constructed Castle as possessing a moral compass, of a kind. Indeed, one of the central themes across publications has been the tension surrounding his willingness to do the wrong thing for the right reason. This is problematic in the case of Vietnam, a conflict that proves a troubling fit as a "dry run" for the Punisher's later war on crime. It is also equally disquieting that creators have consistently allowed Castle to seamlessly transform his enemy from Vietnamese to criminal with few considerations beyond the necessity of their extermination. Doing so not only promotes a particular revisionist memory of the war but also its very meaning for Americans. To reconsider this perspective would require asking critical questions: If the Vietnamese were neither inherently evil nor perhaps even unjust, why were they in need of punishment? If Castle's worldview is black and white and his cause a moral one, why would he fight in an immoral war? These questions remain unanswered.

So, why *did* Frank Castle fight in Vietnam? If the cause was just and the enemy clearly unjust, the answer seems straightforward. However, should interpretations of the war prove more ambiguous or even contrary, the answer is less clear. Even Garth Ennis who so clearly deemed the war a misguided mistake, turned to the existential, perhaps supernatural to account for his motivation to return time and again. Perhaps Frank Castle's true motivation can only be located in the worldview of the character's writers. In the end, why he fought in Vietnam can only be found in the on-going and contested meaning of America's lost war.

Notes

1. Conway, G., & Andru, R. (1974). *The amazing Spider-Man* #129. New York: Marvel Comics. Note the issue carried a cover date of February 1974 but would have been released at an earlier date. Also see Howe, S. (2012). *Marvel Comics: The untold story*. New York: Harper, p. 138.

2. For discussions of Vietnam era comic books more generally see: Wright, B. (2001). *Comic book nation: The transformation of youth culture in America*. Baltimore: Johns Hopkins University Press, pp. 189–199; Scott, C. (2014). *Comics and conflict: Patriotism and propaganda from WWII through Operation Iraqi Freedom*. Annapolis, MD: Naval Institute Press, pp. 17–77; Huxley, D. (1989). "The Real Thing": New images of the Vietnam War in American comic books. In J. Aulich & J. Walsh (Eds.), *Vietnam images war and representation* (pp. 160–170). London: Palgrave Macmillan; Kodosky, R. (2011). Holy Tet Westy! Graphic novels and the Vietnam War. *Journal of Modern Culture*, 44(5), 1047–1066; Young, R. (2017). The "real victims" of the Vietnam War: Soldier versus state in American comic books. *Journal of Modern Culture*, 50(3), 561–584; Vizzini, B. (2016). When (comic) art imitates life: American exceptionalism and the comic book industry in the Vietnam War era. In R. Milam (Ed.), *The Vietnam War in popular culture: The influence of America's most controversial war on everyday life* (pp. 359–378). (Volume 1). Santa Barbara, CA: Praeger; Schlund-Vials, C. (2017). *Comics captured America's opinions about the Vietnam War*. The conversation. https://theconversation.com/comics-captured-americas-growing-ambivalence-about-the-vietnam-war-83756; Rollins, P. (2008). Using popular culture to study the Vietnam War: Perils and possibilities. In P. Collins & J. O'Connor (Eds.), *Why we fought: America's wars in film and history* (pp. 367–389). Lexington: University Press of Kentucky; Maguire, L. (2014). The Avengers always stand ready to do their part: The Avengers and the Vietnam War. In J. Darowski (Ed.), *The ages of the Avengers: Essays on the Earth's mightiest heroes in changing times* (pp. 12–24). Jefferson, NC: McFarland.

3. An excellent definition and explanation of retroactive continuity ("retcon") in comic books is found in Booker, M.K. (2010). *Encyclopedia of comic books and graphic novels* (Two Volumes). Santa Barbara: ABC-CLIO, p. 510.

4. Kruidhof. C. (2016). Crime and Punisher: How the Punisher mediates domestic identity and American ideologies in foreign policies through images of masculinity and vigilantism [Unpublished master's thesis]. Utrecht, NL: Utrecht University; Scully, T. & Moorman, K. (2014). The rise of vigilantism in 1980s comics: Reasons and outcomes. *The Journal of Popular Culture*, 47 (3), 634–653; Allen, J. (2014). Marvel Comics and New York stories: Anti-heroes and street level vigilantes Daredevil and the Punisher [Unpublished master's thesis]. New York: The City University of New York; Lovell, J. (2003). Nostalgia, comic books, & the war against crime: An inquiry into the resurgence of popular justice. *Journal of Popular Culture*, 36, 335–351; Tochterman, B. (2017). *The dying city: Postwar New York and the ideology of fear*. Chapel Hill: The University of North Carolina Press, pp. 145- 210; Heerkens, G. (2018). Justice by any means: The relationship between societal stress and the rise of vigilantism in comic books [Unpublished master's thesis]. Rochester, NY: Rochester Institute of Technology, pp. 13–14, 16, 18–19, 22; Palmer, L. (2013). The Punisher as revisionist superhero western. In C. Hatfield, J. Heer. & K. Worchester (Eds.), *The superhero reader* (pp. 279–294). Jackson: The University of Mississippi Press; DiPaolo, M. (2011). *War, politics and superheroes: Ethics and propaganda in comics and films*. Jefferson, NC: McFarland; Costello, M. (2009). *Secret identity crisis: Comic books and the unmasking of Cold War America*. New York: Continuum, pp. 167–176; Scott, C. (2009). The alpha and the omega: Captain America and the Punisher. In R. Weiner (Ed.), *Captain America and the struggle of the superhero: Critical Essays* (pp. 125–134). Jefferson, NC: McFarland; Scott, C. (2012). Anti-heroes: Spider-man and the Punisher. In R. Peaslee & Weiner (Eds.). *Web-spinning heroics: Critical essays on the history and meaning of Spider-Man* (pp.120–127). Jefferson, NC: McFarland; and Wright (2001), pp. 273–277.

5. Particularly helpful in contextualizing Vietnam era comics are Scott, C. (2014); Murray, C. (2000). *Popaganda: Superhero comics and propaganda in World War Two*. In A. Magnussen & H-C. Christiansen (Eds.), *Comics & culture: Analytical and theoretical approaches to comics* (pp. 141–155). Copenhagen, DK: Museum Tusculanum Press; and Mundey, L. (2012). *American militarism and anti-militarism in popular media, 1945- 1970*. Jefferson, NC: McFarland, pp. 159–208.

6. Also see Elliot. D. (2008). Official history, revisionist history and wild history. In M. Bradley & M. Young (Eds.), *Making sense of the Vietnam Wars: Local, national and transnational perspectives* (pp. 277–304). Oxford: Oxford University Press; Boyle, B. (2016).

Naturalizing war: The stories we tell about the Vietnam War. In B. Boyle & J. Lim (Eds.), *Looking back on the Vietnam War: Twenty-first-century perspectives* (pp. 187–190). New Brunswick, NJ: Rutgers University Press; and Boggs, C., & Pollard, T. (2007). *The Hollywood war machine: U.S. militarism and popular culture* (pp. 99–101). Boulder, CO: Paradigm Publishers.

    7. Also see Allen (2014) and Halevy, A., & Cooper, J. (2016). The noble cause corruption of Frank Castle. *Journal of Theoretical & Philosophical Criminology, 8*(2), 105–123.

    8. While the most significant comic books to emerge were Marvel Comics' *The 'Nam, semper fi: Tales of the Marine Corps*, and Murray, D., & Heath, R. (1991). *Hearts & minds: A Vietnam love story*. New York: Marvel Comics. Also see Scott (2014), pp. 58–77 and Stevens, R. (2015). *Captain America: Masculinity and violence*. Syracuse, NY: Syracuse University Press, pp. 130–132.

    9. Also see Schlund-Vials, C. (2016). Re-seeing Cambodia and recollecting *The 'Nam*. In B. Boyle & J. Lim (Eds.), *Looking back on the Vietnam War: Twenty-first-century perspectives* (pp. 156–157). New Brunswick, NJ: Rutgers University Press. For a fuller discussion of conflict era Vietnam war comics see Connor, S. (forthcoming, 2020). Victor Charles and Marvin the ARVN: Vietnamese as enemy and ally in American war comic books. In D. Hall & M. Goodrum (Eds.), *Drawing the past: Comics and the historical imagination*. Jackson: University of Mississippi Press.

    10. Also see Voger, M. (2006). From Vietnam to The 'Nam: Doug Murray's journey. In M. Voger, *The dark age: Grim, great & gimmicky post-modern comics* (pp. 30–32). Raleigh, NC: Two Morrows Publishing; Blackmore, T. (1994). Doug Murray's *The 'Nam*, a comic battle for Vietnam at home and abroad, *Lit: Literature Interpretation Theory, 5*(3–4), 213–225; Murray, D. (2001). Interview with Brian Jacks. Slush Factory. http://www.slushfactory.com/features/articles/052502-murray.php; Murray, D. (1987). Interview with Charlie Rose. CBS News. https://www.youtube.com/watch?v=qwfB9bCs4kw; Span, P. (1986, September 10). Vietnam: The comic book war: Marvel brings out a dark, gritty and popular series. *Washington Post*; and Sandy, J. (2016). A paneled perspective: The United States and the Vietnam War examined through comic books. In R. Milam (Ed.), *The Vietnam War in popular culture: The influence of America's most controversial war on everyday life* (p. 216). (Volume 2). Santa Barbara, CA: Praeger.

    11. Also see Young, R. (2015). There is nothing grittier than a "grunt's eye view": American war comic books and the popular memory of the Vietnam War. *Australasian Journal of American Studies, 34*(2), 75–93; Issacs, A. (1997). *Vietnam shadows: The war, its ghosts, and its legacies*. Baltimore: Johns Hopkins University Press, pp. 1–8; Span (2016).

    12. Doug Murray claimed that the book was "the real thing—or at least as close to the real thing as we can get-in a newsstand comic bearing the Comics Code seal." The series, intended initially to be published in real time, promised both historical accuracy and to present "what the war was really like for those who fought in it." Murray purported that "every action, every fire fight … [was] based on fact." See Murray, D. & Golden, M. (1986, December), *The 'Nam* #1.

    13. The decision for a Punisher guest appearance in *The 'Nam* proved popular with readers. Beyond positive "critical …response, the book's commercial success prompted Marvel to publish a second printing featuring an alternate cover and 'a special metallic ink.'"

    14. Also see Wright (2001), pp. 30–55, 110–121; Field, C. (2012). "He was a living breathing human being": Harvey Kurtzman's war comics and the "Yellow Peril" in 1950s containment culture. In C. York & R. York (Eds.), *Comic books and the Cold War, 1946–1962: Essays on graphic treatment of communism, the code and social concerns* (pp. 45–52). Jefferson, NC: McFarland; and Scott, C. (2014). pp. 41–47, 49–52.

    15. Also see Madison, N. (2013). *Anti-foreign imagery in American pulps and comic books*. Jefferson, NC: McFarland; Ma, S. (2000). *The deadly embrace: Orientalism and Asian American identity*, Minneapolis: University of Minnesota; and Mayer, R. (2014). *Serial Fu Manchu: The Chinese supervillain and the spread of Yellow Peril ideology*. Philadelphia: Temple University Press.

REFERENCES

Aaron, J. (2007). *The other side*. New York: Vertigo.
Allen, J. (2014). *Marvel Comics and New York stories: Anti-heroes and street level vigilantes Daredevil and the Punisher* [Unpublished master's thesis]. New York: The City University of New York.
Blackmore, T. (1994). Doug Murray's *The 'Nam*, A comic battle for Vietnam at home and abroad. *Lit: Literature Interpretation Theory*, 5(3–4), 213–225.
Boggs, C. & Pollard, T. (2007). *The Hollywood war machine: U.S. militarism and popular culture*. Boulder, CO: Paradigm Publishers.
Boyle, B. (2016). Naturalizing war: The stories we tell about the Vietnam War. In B. Boyle & J. Lim (Eds.), *Looking back on the Vietnam War: Twenty-first-century perspectives* (pp. 175–192). New Brunswick, NJ: Rutgers University Press.
Bush, G. (1991). *Remarks to the American Legislative Exchange Council*. The American presidency project. https://www.presidency.ucsb.edu/documents/remarks-the-american-legislative-exchange-council-0.
Conway, G., & Andru, R. (1974). *The amazing Spider-Man* #129. New York: Marvel Comics.
Conway, G., & DeZuniga, T. (1975). *Marvel preview* #2. New York: Marvel Comics.
Costello, M. (2009). *Secret identity crisis: Comic books and the unmasking of Cold War America*. New York: The Continuum International Publishing Group.
Dagilis, A. (1990). Uncle Sugar vs. Uncle Charlie: An interview with *The 'Nam's* creator, Doug Murray. *The Comics Journal*, 136, 62–85.
DiPaolo, M. (2011). *War, politics and superheroes: Ethics and propaganda in comics and films*. Jefferson, NC: McFarland.
Dixon, C., & Kobasic, K. (1992, April). *The 'Nam* #67. New York: Marvel Comics.
Dixon, C., & Kobasic, K. (1992, May). *The 'Nam* #68. New York: Marvel Comics.
Dixon, C., & Kobasic, K. (1992, June). *The 'Nam* #69. New York: Marvel Comics.
Dixon, C., & Vansant, W. (1991). *The 'Nam* #54. New York: Marvel Comics.
Dower, J. (1986). *War without mercy: Race and power in the Pacific War*. New York: Pantheon Books.
Elliot. D. (2008). Official history, revisionist history and wild history. In M. Bradley & M. Young (Eds.), *Making sense of the Vietnam Wars: Local, national and transnational perspectives* (pp. 277–304). Oxford, UK: Oxford University Press.
Ennis, G., & Parlov, G. (2013). *Fury: My war gone by* #7–9. New York: Marvel Comics.
Ennis, G., & Parlov, G. (2017—2018). *Punisher: The platoon* #1–6. New York: Marvel Comics.
Ennis, G., & Robertson, D. (2003). *Born* #1–4. New York: Marvel Comics.
Field, C. (2012). "He was a living, breathing human being": Harvey Kurtzman's war comics and the 'Yellow Peril' in 1950s containment culture. In C. York and R. York (Eds.), *Comic books and the Cold War, 1946-1962: Essays on graphic treatment of communism, the code and social concerns* (pp. 45–54). Jefferson, NC: McFarland.
Goodwin, A., & DeZuniga, T. (1976). *Marvel super action*, #1. New York: Marvel Comics.
Halevy, A., & Cooper, J. (2016). The noble cause corruption of Frank Castle. *Journal of Theoretical & Philosophical Criminology*, 8(2), 105–123.
Heerkens, G. (2018). *Justice by any means: The relationship between societal stress and the rise of vigilantism in comic books* [Unpublished master's thesis]. Rochester, NY: Rochester Institute of Technology.
Howe, S. (2012). *Marvel Comics: The untold story*. New York: Harper.
Huxley, D. (1989). The real thing: New images of the Vietnam War in American comic books. In J. Aulich & J. Walsh (Eds.), *Vietnam images: War and representation* (pp. 160–170). London: Palgrave Macmillan.
Issacs, A. (1997). *Vietnam shadows: The war, its ghosts, and its legacies*. Baltimore: Johns Hopkins University Press.
Klein, M. (1990). Cultural narrative and the process of re-collection: Film, history and the Vietnam era. In M. Klein (Ed.), *The Vietnam era: Media and popular culture in the U.S. and Vietnam*. London: Pluto Press.

Kodosky, R. (2011). Holy Tet Westy! Graphic novels and the Vietnam War. *Journal of Modern Culture, 44*(5), 1047–1066.
Kraft, D. (1985). Interview with Gerry Conway. *Comics Interview,* 75.
Kruidhof. C. (2016). Crime and Punisher: How the Punisher mediates domestic identity and American ideologies in foreign policies through images of masculinity and vigilantism [Unpublished master's thesis]. Utrecht, NL: Utrecht University.
Lawrence, M.A. (2008). *The Vietnam War: A concise international history.* New York: Oxford University Press.
Lomax, D., & Saichann, A. (1994). *Punisher invades The 'Nam: Final invasion.* New York: Marvel Comics.
Lovell, J. (2003). Nostalgia, comic books, & the war against crime: An inquiry into the resurgence of popular justice. *Journal of Popular Culture,* 36, 335–351.
Ma, S. (2000). *The deadly embrace: Orientalism and Asian American identity,* Minneapolis: University of Minnesota.
Madison, N. (2013). *Anti-foreign imagery in American pulps and comic books.* Jefferson, NC: McFarland.
Maguire, L. (2014). The Avengers always stand ready to do their part: The Avengers and the Vietnam War. In J. Darowski (Ed.), *The ages of the Avengers: Essays on the Earth's mightiest heroes in changing times* (pp. 12–24). Jefferson, NC: McFarland.
Mayer, R. (2014). *Serial Fu Manchu: The Chinese supervillain and the spread of Yellow Peril ideology.* Philadelphia: Temple University Press.
Mundey, L. (2012). *American militarism and anti-militarism in popular media, 1945–1970.* Jefferson, NC: McFarland.
Murray, C. (2000). *Po*paganda: Superhero comics and propaganda in World War Two. In A. Magnussen & H-C. Christiansen (Eds.), *Comics & culture: Analytical and theoretical approaches to comics* (pp. 141–155). Copenhagen, DK: Museum Tusculanum Press.
Murray, D. (1987). *Interview with Charlie Rose* [Video]. CBS News. https://www.youtube.com/watch?v=qwfB9bCs4kw.
Murray, D. (2001). *Interview with Brian Jacks.* Slush Factory. http://www.slushfactory.com/features/articles/052502-murray.php.
Murray, D., & Golden, M. (1986). *The 'Nam,* #1. New York: Marvel Comics.
Murray, D., & Heath, R. (1991). *Hearts & minds: A Vietnam love story.* New York: Marvel Comics.
Palmer, L. (2013). The Punisher as revisionist superhero western. In C. Hatfield, J. Heer & K. Worchester (Eds.), *The superhero reader* (pp. 279–294). Jackson: The University of Mississippi Press.
Reagan, R. (1978). *America's purpose in the world.* (March 27, 1978, 5th Annual CPAC Conference). The Patriot Post. https://patriotpost.us/pages/431-ronald-reagan-americas-purpose-in-the-world
Reagan, R. (1980). *Peace: Restoring the margin of safety.* Ronal Reagan Presidential Library and Museum. https://www.reaganlibrary.gov/8-18-80
Rollins, P. (2008). Using popular culture to study the Vietnam War: Perils and possibilities. In P. Collins & J. O'Connor (Eds.), *Why we fought: America's wars in film and history* (pp. 367–389). Lexington: University Press of Kentucky.
Salick, R., & Harris, M. (1991, January). *The 'Nam,* #52. New York: Marvel Comics.
Salick, R., & Harris, M. (1991, February). *The 'Nam,* #53. New York: Marvel Comics.
Sandy, J. (2016). A paneled perspective: The United States and the Vietnam War examined through comic books. In R. Milam (Ed.), *The Vietnam War in popular culture: The influence of America's most controversial war on everyday life.* (Volume 2). Santa Barbara, CA: Praeger.
Schlund-Vials, C. (2016). Re-seeing Cambodia and recollecting *The 'Nam.* In B. Boyle & J. Lim (Eds.), *Looking back on the Vietnam War: Twenty-first-century perspectives.* (pp. 156–174). New Brunswick, NJ: Rutgers University Press.
Schlund-Vials, C. (2017). *Comics captured America's opinions about the Vietnam War.* The conversation. https://theconversation.com/comics-captured-americas-growing-ambivalence-about-the-vietnam-war-83756

Scott, C. (2009). The alpha and the omega: Captain America and the Punisher. In R.G. Weiner (Ed.), *Captain America and the struggle of the superhero: Critical essays* (pp. 125–134). Jefferson, NC: McFarland.

Scott, C. (2012). Anti-heroes: Spider-man and the Punisher. In R. Peaslee & R.G. Weiner (Eds.), *Web-spinning heroics: Critical essays on the history and meaning of Spider-Man* (pp.120–127). Jefferson, NC: McFarland.

Scott, C. (2014). *Comics and conflict: Patriotism and propaganda from WWII through Operation Iraqi Freedom*. Annapolis, MD: Naval Institute Press.

Scully, T., & Moorman, K. (2014). The rise of vigilantism in 1980s comics: Reasons and outcomes. *The Journal of Popular Culture, 47*(3), 634–653.

Span, P. (1986, September). Vietnam: The comic book war: Marvel brings out a dark, gritty and popular series. *Washington Post*.

Stevens, R. (2015). *Captain America: Masculinity and violence*. Syracuse, NY: Syracuse University Press.

Tochterman, B. (2017). *The dying city: Postwar New York and the ideology of fear*. Chapel Hill: The University of North Carolina Press.

Vizzini. B. (2016). When (comic) art imitates life: American exceptionalism and the comic book industry in the Vietnam War era. In R. Milam (Ed.), *The Vietnam War in popular culture: The influence of America's most controversial war on everyday life* (pp. 359–378). (Volume 1). Santa Barbara, CA: Praeger.

Voger, M. (2006). From Vietnam to *The 'Nam*: Doug Murray's journey. In M. Voger, *The dark age: Grim, great & gimmicky post-modern comics* (pp. 30–32). Raleigh, NC: Two Morrows Publishing.

Wein, L., & Andru, R. (1977, November). *The amazing Spider-Man*, #174. New York: Marvel Comics.

Wein, L., & Andru, R. (1977, December). *The amazing Spider-Man*, #175. New York: Marvel Comics.

Worcester, K. (2012). The Punisher and the politics of retributive justice. *Law Text Culture, 16*(1), 329–352.

Wright, B. (2001). *Comic book nation: The transformation of youth culture in America*. Baltimore: Johns Hopkins University Press.

Young, R. (2015). There is nothing grittier than a 'grunt's eye view': American war comic books and the popular memory of the Vietnam War. *Australasian Journal of American Studies, 34*(2), 75–93.

Young, R. (2017). The "real victims" of the Vietnam War: Soldier versus state in American comic books. *Journal of Modern Culture, 50*(3), 561–584.

Youngquist, J. (2012). *The Punisher: Official index to the Marvel Universe*. New York: Marvel Comics.

Section IV
Politics and Gun Violence

Bullet-Riddled Production

The Punisher's Influence on Violence in Decades of Tragedy

Rob E. King

The character of Marvel Comics' *The Punisher* has been researched on the merits of his statements on law and vigilantism. Two instances, J. Allen's "Marvel Comics and New York Stories: Anti-heroes and Street Level Vigilantes Daredevil and The Punisher" and A.E. Taslitz's "Daredevil and the Death Penalty," are cited in this essay. The question asked here is whether or not the character has been or remains a necessary vehicle for revenge fantasy as a caricaturized avatar for that violence in environments of frequent mass shooting. The character's three-season series premiered on Netflix in 2017 and ran until 2019, adding to the timeliness of this research. Does the revenge fantasy end with serialized narratives of *The Punisher,* or does it feed into a personal narrative that gets acted out through real-world aggression? If the character started as an extension of male fantasy and adventure serials (i.e., *The Executioner* novels) targeting juvenile as well as adult audiences through comics books in the 1970s, how did his portrayal adapt to changing environments specific to gun violence? To judge such requires the researcher to examine the character of Frank Castle throughout the decades, to cite notable instances of mass shootings during periods of the character's popularity, and to turn a lens to media's effect on violence.

Frank Castle's most recent popularity began when he was introduced to Netflix audiences in *Daredevil* Season 2, which premiered in March of 2016. It was ordered on April 2015. According to a Mother Jones database—corroborated by Harvard researchers and a 2013 study by the FBI—tallying American mass shootings, instances where four or more were injured or killed by a shooter, dating back to 1982, there had been a brief lull in American mass shootings from October 2014 until June 2015 (Follman, 2018, Excel database section), placing the production of *Daredevil* Season

155

2 during a period of increasing incidents of gun violence but only after a time of reprieve from the violence. On June 17, 2015, Dylan Roof, 21, shot and killed nine people, injuring one other. A *Deadline Hollywood* article from June 26, 2015, reads "The Punisher to Loom Large in 'Daredevil' Season 2" (Lincoln, 2015, from title). Shortly thereafter, on July 16, Mohammod Youssuf Abdulazeez, walked into two military recruitment centers, killing five and injuring two. Leaked set photos and a bullet-riddled logo teasing the coming of the Punisher appeared in a reveal piece for *Daredevil* Season 2 by BleedingCool.com on July 6. The following October saw Chris Harper-Mercer open fire at a school killing nine and injuring nine others. Colorado Springs would suffer two incidents, one in October and another at a Planned Parenthood center that November, adding up to a total of six more killed and nine injuries. Co-showrunner Doug Petrie is quoted in an article on UPI from October 13, 2015, saying "With the Punisher and Elektra, we get to take it darker and further" (Martin, 2015, para. 2). The San Bernardino mass shooting was in December, where fourteen were killed with twenty-one injuries. ITM.com reports from that December:

> For those unaware, Frank Castle, a.k.a. The Punisher, is one of the meanest and most dangerous vigilantes in comic book history. While Castle is righteous and dangerous, he often ignores the law to accomplish his goal. In fact, the Punisher kills his victims, making him in many ways a strong foil for Matt Murdock's journey [French, 2015, para. 4].

Still, two more mass shooting incidents would occur that February 2016 before the *Daredevil* series release in March. The notation of these dates and incidents are not related or an indictment of Netflix, yet they highlight the violent environment surrounding the production of the character's return to the screen and emphasize the question at the crux of this essay—does violent media, specific to the Punisher in this instance, have an influence on gunmen?

Frank Castle appears in the series leading to his capture and a trial, where PTSD is weighed as part of his narrative. His character refuses the notion out of respect for those truly suffering the illness and reminding us of his cognitively stable and premeditated intent, the former of the two debatable. *The Punisher* was ordered to series on April 2016 for release on November 17, 2017. Following the April order of the show, a new slew of gun violence would begin that June at an Orlando, Florida, nightclub, where Omar Mateen, 29, slayed 49 and injured 53 people. And while no value can be placed on a single life over another, the nine mass shootings that followed were minimal in comparison until October 1, 2017, just a month and a half before the release of Netflix and Marvel's *The Punisher*. The following is from an Associated Press article reported by Southern California's 89.3 KPCC.

The Las Vegas gunman meticulously planned how to carry out the worst mass shooting in modern U.S. history, researching SWAT tactics, renting other hotel rooms overlooking outdoor concerts and investigating potential targets in at least four cities, authorities said Friday. But months after Stephen Paddock killed 58 people and wounded more than 800 others with a barrage of bullets from the Mandalay Bay casino-hotel, investigators still have not answered the key question: Why did he do it? [Ritter & Balsamo, 2018, para. 1]

Pre-meditated and thoroughly researched, the violent act that killed 59 women, men, and teenagers, injuring over 527 more (Follman, 2018, Excel fig.), leaves the public with no understanding of its motivation. Stephen Craig Paddock was 64 years old. Once again, these bloody tragedies are not ascribed to *The Punisher* comic books, video games, films, or television appearances, but they illustrate the environment of that media's production. Is it responsible to produce such a character in this environment? It is the goal of this paper to find out.

Back to the history, *The Punisher* did not begin on the screen. The slightest research tells us that he appeared first in *The Amazing Spider-Man* comic books in February 1974. According to a study titled "At what age did you start reading comic books?" conducted by Comic Book Resources from June 6–13, 2013, out of respondents with an age group of 0–59, 60 percent claimed they began reading comic books before the age of ten. Twenty-six percent began between the ages of ten and fourteen, and 13 percent between the ages of fifteen and twenty-nine (Comic Book Resources, 2013 June, fig.). If a similar spread of numbers could be applied across decades, it appears that comic book reading occurs at impressionable and formative ages with the highest ages being between birth and 14 years old. Frank Castle initially appeared with cartoonish, Dracula-like styling—thick, black, angular eyebrows and slicked back hair. His character was to be consumed by readers of all ages but certainly those young readers of *Spider-Man* as well as those of adults. While by comic's end he defied their end goals, he commonly teamed with the likes of Spider-Man villains like the Jackyl or added to Spider-Man's tensions while fighting the Tarantula. His Vietnam War background was present early in his introduction, a trait that connects him back to creator Gerry Conway's inspiration by serialized *Executioner* novels. Howe (2013) admits to some propaganda:

> But Conway began sliding a patina of political content into his work. Drawing inspiration from Don Pendleton's popular Executioner novels, Conway created a new character called the Punisher. Like Pendleton's Mack Bolan, the Punisher was a Vietnam War veteran who exacted revenge on the mob after it murdered members of his family. But where Bolan—lusty, unrepentantly vicious, and charmless—was cast as a hero, Conway framed the Punisher as a paranoid and dangerous, if somewhat sympathetic, antagonist. It was the vigilante adventure as cautionary tale [p. 138].

As his character evolved from antagonist to vigilante hero, the character would eventually encourage audiences to ask the question: how far should a vigilante hero go to be effective? There were other vigilante characters similarly inspired in the mid-seventies, the most memorable being Charles Bronson's Paul Kersey in *Death Wish* and Clint Eastwood's *Dirty Harry*. *Dirty Harry* was released before the Punisher character, while *Death Wish* was released in the same year. Cline (2010) touched on the subject, explaining "First appearing in 1974 (the same year *Death Wish* was released) both Marvel Comics' character and Michael Winner's film owe a great deal of their sensibility—like western films before them—to pulp fiction, particularly Vietnam-era urban vigilante narratives" (p. 125). While audiences took to the gritty character of the Punisher alongside Paul Kersey, for most of the 1970s he remained a guest character in the comics.

Still, vigilantism is central to note here. Out of a sense of complete desperation in the wake of helplessness against an environmental onslaught of terrorism, it is easy to cheer these characters on, exclaiming "The Punisher would have stopped him." Taslitz (2004) defines the notion of this form and necessity for vigilantism in his study "Daredevil and the Death Penalty" asking, "But what exactly is a 'vigilante?'" A whirlwind review of the history of vigilante violence in America reveals that vigilantism, properly understood, involves the use of violence on behalf of the local community when it perceives itself no longer to be adequately protected by the state. Vigilantism is thus generally "extra-legal" (p. 1). Agreeing that audiences for *Death Wish* and *Dirty Harry* might have approached the material with a maturity that understood that condition, in not necessarily those exact words, could one also claim that a majority audience before the age of fourteen might interpret it the same? What is the defining line between acting out in the interest of a community and acting out of one's self-justifications?

The character would finally have enough development to receive his first solo title in 1986. Researcher Jesse Allen (2014), in his master's thesis, suggests a reason for the popularity of these characters, indeed, an impetus for the inevitability of such characters during this specific time period. What he argues is that vigilante heroes, the Punisher and Daredevil, reflected the socio-economic environment of New York City in real time. As scholar Alex Vitale explains:

> "everyday [people saw] ... the growth of disorder. Dirt, vandalism, visible homelessness, panhandling, prostitution, and graffiti were all daily indignities to be managed by city residents." Magazine and newspaper headlines reflected this frustration with the quality of life for residents, and the threat of becoming a victim of living in New York City. A distrust of police by minority residents arose in several neighborhoods in Harlem, the Bronx and Brooklyn as well as the Lower East Side of Manhattan as youth gangs and criminal organizations

terrorized and exploited residents. Police were also at odds with a city that could not afford to pay them [Allen, 2014, p. 13].

The popular case cited in both Taslitz and Allen's research is that of Bernard Goetz, who shot four African American teenagers, one critically, in 1984. Popular opinion hoisted Goetz as a hero, and he would be acquitted of charges related to attempted murder in a 1987 criminal trial. Allen points out a detail that pertains to the production environment in that "One year after the Goetz shooting, Marvel comics released a 5-issue mini series featuring one of its guest characters, The Punisher" (Allen, p. 5). As noted above, his first major solo outing was in 1986, billed as "America's Greatest Crime Destroyer: The Punisher."

In the Punisher's solo outings of the late 1980s, his foils became more focused. He would gain a partner in Microchip, who would join him in his fully established next series, which began in 1988 and ran through 1995. But before that, in another mini-series in 1987, realism was applied to his missions as he began to seek out crack cocaine dealers and cited a mission to "destroy organized crime" (Baron, 1987, p. 25). This is an altogether different type of villain from his *Amazing Spider-Man* days. With this new mission and series, he became popular enough to see his first screen time in 1989 portrayed by Dolph Lundgren in a widely panned rated-R movie co-starring Louis Gossett, Jr., as his one-time police partner. In this version, the new standard for realistic crime villains remained. As Frank Castle sought out New York's crime families, he is soon forced to team with a Family head after the crime boss' children are kidnapped by a new, particularly sadistic, branch of the Yakuza. He saves the children, then kills the father, explaining to the son that if he grows up to be like his father, he'll be waiting to kill him, too (Yakin, *The Punisher*, 1989). And while that does read like a deranged after-school special, the point is the connection to realistic villains. Scott (2016) explains the shortcomings of the still-violent film:

> This movie failed for a variety of reasons. The most glaring of these reasons was the lack of the trademark Punisher skull logo on Castle's shirt, which left many established readers unimpressed even by the mere appearance of the character. While the film was based on the comic books and even had Stan Lee listed as an executive producer, it was nonetheless a tepid version of the story [p. 232].

Regardless of its success, Allen's socio-economic point shines through in these late '80s iterations as Frank Castle is taking on avatars of actual crime occurring in the streets. Crime was at an all-time high in the United States during this time period. As shown in a report by the FBI titled "Reported violent crime rate in the United States from 1990 to 2016," in 1990 there were 729.6 cases of crime per 100,000 of the population. That increased to

758.2 in 1991 sustaining to 747.1 in 1993 before a sharp decrease, reaching an all-time low in 2014 of 361.6 (FBI, 2017, graph). Allen (2014) points out as well that "From 1985 to 1990, murders increased by over 60 percent from 1,384 to 2,245, an all-time high. Several notable events affected how New Yorkers as a public body viewed crime that influenced their daily lives as well as popular culture that represented New York as 'Fear City'" (p. 9). This moves our timeline into the 1990s, where a curious change occurs.

The comics begin to see the Punisher integrated back into the more fantastic elements of the Marvel Universe as opposed to the gritty streets of common crime. The movement is one from fighting realistic street-level cartels back into the trumped-up world of Kingpin and Doctor Doom's larger schemes. Once reintegrated, there was one detour that positioned Castle for engagement with. In January of 1991, "CBS's Charles Osgood (1/17/91) described the early bombing of Iraq as 'a marvel,' while the same network's Jim Stewart (1/17/91) spoke of 'two days of almost picture-perfect assaults'" (Naureckas, 1991, para. 2). This was in regard to the Persian Gulf War. On the cover of *The Punisher* issue 47 from April 1991, Frank Castle wields an Uzi in his left hand, while in his right, he hefts the weight of a newly knocked out, limp-bodied Iraqi, whose scimitar falls from his defeated hand. The illustrated and adventurous font reads "Caught—in a Desert Storm." It has a pulp quality, like Robert E. Howard's *El Borak*. To further illustrate the point, on the cover of issue 48 Frank is strapped to the end of a missile-launching barrel with the tagline "Next Stop: Baghdad."

In the issue, the political undertones are less than subtle, akin to Captain American punching Hitler. There is a Trafian leader who is a Saddam Hussein look-alike. There is almost no doubt that Trafia is Saudi Arabia, while the issue's Zukistan is a stand-in for Iraq. The Trafian leader bemoans his weapon recently destroyed by the Punisher, while the Zukistan leader thanks Microchip and the Punisher for destroying it. Only now, the Zukistan leader boasts that the weapon's creator, Dr. Brattle, is building him an even larger weapon to humiliate the West. The final page offers readers Frank Castle back in New York two weeks later. Frank has tracked down said weapon creator and war lord, Dr. Brattle. With an illustrated barrel of a gun silencer and the "Phut, phut, phut" illustrated font, the message is clear—the Punisher was reminded that as with Vietnam (an influence on his origin), interference in overseas conflicts achieves nothing. Damned if you do, damned if you don't. This leaves exception for his personal war, of course. So, *The Punisher* series can be said to offer at least one more instance of propaganda as well as a promotion of self-motivated violence.

A fascinating characteristic about *The Punisher* rarely commented upon is caricature. The Punisher's placement in Baghdad as propagandist commentary was equally ridiculous, equally coping mechanism, and all caricature.

Writers of *The Punisher* either consciously or subconsciously needed him to have his own arch enemy at this time to be truly incorporated into the more fantastic Marvel Universe as its own title. Captain America had the Red Skull; Spider-Man had Doctor Octopus and the Green Goblin. Kingpin largely belonged to the *Daredevil* title. Before these, though, he would take on a cast of characters like the Rev, a violent, religious zealot who suffered traumas in Vietnam but brought his violence to bear on others. Much like Spider-Man's Hammerhead with his on-the-nose nomenclature, one is reminded that these gangsters take on a similar role to those of the villains in *Dick Tracy*. Like Pruneface, Flattop, or Mumbles, they are caricatures of gangsters. The violence is also caricatured, made to be so bombastic with knives disarmed every three panels and explosions every five, that it is difficult to digest it as reality. Some of that motivation is noted by Howe (2013):

> With pressure to beat 1991's astronomical sales figures, DeFalco and the editorial staff focused on its big launches: "Big Guns" was a campaign to publicize new titles like Silver Sable, Nomad, and Punisher: War Zone, each of them starring characters who were, literally, armed with "big guns" [p. 341].

The Punisher was given equally gaudy villains to match his larger than life weaponry.

The Punisher would find his archenemy in an older character revived in Jigsaw. At this time in the 1990s, it was a time of crossover revivals coinciding with Spider-Man's thirtieth anniversary in 1992. As further stated by Howe (2013), "When Terry Stewart and Richard Rogers decided that Spider-Man's thirtieth anniversary was the perfect opportunity for 3-D hologram covers and more crossovers and double-sized issues, editor Danny Fingeroth voiced resistance, worrying about workload and compromises in quality" (p. 343). The Punisher wasn't immune to those compromises, having such disparately paired villains like the Kingpin and Dr. Doom for a single issue to crossovers like "Lifeform" with enemies like A.I.M. from *The Avengers* or the foil-covered "Double Edge," a series bestowed by CBR.com as "likely best left forgotten" (Cronin, 2016, para. 1) wherein Castle kills the original Nick Fury. The last series occurred in 1994, a year most noted in popular culture as the year Kurt Cobain, front man for the band Nirvana, committed suicide with a shotgun, but also a year wherein the drop in crime rates began its steady descent. In 1994, the crime rate had dropped from 747.1 per 100,000 population to 713.6 and steeply to 684.5 by 1995 (FBI, 2017, fig.), the year Punisher's solo title was cancelled due to poor sales. For all of that descent in crime, media like video games and characters like the Punisher, who had two early games—*The Punisher* for the Nintendo Entertainment System and *The Punisher: The Ultimate Payback!* for Nintendo's Game Boy—would come under new scrutiny following the Columbine High School massacre in 1999, which left 15 dead with 24 injured. The crime rate had dropped to 523 per 100,000 that particular year, but the public was left particularly shocked by the attackers' onslaught, which appeared to be executed with the detachment of someone trained and desensitized by first-person shooter video games. In the following year, the Punisher would see a popular return in a twelve-issue mini-series penned by gritty author Garth Ennis of *Preacher* fame.

Given all of this, what is the actual effect of the media on the minds of its audience? The Game Boy game was a first-person shooter. That is a game comprised solely of moving crosshairs around on a screen to shoot random enemies as the screen pans to the end of the level, a poor example of simulation, but a simulator nonetheless. Would its players then become real life aggressors? According to an article by Kaplan (2012) in an issue of *Psychiatric Times*:

> A 2002 report by the US Secret Service and the US Department of Education, which examined 37 incidents of targeted school shootings and school attacks from 1974 to 2000 in this country, found that "over half of the attackers demonstrated some interest in violence through movies, video games, books, and other media" [p. 7].

That study reminds one of the conspiratorial *Catcher in the Rye* speculation based on John Hinckley and Mark David Chapman connections. Did the novel have some connection to their motivations? Still, what that particular study brings to question is: what is the gauge for "some interest?" Kaplan looks to another study for more context:

> Douglas Gentile, PhD, Associate Professor of Psychology, along with Brad Bushman, PhD, Professor of Communication and Psychology at Ohio State University and Professor of Communication Science at the VU University in Amsterdam, recently published a study that identifies media exposure as 1 of the 6 risk factors for predicting later aggression in 430 children (aged 7 to 11, grades 3 to 5) from Minnesota schools. Besides media violence, the remaining risk factors are bias toward hostility, low parental involvement, participant sex, physical victimization, and prior physical fights [Kaplan, 2012, p. 11].

What this tells us is that media influence is only one of six potential risk factors. What we can take from that is that the influence of violence in *The Punisher* is not a sole influence on enacted real-world violence. What should be answered following that is: what is the actual influence of that one factor? What is the human reaction to those depictions? Researchers Ashworth, Pancer, and Pyle (2011) of Queens University, Canada performed a study that looked at men and women's reactions to violence in three separate experiments: (1) designed to address the question of whether consumers preferentially approach media with violent content; (2) designed to investigate the role of vicarious reactions to domination in the actual enjoyment of violent depictions through teaser-trailer clips, in-game cut scenes, and actual gameplay; (3) designed to investigate the role of justice in the enjoyment of violence using manipulated book text (p. 872). Their findings are cited below:

> [Experiment 1:] An ANOVA revealed a Violence X Gender interaction ... that indicated men thought they would enjoy the movie more when it appeared to be more violent, ... whereas women thought they would enjoy it less. ... [Experiment 2:] Follow-up analyses within gender revealed that women liked the game less when it contained any violence ... whereas men liked the game less only when the protagonist was dominated. ... [Experiment 3:] Overall, our results suggest that men, but not women, approach violent content in media. The violence itself, however, appears to reduce enjoyment in both men and women unless it satisfies some other motive. Both men and women enjoyed violence that satisfied the justice motive, although they responded to quite different forms of violence. Men enjoyed extreme justified violence; women only enjoyed reduced forms of justified violence [Ashworth, Pancer, & Pyle, 2011, pp. 872–873].

It is likely, according to this study, that men are more likely to gravitate to the violent content of *The Punisher*. It also tells us that how the violence is digested matters as both sexes prefer some element of just justification to exist for the violence to exist. Perspective on justice is the issue. Antiheroes always leave us with much to reconcile, not as mass shooters but often as sympathizers of violence. As gun violence continues in the United States with little to convince us it is ending, Frank Castle is a character that plays out revenge scenarios some might wish for as a kind of narrative catharsis. Evidence suggests that his character is an avatar for the frustrations of the helpless and less a catalyst for enacted aggression. In decades where crime has steadily decreased but inexplicable tragedy occurs too often in mass spurts of gun violence, we see larger and increased heroes in Hollywood. As the Avengers burst onto the screen to boast super-heroism against the cosmic dangers of the universe, the Punisher meets his audience on the streets, hoisting the weaponry used against us. Ultimately, audiences get to choose which justice they need to virtually filter their emotions through in response to the violence around them, be that on the news, in sequential art, or on the screen. The Punisher is only one of many, seemingly necessary, options.

REFERENCES

Allen, J. (2014). *Marvel Comics and New York stories: Anti-heroes and street level vigilantes Daredevil and the Punisher* [Master's thesis.] New York: City University of New York.
Ashworth, L., Pancer, E., & Pyle, M. (2011). Buying violence: Understanding the appeal of violence in popular media. *ACR North American Advances, 39*, 872–873.

Baron, M. (1987). *The Punisher,* #2 In J.F. Gabrie (Ed.), *Essential the Punisher,* 2 (p. 25). New York: Marvel Comics.
Baron, M. (1991). *The Punisher,* #48. In S. Crespi (Ed.), *Essential the Punisher,* 4 (p. 236). New York: Marvel Comics.
Cline, J. (2010). Bernie's "deathwish": History and transgression in New York City. In R. Weiner, J. Cline, & D. Cline (Eds.), *Cinema inferno: Celluloid explosions from the cultural margins.* https://ebookcentral.proquest.com.
Comic Book Resources. (2013, June). *At what age did you start reading comic books?* Statista. https://www-statista-com.lib-e2.lib.ttu.edu/statistics/299862/comic-book-reading-age/.
Cronin, B. (2016, March 19). *Remember to forget—That time the Punisher killed Nick Fury.* CBR. https://www.cbr.com/remember-to-forget-that-time-the-punisher-killed-nick-fury/.
FBI. (2017, September). *Reported violent crime rate in the United States from 1990 to 2016.* Statista. https://www-statista-com.lib-e2.lib.ttu.edu/statistics/191219/reported-violent-crime-rate-in-the-usa-since-1990/.
Follman, M., Arnosen, G., & Pan, D. (2018, May 18). *U.S. mass shootings, 1982–2018: Data from Mother Jones' investigation.* Mother Jones. https://www.motherjones.com/politics/2012/12/mass-shootings-mother-jones-full-data/
French, A. (2015, December 29). *Updated: The Punisher and Elektra in "Daredevil" season 2.* Inside the Magic. https://insidethemagic.net/2015/12/first-look-the-punisher-and-elektra-in-daredevil-season-2/
Goldblatt, M. (Director) (1989). *The Punisher* [Film]. United States: New World Pictures.
Howe, S. (2013). *Marvel Comics: The untold story.* New York: Harper Perennial.
Kaplan, A. (2012). Violence in the media: What effects on behavior? *Psychiatric Times, 29*(10), 1–5.
Martin, A. (2015, October 13). *'Daredevil' season 2 trailer previews Elektra, the Punisher.* UPI. https://www.upi.com/Entertainment_News/TV/2015/10/13/Daredevil-Season-2-trailer-previews-Elektra-the-Punisher/2481444762134/.
Naureckas, J. (1991, April). *Gulf War coverage: The worst censorship was at home.* FAIR. https://fair.org/extra/gulf-war-coverage/.
Ritter, K. & Balsamo, M. (2018, January 19). *Las Vegas shooting suspect's motive remains a mystery.* 89.3 KCPP. https://www.scpr.org/news/2018/01/19/79966/no-motive-uncovered-for-las-vegas-mass-shooting/.
Scott, C.A. (2016). Punishing the Punisher: Can Hollywood ever capture the essence of the character? In M. McEniry, R. Peaslee, & R. Weiner (Eds.), *Marvel comics into film: Essays on adaptations since the 1940s.* Jefferson, NC: McFarland.
Taslitz, A.E. (2004). Daredevil and the death penalty. *Ohio State Journal of Criminal Law,* 1, 699.

"When is the right moment to release a TV series about a heroic mass shooter?"
Contemporary American Politics and the Reception of Netflix's The Punisher

MIRIAM KENT

Netflix's series *Marvel's The Punisher* (2017–) is a live-action adaptation of the enduring gun-wielding anti-hero who first appeared in Marvel comics in 1974. The Punisher has spoken to different political contexts according to when—and in what medium—he has appeared, from Reaganite politics (Browning, 2014) to the War on Terror (DiPaolo, 2011). Due to his unyielding methods of exacting violent justice upon criminals, he is often characterized as a deeply conservative figure.

Surrounded by controversy and conflict, the Netflix series, like the character on which it is based, can shed light on issues that emerge when considering a text about a white, masculine anti-hero seeking revenge on those who killed his family. *Marvel's The Punisher* attempts to mediate debates around gun control and masculine post-traumatic stress as the result of war, indicating a cultural awareness of the limitations of hegemonic masculinity. The critical reception of the series is a means to discern how gender, race and class politics converge through themes of gun violence and revenge within broader popular discourses. It also examines how complex questions of contemporary masculine identity have been made sense of by cultural commentators during a polarized political era. What is the place of the Punisher within contemporary American politics? Moreover, how have audiences made sense of the series within this context?

Masculinity and Trump-Era Politics: Marvel's The Punisher *in Context*

This iteration of Frank Castle (Jon Bernthal) previously appeared in Netflix's *Marvel's Daredevil* (2015–) as a paramilitary officer hunting down mafia criminals, acting as an antithesis to the titular superhero character. While both characters have distinct moral values, they differ in their approach to dealing with criminals—whereas Daredevil believes it is wrong to kill, Castle views it as an often necessary solution to crime, even relishing the revenge he takes on those who murdered his wife and daughter. In *Marvel's The Punisher*, Castle discovers that the violence enacted against his family was part of a bigger conspiracy relating to his time served in Afghanistan.

Here, Castle is a war veteran who was hand-selected by corrupt CIA agent William Rawlins (Paul Schultze) to join a Black Ops unit funded by the illegal drugs trade. In Kandahar, Afghanistan, he was part of a task force ordered to torture and kill an Afghani police officer. This was filmed by another soldier on a tape leaked to NSA employee David Lieberman (Ebon Moss-Bachrach). The leader of the Black Ops unit aimed to eliminate both Castle and Lieberman (who names himself Micro) because of the leak. Castle's family was resultantly killed, and Micro faked his own death.

Conceptions of post-traumatic stress disorders (PTSD) associated with war are inherently gendered due to the social pressures experienced by men within the hegemonic masculine setting of the military. Military contexts require masculine ideals of stoicism, courage, competitiveness and physical strength, prohibiting emotional expression and vulnerability—deemed feminine—called for in therapeutic recovery processes. The masculine trauma of war is at the heart of *Marvel's The Punisher*—many scenes take place at a mental health support group for veterans led by Curtis Hoyle (Jason R. Moore). Young veteran Lewis Wilson (Daniel Webber) becomes a terrorist in support of the right to bear arms and is portrayed as vulnerable after his service, being radicalized by an older man (a clear stand-in for the alt-right extremists). Likewise, both Castle and Micro are traumatized: Castle has continuous flashbacks and dreams of his wife and daughter, while Micro is a desperate man yearning for his past life through surveilling his family with hidden cameras.

The series thus presents converging masculinities in its male characters, attempting to make sense of men's trauma from distinct points of view. This is noteworthy within a contemporary postfeminist media context, which accounts for performative approaches towards gender. That is, gender is acknowledged to be a social construct, rather than an essential or innate quality of people assigned male at birth. However, the series also reinscribes hegemonic gender roles and attributes, while absorbing, or taking account of, of feminist critiques of those very essentialist conceptualizations of masculinity, as is characteristic of postfeminist media representations of gendered subjectivities (Tasker & Negra, 2007, p. 2). Indeed, contemporary developments in postfeminist media culture are characterized by a continued taking account of feminist goals so as to suggest political feminisms have fulfilled their purpose (McRobbie, 2007, p. 28) and also moves towards a widespread embrace of (certain) feminisms, such as within the #MeToo movement against sexual harassment. Indeed, according to Rosalind Gill, recent postfeminist culture maintains its complex intertwining of the empowerment of women and its reinforcing of neoliberal individualism by which those women are expected to empower themselves (Gill 2017). Rosalind Gill and Shani Orgad have since highlighted the continued reliance of #MeToo on enduring, essentialist notions of gender and the privileging of white, affluent femininities, concluding that "many of the fundamental problems identified in relation to the sexualization debate persist in the context of #MeToo, and are manifest in old as well as new and troubling ways" (Gill & Orgad, 2018, pp. 1318–19). This illustrates that mainstream media culture ostensibly embraces what might be referred to as a liberal, progressive politics while remaining embroiled in negotiations with the status quo that structure American society, including (the gendered politics of) neoliberal capitalism.

The cast of Netflix's *The Punisher* is predominantly white, heterosexual and non-disabled—apart from certain supporting characters: veteran Curtis, who is black and has had a leg amputation due to injuries sustained in the war; and Homeland Security Agent Dinah Madani, whose parents are Persian. Importantly, the series aligns with neoliberal individualism in its conception of military men through its highlighting of individual masculine traumas and lack of critique towards the neoliberal capitalist structures that result in war that causes this kind of trauma. As Catherine Scott has noted, in American society, "the travails of soldiers are understood through personal solutions to be found in responsibility and coping" (C.V. Scott, 2018, p. 221). *The Punisher* therefore emphasizes how (predominantly male) soldiers cope, rather than offering a critique of the institutions that result in the *necessity* for them to cope.

The series occupies a distinct space in Netflix's catalogue, following the platform's tradition of Marvel adaptations that feature a street-level hero rather than a godlike superbeing. This is akin to previous Netflix content such as *Marvel's Jessica Jones* (2015–2019), which was lauded by critics for its "realistic" rendering of superhero trauma (this was also highly gendered due to its feminist themes of sexual assault and women's agency). Indeed, Julia Havas has discussed how Netflix content makes use of and reworks familiar conventions of quality television in its utilization of genre transgressions and feminist discourses (Havas, 2017, p. 249). Both *Jessica Jones* and *The Punisher* are concerned with post-traumatic stress, although how these themes materialize are inevitably gendered. In this sense, *The Punisher* draws the focus back to the quality TV domain of white manhood (Lagerwey, Leyda & Negra, 2016). Likewise, *The Punisher*'s focus on the disenfranchisement of working-class white men is in line with the continuing discursive practice of characterizing masculinity as "in crisis" (Negra & Tasker, 2014, p. 2; Walker and Roberts, 2018, p. 2). Within these practices, in which feminism often occupies an almost authoritarian representational space, "men experience a crisis because the resources through which their masculinities were articulated are no longer available," resulting in a symbolic reassertion of masculinity through violence (Haywood et al., 2017, p. 128). This simultaneously acknowledges gender as a construct *and* essential essence in line with continuing postfeminist discourses.

Indicating the political significance of the character, Castle's introduction to comics in the 1970s was part of a wider turn towards darker stories in Marvel superhero comics characterized by stories in which wives and girlfriends of superheroes are killed, tortured or otherwise victimized by villains as a prompt for the hero's vengeful action (Blumberg 2003). Jeffrey Johnson has noted that at this time "comic books entered a darker period in which creators presented more realistic stories as American society and popular culture was filled with many stark and unhappy images" (Johnson, 2012, p. 64). In the comics, Castle, a former Marine sniper, seeks revenge on the mobsters who murdered his wife and children while out on a picnic (Conway & DeZuniga, 1975). There are distinct gendered and political qualities to this character as an aggrieved man who takes action on account of vulnerable family members through violent, militaristic means. The Punisher has subsequently been thought of in relation to wider popular cultural trends portraying vengeful anti-heroes and fits into the mold of 1970s vengeance thrillers *Dirty Harry* (1971) and *Death Wish* (1974), which have likewise been discussed in terms of conservative politics (Ryan & Kellner, 1988, pp. 45–46, 89–90). Regarding the Punisher's political leanings specifically, Marc DiPaolo summarizes that:

> most vigilante narratives are not angry liberal screeds, but angry conservative screeds. Unconcerned with corporate excess, or crimes committed by good, white, Christian men, most "Punisher" tales are instead interested in seeing the dangerous hippies and brown people of the world brought to the sword for leading a fundamentally corrupt life [2011, p. 121].

Netflix's series premiered during a precarious era in American politics marked by a turn to conservatism, right-wing populism and the alt-right, which can be thought of as a far-right hate group often associated with working-class white masculinity and the political policies of Trump (Main, 2018, p. 227). This is interesting in relation to the potentially right-leaning politics of Castle, whose ends-justify-the-means approach to justice (and the right to bear arms) may resonate with conservative audiences. Highlighting the ongoing cultural significance of the character, the Punisher skull logo has been appropriated with political implications at different points in history, for instance, it was used by the 24th Infantry Regiment that served in Iraq (2005–06), and Navy SEAL Team 3 and famous veteran Chris Kyle, subject of the autobiographical book *American Sniper* (2012) and its film adaptation (2014). More recently, Iraqi soldiers fighting ISIS have adopted the skull logo as an insignia. The symbol is also said to have been used by far-right and white nationalist marchers at a rally in Charlottesville, Virginia, 2017. This prompted Punisher actor Jon Bernthal, himself a gun owner, to issue a statement declaring "fuck them" regarding alt-right Punisher fans and that "a guy with mental issues like the asshole in Texas" should not have had access to guns (as cited in Alexander, 2018). Again, the surrounding context of the series is emblematic of the convoluted political (and gendered) discourses circulating through American culture.

Guns, described by Amy Ann Cox as a "cultural symbol of masculinity" within American society (Cox, 2007, p. 141), feature prominently in the series. The association between masculinity and guns has shifted throughout history but is often linked to the traditional need for a man to fulfill his role as the provider of food and protection for his family (Cox, 2007, p. 142). Underlining the importance of guns, the opening credits of *The Punisher* portray a kaleidoscopic black and white sequence with guns firing in slow motion and close-ups of gun components, as well as the skull logo made up of guns. This is to the sound of a sinister country-inflected theme tune, which itself has white masculine connotations despite the genre's complicated relationship with race and the Deep South (Mather, 2017). Though singular readings of the series are not necessarily useful, *Marvel's The Punisher*'s insistence on the unabashed display of guns may be considered fetishistic.

Nonetheless, the series itself is convoluted in terms of politics and attempts to include characters with converging political stances regarding gun control that are difficult to pin down in terms of polarized notions of conservative and liberal. For instance, Castle's ally, journalist Karen Page, is pro-gun control but carries a legal firearm to protect herself after being attacked. These gun control debates are gendered within the series and in wider social contexts. For instance, Jennifer Carlson has examined the widespread discourses of guns as gender "equalizers" in confrontations between weak, victimized women and strong, predatory men, a position that assumes a universal victimhood that erases women's experiences of vulnerability within patriarchal societies (Carlson, 2013). Guns remain an integral site of American political debate and were the focus of widespread discussions during the 2016 election campaigns of Republican candidates—including Trump, Ted Cruz, Marco Rubio and Rick Santorum—and continue to dominate the news in the light of mass shootings (Yuill & Street, 2017).

Balancing Guns, Masculinity and Quality: Critical Reception of Marvel's The Punisher

Cord Scott has argued that the core characteristics of the Punisher (his military training, experiences in war and vigilante values) have always narratively responded to ongoing political developments, regardless of medium (C.A. Scott, 2016). However, Scott has also noted that critical responses to the character are likewise dependent on political contexts, suggesting that "the biggest problem with bringing the Punisher to screen is that, at its core, the story is inherently violent" (C.A. Scott, 2016, p. 250). This means that critics' judgments of the character's "quality" are fundamentally political, despite attempts by some to separate "quality" from politics.

Given *Marvel's The Punisher*'s centralizing of masculinity, guns and trauma, I argue that the political sentiments within the textual baggage of the character were attuned to the complexities of contemporary Trump-era politics, commenting on gun control and (white, working-class) masculinity in American society. Some comic book writers who have contributed to Punisher comics maintain that their objective was to critique the chaos of war and the pitfalls of bloody revenge. Punisher creator Gerry Conway, while acknowledging that other creators have taken the character in different directions, has stated that his conceptualization of the Punisher was as "a guy who was driven by his need for vengeance but was not so driven that he couldn't see what was going on around him" (as cited in DiPaolo, 2011, p. 125). Indeed, DiPaolo suggests that for many writers, the goal of Punisher stories is to "see him as an average citizen who has been pushed too far. Inside all of us lurks a potential Punisher, once someone harms our family" (DiPaolo, 2011, p. 124). However, neither of these viewpoints considers the specificities of the "average citizen" as inhabiting a masculine subjectivity informed by wider gendered, racial and classed discourses. The ongoing popularity and rejuvenation of the character throughout different eras and in different media thus speak to issues concerning masculinity and violence relevant at those times. This is further indicated within the critical reception of the series.

Castle's traumas were picked up on by critics who referred to him as tragic or traumatized (Dibdin, 2017; Gilbert, 2017; Saraiya, 2017). These discourses act as explanations (or perhaps justifications) for his ruthless approach to crime. One critic, for instance, wrote "It's whack-a-mole vigilante justice, but Frank doesn't care because his pain is bottomless" (Gay, 2017). Many of these discussions refer to the character's comic book origins and backstory here. However, critics were divided over how appropriate Castle's "simplistic" approach to justice was for a supposedly more "complex" format such as a Netflix TV series. Kevin Yeoman of *Screen Rant* suggested that

> the inherent problems with the character are amplified by the season's excessive length and garden-variety approach to the Punisher's way of doing things. At this point, the methods of operation for both Frank Castle and Netflix's corner of the MCU could stand to be refreshed [2017].

The interpretation of Castle's defining characteristics (cold-blooded revenge enacted on criminals via violent gunfire in the name of justice) as inherently problematic indicate the perceived tensions present in representing such a character on-screen rather than in comic books. Indeed, Yeoman states that while "that kind of straightforward simplicity works well in the two-dimensional world of the comics, it's proven less successful in live-action adaptations," indicating that the ethical and political issues presented in *The Punisher* are transcribed onto genre and medium, perhaps diffusing the pro- or anti-gun argument entirely.

In another example, Darren Franich suggests that the Punisher character worked in the comics because he was an over-the-top parody, but that the Netflix series is ineffective:

> So this show wants to be different, wants to be a thoughtful version of the Punisher story? It wants to ground him, take seriously the idea of this man as one emotionally bruised veteran among many? Interesting! But you have to *actually* take him seriously [2017, original emphasis].

Franich's sarcasm-laden response suggests that Castle's core characteristics are unsuitable for serious television, again negotiating questions of formal quality and specific narrative content. Indeed, the notion that the premise of the show is too simplistic repeatedly appeared in reviews, illustrating the hierarchical nature of discussions around comic books and quality TV—supposedly quality TV is much too complex to be able to carry the Punisher.

The issue therefore discursively shifts from critics questioning whether the Punisher's actions are appropriate or ethical to wondering whether the Punisher's actions are appropriate or ethical to *this particular genre* (superhero) and *medium* (live-action TV). This ultimately displaces the politics of the character onto formal and implicitly gendered elements.

The premiere of the series was delayed due to the Las Vegas mass shooting in October 2017, prompting responses from cast and crew of the show and contributing to its controversial context (Lee, 2017). Mass shootings carried out by white male shooters have themselves been discussed in terms of their linkage to hegemonic masculinity, notably by Michael Kimmel. Castle's crisis-stricken masculinity—regardless of the medium in which he appears—depends on the affective dynamics encapsulated in what Kimmel defines as "aggrieved entitlement" (Kimmel, 2017).

Kimmel's term is appropriate here due to the vengeful nature of Castle's motives and his singular vision of fairness as hinging on his own trauma (and through the use of guns). Noting the turn towards masculinity in crisis in popular discourses, Kimmel had referred to widespread ideas that men have been let down by a system that should supposedly serve their needs (partly due to the successes of feminism). Like Castle and his fellow veterans, these men have been "betrayed by the country they love, discarded like trash on the side of the information superhighway" (Kimmel, 2013, p. 3). Due to the intersections of class, gender and race, these men can be defined as America's Angry White Men. Because a key component of their masculinity has been, in their eyes, taken away (for instance by an authority figure who seeks to exploit the military for his own corrupt ends, as in *Marvel's The Punisher*), these men are positioned as entitled to some form of payback or revenge. Essentially, this makes Castle an Angry White Man, a version of masculinity that has arguably been emboldened during the Trump era. Castle's aggrieved entitlement may even be justified according to some critics (he is traumatized; therefore, his actions are understandable). This illustrates the highly complex discursive mechanics at work when violent white masculinity is made sense of and points to a need for nuanced discussion.

Critics thus wrestled with reconciling the idea that *The Punisher* might be a quality series with the notion that his methods might not be ethical. They did this by referring to wider social and political contexts. Philip Owen of *The Wrap* stated that "it seems like somewhat of a bad idea to give a character like Punisher (or as he's traditionally known in my home, 'Murder Guy') his own show" and yet concluded that "This version of Frank Castle … is a real human character who has far more depth than just 'Murder Guy'" (Owen, 2017), suggesting that the series offers enough emotional nuance to make "Murder Guy" compelling. Franich similarly stated that:

> Frank Castle is a man with a skull shirt who fires big guns at bad guys. So you could say the new Netflix Punisher show is ill-timed—but when is the right moment to release a TV series about a heroic mass shooter? [Franich, 2017]

The prospect that there may never be a "right moment" for the Punisher here deflects the ethical dimensions of the critic's value judgment.

Likewise, Lorraine Ali writing for the *Los Angeles Times* argued that "It's unlikely there was ever going to be an opportune time for 'The Punisher' to be released after the Oct. 1 tragedy given that there's been at least 35 mass shootings since then, according to recent reports" (Ali, 2017), while another critic argued that "It's hard to root for a fictional sniper ... after a real-life one has orchestrated this level of awfulness" (Miller, 2017). These critics, then, while noting that Punisher might be inappropriate within the contemporary social and political landscape, also resigned to the idea that gun violence is an enduring presence ingrained within American society with ambivalent results.

Critics also had diverging opinions regarding the show's political stance in terms of conservatism versus liberalism, which I have characterized as ambiguous and conflicted. For some, the ambiguity, often read as complexity, was considered a positive aspect of the show. Interestingly, Owen argued that:

> this show is not really thinking much about being left or right.... The show isn't trying to make some kind of grand, obvious statement, and it's also not trying to avoid politics completely. Instead it has a laser-like focus on the humans involved [2017].

To this critic the series is about *people* rather than politics, thereby depoliticizing the series entirely. Meanwhile, Daniel Feinberg characterized the ambiguity as such:

> *The Punisher* has things on its mind, including that side-eyed glance at the depersonalized military industrial complex, how it turns boys into killing machines and then too often doesn't help them assimilate back into society, leaving them weaponized and unguided [2017].

While David Griffin of *IGN* noted that:

> *Marvel's The Punisher* is not an easy story to tell, especially in the current political climate.... The series could have easily turned into an indulgence for senseless acts of violence, but it doesn't. Instead of shying away or ignoring the harsh realities of the real world, *The Punisher* dives face-first into the debate [2017].

In such statements, the quality of the series is therefore elaborated through distinctions of "complexity" and how that links with the representation of the politics of gun violence.

On the other hand, some critics thought the series was not complex enough, as mentioned earlier. One writer maintained that "It may seem like *The Punisher* wants to live in gray areas, but it ends up lamely sticking to black and white" (Lawler, 2017), while another piece by Laura Hudson was titled "Netflix's Punisher would be timely if it had anything coherent to say about gun violence" (Hudson, 2017). Hudson consequently characterizes the series' portrayal of gun politics and PTSD as "a thin sheen of social consciousness," suggesting that there is an insincerity about the handling of these topics and drawing hierarchical distinctions of realism and authenticity in representations of "serious" subjects.

Therefore, there is a fissure within *The Punisher*'s reception: it may be "good" due to its moral complexities or "bad" because of its simplicity. These discourses feed into wider questions around who is perceived to be entitled to kill whom and why (e.g., according to gender, race and class), and with what kind of weapons (guns), bringing the focus implicitly back to gun politics and identity.

Conclusion

Issues that came to light within these reviews often pointed towards questions of genre, format and quality, and converged with politics and gender. For some critics, elements of the series were not politically complex enough to be deemed of quality, whereas for others, the series' supposed lack of distinct engagement with political sides (which in itself is a political position to take) was a strength of the show. For other critics, it offered a nuanced critique of corrupt political systems. Meanwhile, a number of critics demonstrated an awareness of the problematics of representing an Angry White Man as hero but did not engage in-depth with the ethical and political dilemmas of the character, focusing instead on the opportunities offered by the series to represent masculine trauma.

These reviews point towards a multiplicity in the way in which violent white masculinities (and the politics that accompany them) are made sense of. They also provide an insight into shifting definitions of justified violence and what sort of people are represented as having the privilege to enact it. Regardless of the political position of the series, the converging discourses of the series, which represent varying models of heroism pertaining to masculine subjects, must be approached with nuance. With this in mind, a fruitful topic of inquiry for the future may be to address the responses of veterans and military personnel to the series, for these would offer yet further nuance to the discussion. This essay scratches the surface of the potential positioning of a contentious character within critical spheres; however, an audience study would prove equally compelling.

If Carlson's objective to make a fairer, safer, more equal society by making the (itself gendered) need for guns irrelevant (Carlson, 2015) is to be fulfilled, Netflix's *The Punisher* offers few solutions due to its centralizing (or fetishizing) of guns. Meanwhile, the critical reception of the series demonstrates that readings on both sides of the political spectrum continue to address gun violence in terms of long-standing debates that link to gender, race and class.

References

Alexander, J. (2018, January 4). *The Punisher's Jon Bernthal condemns alt-right's co-opting of character's imagery*. Polygon. https://www.polygon.com/tv/2018/1/4/16849080/punisher-jon-bernthal-alt-right-gun-control.
Ali, L. (2017, November 17). Marvel's the Punisher packs a punch but still suffers from bad timing. *Los Angeles Times*. http://www.latimes.com/entertainment/tv/la-et-st-marvel-the-punisher-review-20171116-story.html.
Browning, G. (2014). Crime. In M.K. Booker (Ed.), *Comics through time: A history of icons, idols, and ideas* (pp. 88–93). Santa Barbara, CA: Greenwood.
Carlson, J. (2013). The equalizer? Crime, vulnerability, and gender in pro-gun discourse. *Feminist Criminology*, 9(1), 59–83.
Carlson, J. (2015). *Citizen-protectors: The everyday politics of guns in an age of decline*. Oxford: Oxford University Press.
Conway, G., & DeZuniga, T. (1975, August). Death sentence. In *Marvel preview*, #2. New York: Marvel Comics.
Cox, A.A. (2007). Aiming for manhood: The transformation of guns into objects of American masculinity. In C.F. Springwood (Ed.), *Open fire: Understanding global gun cultures* (pp. 141–152). London: Berg.
Dibdin, E. (2017, November 21). The Punisher *is an effective horror story about the American military*. Esquire. https://www.esquire.com/entertainment/tv/a13812745/marvels-the-punisher-netflix-review/.
DiPaolo, M. (2011). *War, politics and superheroes: Ethics and propaganda in comics and film*. Jefferson, NC: McFarland.
Eastwood, C. (Producer/Director). (2014). *American Sniper* [Film]. United States: Warner Bros. Pictures.
Feinberg, D. (2017, November 13). *Marvel's 'The Punisher': TV Review*. The Hollywood Reporter. https://www.hollywoodreporter.com/review/marvels-punisher-review-1057289.
Franich, D. (2017, November 13). *Marvel's* The Punisher *is sensitive, thoughtful, and boring: EW review*. Entertainment Weekly. https://ew.com/tv/2017/11/13/the-punisher-is-sensitive-thoughtful-and-boring-ew-review/.
Gay, V. (2017, November 16). *'The Punisher' review: Jon Bernthal makes the best of a bad character*. Newsday. https://www.newsday.com/entertainment/tv/the-punisher-review-1.14999753.
Gilbert, S. (2017, November 19). The Punisher *is rooted in American trauma*. The Atlantic. https://www.theatlantic.com/entertainment/archive/2017/11/the-punisher-review-netflix/546182/.
Gill, R. (2017). The affective, cultural and psychic life of postfeminism: A postfeminist sensibility 10 years on. *European Journal of Cultural Studies*, 20(6), 606–626.
Gill, R. & Orgad, S. (2018). The shifting terrain of sex and power: From the "sexualization of culture" to #MeToo. *Sexualities*, 21(8), 1313–1324.
Griffin, D. (2017, November 20). *Marvel's The Punisher: Season 1 TV review*. IGN. https://me.ign.com/en/marvels-the-punisher-season-1/140344/review/marvels-the-punisher-season-1-review.
Haywood, C., Johansson, T., Hammarén, N., Herz, M., & Ottemo, A. (2017). *The conundrum of masculinity hegemony, homosociality, homophobia and heteronormativity*. New York: Routledge.
Hudson, L. (2017). *Netflix's Punisher would be timely if it had anything coherent to say about gun violence*. The Verge. https://www.theverge.com/2017/11/17/16670940/punisher-review-netflix-marvel-jon-bernthal-gun-violence.

Kimmel, M. (2013). *Angry white men: American masculinity at the end of an era*. New York: Nation Books.

Kyle, C., McEwen, S., & DeFelice, J. (2012). *American sniper: The autobiography of the most lethal sniper in U.S. military history*. New York: William Morrow & Company.

Lagerwey, J., Leyda, J., & Negra, D. (2016). Female-centered TV in an age of precarity. *Genders Online Journal*, *1*(1). https://www.colorado.edu/genders/2016/05/19/female-centered-tv-age-precarity.

Lawler, K. (2017, November 16). Review: Netflix's gory new Marvel series 'The Punisher' misses the mark. *USA Today*. https://eu.usatoday.com/story/life/tv/2017/11/16/punisher-review-marvel-netflix-series-jon-bernthal/849284001/.

Lee, B. (2017, November 8). *Jon Bernthal confirms The Punisher was delayed because of Las Vegas shooting*. Digital Spy. http://www.digitalspy.com/tv/the-punisher/news/a842581/jon-bernthal-the-punisher-delayed-las-vegas-shooting/.

Lightfoot, S. (Executive Producer). (2017–2019). *Marvel's The Punisher* [Streaming series]. Netflix.

Main, T.J. (2018). *The rise of the alt-right*. Washington, D.C.: Brookings Institution Press.

Mather, O.C. (2017). Race in country music scholarship. In T.D. Stimeling (Ed.), *The Oxford handbook of country music* (pp. 327–354). Oxford: Oxford University Press.

McRobbie, A. (2007). Post-feminism and popular culture. In Y. Tasker & D. Negra (Eds.), *Interrogating postfeminism: Gender and the politics of popular culture* (pp. 27–39). Durham, NC: Duke University Press.

Miller, L.S. (2017, November 13). *'The Punisher' season 1 review: Marvel's least superhero-y show ever fails to find a spark*. IndieWire. https://www.indiewire.com/2017/11/the-punisher-season-1-review-marvel-netflix-1201896825/.

Negra, D. & Tasker, Y. (2014). Introduction: Gender and recessionary culture. In D. Negra & Y. Tasker (Eds.), *Gendering the recession: Media and culture in an age of austerity* (pp. 1–30). Durham, NC: Duke University Press.

Owen, P. (2017, November 13). *Marvel's The Punisher TV review: It's actually pretty great*. The wrap. https://www.thewrap.com/the-punisher-tv-review-its-actually-pretty-great/.

Ryan, M., & Kellner, D. (1988). *Camera politica: The politics and ideology of contemporary Hollywood film*. Bloomington: Indiana University Press.

Saraiya, S. (2017, November 13). TV review: 'Marvel's The Punisher,' starring Jon Bernthal. *Variety*. Retrieved from https://variety.com/2017/tv/reviews/punisher-review-marvel-netflix-jon-bernthal-1202610451/.

Scott, C.A. (2016). Punishing the Punisher: Can Hollywood ever capture the essence of the character? In M.J. McEniry, R.M. Peaslee & R.G. Weiner (Eds.), *Marvel Comics into film: Essays on adaptations since the 1940s* (pp. 243–251). Jefferson, NC: McFarland.

Scott, C.V. (2018). *Neoliberalism and U.S. foreign policy: From Carter to Trump*. New York: Springer.

Siegel, D. (Producer/Director). (1971). *Dirty Harry* [Film]. United States: Warner Bros.

Tasker, Y., & Negra, D. (2007). Introduction: Feminist politics and postfeminist culture. In Y. Tasker & D. Negra (Eds.), *Interrogating postfeminism: Gender and the politics of popular culture* (pp. 1–25). Durham, NC: Duke University Press.

Walker, C., & Roberts, S. (2018). Masculinity, labour and neoliberalism: Reviewing the field. In C. Walker & S. Roberts (Eds.), *Masculinity, labour, and neoliberalism: Working-class men in international perspective* (pp. 1–30). London: Palgrave MacMillan.

Winner, M. (Director). (1974). *Death Wish* [Film]. United States: Paramount. Film.

Yeoman, K. (2017, November 17). *Marvel's The Punisher isn't bad, but the Netflix formula is wearing thin*. Screen rant. https://screenrant.com/marvel-the-punisher-netflix-season-1-review/.

Yuill, K. & Street, J. (2017). Introduction. In K. Yuill & J. Street (Eds.), *The second amendment and gun control: Freedom, fear, and the American Constitution* (pp. 1–6). London: Routledge.

About the Contributors

Ryan **Cassidy** is an associate librarian at Texas Tech University, where he runs the University Library's Makerspace and Virtual Reality Lab. He received his BA in English from the University of Texas at Arlington and his MS in library and information science from the University of North Texas.

Stephen **Connor** holds a Ph.D. from Wilfrid Laurier University. He is an assistant professor of history and co-founder and associate director at the Centre for the Study of War, Atrocity at Nipissing University (North Bay, Canada). He is the recipient of numerous awards for teaching excellence, and also serves as regimental historian for the Algonquin Regiment (Canadian Army).

Alicia M. **Goodman** has a Ph.D. in fine arts: theatre with foci in arts administration and history/theory/criticism. Her research interests include theater administration/management, arts advocacy, intersectional representation of gender and violence in popular culture, and stage combat pedagogy. She has more than ten years of experience in designing theatrical violence and teaching stage combat.

John **Harnett** is an independent post-doctoral researcher from Limerick City (Ireland). His research interests combine elements of symbolism, mythology, and psychoanalytic discourse with multimodal design theory to explore how comics convey different emotional states. He has presented internationally on a wide range of comics-oriented topics and has published on the orchestration of memory in comics.

Elizabeth **Jendrzey** is a Ph.D. student of rhetoric and composition at Purdue University, where she also teaches composition and professional writing. Her previous projects include conference presentations on the nature and usage of fanfiction and a master's thesis on the rhetoric of adaptation in the theater. Her research interests also explore writing in the digital sphere and the writing process itself.

Kelly **Kanayama** is a Ph.D. candidate at the University of Dundee, where her research focuses on British authors' portrayals of America in contemporary comics. She is working on a book about the comics of Garth Ennis, to be published by Sequart, and is a contributor to the comics criticism website Mindless Ones.

Miriam **Kent** has a Ph.D. in film studies with a focus on Marvel superheroes and has taught a wide range of film, media and gender studies university courses. She has published on superhero media with an interest in gender, representation and adaptation, including a monograph, *Women in Marvel Films*. Her work has appeared in academic journals and edited volumes.

About the Contributors

Rob E. **King** is an associate librarian at Texas Tech University's Southwest Collection/Special Collections Library and a doctoral student in English at Texas Tech University. He is coeditor of a collection of essays on David Lynch, the American West and *Twin Peaks*, which is forthcoming from McFarland. His research interests include American cultural studies, paratextuality, radical cataloging, and archival futures.

Mike **Lemon** earned a Ph.D. from Texas Tech University, where he works as an instructor. He has taught a seminar on race and the immigrant experience in American comics; he has also been an invited lecturer on gender and comics for college classes and public round tables. His research interests include comic books and fandom and place-based American literature. His research explores depictions of the African American West in comics.

Ryan **Litsey**, Ph.D., is the associate librarian and head of Information Access and Delivery at Texas Tech University. He has a Ph.D. in educational psychology and leadership from Texas Tech University. He has spent most of his academic career developing groundbreaking technologies that have transformed resource sharing.

Anders **Lundgren** is a freelance writer and lecturer. His work has been published in journals and in *The Mignolaverse* (edited by S.G. Hammond). He is the co-producer of the Stockholm International Comics Festival and founder of the Stockholm H.P. Lovecraft Festival. With Anton Bjurvald and Freddie Kaplan, he makes up the triumvirate behind long-running podcast *High on Comics* (*Hög av serier*).

Kathleen **McClancy** is an associate professor of media studies at Texas State University. She has published articles in *Film & History* and *ImageTexT*, and the chapter "Black Skin, White Faces" in *New Perspectives on the War Film* (Palgrave Macmillan). She is engaged in a research project studying Cold War nostalgia after September 11. She is the primary organizer of the Comics Arts Conference.

Matthew J. **McEniry** is an associate librarian at Texas Tech University and the director of the Digital Scholarship Lab. He was a coeditor on *Marvel Comics into Film* and has a published chapter in *The Super Villain Reader*. His research interests include digital scholarship, science fiction, and comic studies.

Meredith **Pasahow** is a Ph.D. student at Texas Woman's University, where she also teaches first year composition as a graduate assistant. She has a master's degree in English literature. Her research interests include British literature with a concentration on monstrosity and the grotesque, though the main focus of her work is in the field of dystopian science-fiction.

Robert G. **Weiner** is the popular culture librarian at Texas Tech University and teaches courses on popular culture for the Honors College. He has published extensively on a wide variety of pop culture topics, in the *International Journal of Comic Art*, *Gospel According to Superheroes*, *Secret History of Comic Studies*, *Routledge Companion to Comics*, and many others. He is the author/editor/coeditor of 15 plus books.

Kent **Worcester** is a professor of history and political science at Marymount Manhattan College. His books include *C.L.R. James: A Political Biography* (1996), *A Comics Studies Reader* (2008, coedited with Jeet Heer), and *The Superhero Reader* (2013, coedited with Charles Hatfield and Jeet Heer).

Index

the A-Team 132
Aaron, Jason 7, 35, 42, 144; *see also The Other Side*
Abraham, Phil 117
Abulazeez, Mohammod Youssuf 156
Afghanistan 7, 9, 62, 106, 117, 119, 134, 166
Agent Orange 33
A.I.M 161
Alexander, Lexi 95; *see also Punisher: War Zone* (film)
Allen, Jesse 158–159
Alonso, Axel 76
alt-right 166, 168–169
alternate universe 19, 78, 92, 100, 143
Amazing Spider-Man (comic) 54, 136, 157, 159; *Amazing Spider-Man* #129 1, 50, 136; *Amazing Spider-Man* #135 133; *Amazing Spider-Man* #174 138; *Amazing Spider-Man* #175 138; *Amazing Spider-Man* #574 63; *Amazing Spider-Man* #654 63; "Big Apple Battleground" 138; "The Hitman's Back in Town" 138
American Sniper 134, 169
Andru, Ross 129, 137
anti-hero 2, 4, 6–8, 15, 24, 35, 45–46, 62, 82–83, 88, 155, 163, 165, 168
Antisocial Personality Disorder 57
anti-war movement 53, 103, 131
Apocalypse Now 103
Archie 2, 24
Archive of Our Own 96
atheism 22
Athenians 30
The Avengers 4, 63, 66, 161, 163
Avengers Confidential: Black Widow & The Punisher 2

Baghdad 160
Barbarian with a Gun 57
Barnes, Bucky 68–69
Baron, Mike 55, 58
Baron Strucker 19
Baron Zemo 68, 70
Barracuda 5
Batman 5, 24, 33, 75

Benjamin, Paul 49
Bernthal, Jon 94–96, 116, 166, 169
Bickle, Travel 44, 138
Black Lightning 4
Black Widow 2–3, 68–69, 81
Blake, William 35–36, 38–39, 41
Blue Beetle #1 51
Blue Devil 4
body count 16, 23, 94, 108, 140
Bolan, Mack *see The Executioner*
Born 7, 37, 39–42, 103, 144–145
Bosnia 109
Bridge, G.W. 4
Brock, Eddie 71
Bronson, Charles 50, 158
Bulat, Cristu 108, 110
Bulat, Tiberiu 108, 110
Bullseye 42–43
Burnett, Dylan 49
Bush, George H.W. 141
Bush, George W. 104
Buvoli, Private Sal 36

Cage, Luke 55
Campbell, Joseph 8, 38, 46
Campbell, Laurence 41; *see also Girls in White Dresses*; Hurwitz, Gregg
capitalism 127, 167
Captain America (character) 2–3, 17–20, 22, 24, 54, 65, 68, 75, 91, 115, 160–161
Captain America #241 17
Captain Marvel 67–68, 75
Carnage (character) 65
cartel 142, 160
Castiglione, Francis 48, 137, 140
Castle, Cossandra 8, 75–76, 78, 82–86, 88
Castle, Frank, Jr. 2, 41, 97; *see also* Castle, Lisa; Castle, Maria; family
Castle, Lisa 2, 32, 41, 97, 166; *see also* Castle, Frank Jr.; Castle, Maria; family
Castle, Maria 2, 9, 41, 88, 94, 97, 99, 166; *see also* Castle, Frank Jr.; Castle, Lisa; family
Catcher in the Rye 162
Cates, Donny 49
CBS Evening News 127

179

180 Index

Central Park 42, 56, 94, 137, 146
Cerberus Group 33
Chapman, Mark David 162
Charlottesville, Virginia 169
Charlton Comics 51–52
Charnel 19
Chernaya 66
CIA (Central Intelligence Agency) 32, 106, 134, 166; *see also* FBI (Federal Bureau of Investigation); law enforcement; New York Police Department; police
The City and Man 7; *see also* Strauss, Leo
Civil War 20
Clarke, Stuart 5
class 165, 168–170, 172, 174–175
Cloak 24
Cloonan, Becky 53, 93, 96
Cobain, Kurt 161
The Cold War 141, 143
Cole-Alves, Rachel 85
Colonel Howe 45
Colonel No-Name 142
Colonel Ottman 39
Colorado Springs 156
Columbine High School 162
Comics Code Authority 51–52, 54
Commando 59
Congressional Medal of Honor 142
Connor, Stephen 9
Conrad, Joseph 37–39
conservatism 57, 119, 165, 168–169, 173
Conway, Gerry 1, 49, 51, 54, 62, 136–137, 157, 170
Cooke, Jen 108–109
Cosmic Ghost Rider (character) 69–71
Cosmic Ghost Rider (series) 8, 49
Cosmic Ghost Rider Destroys Marvel History 70
Council for Public Safety 53
courts 17, 23, 32; *see also* criminal justice system
Cox, Charlie 117
Crais, Robert 5, 41, 44
crime rate 53, 159–162
criminal justice system 1, 3, 16–17, 21, 54, 132; *see also* courts
criminal underworld 1, 3, 21, 33, 44, 145
Cronkite, Walter 127

Dagger 24
Daredevil (character) 2, 3, 17, 20–22, 24, 54, 64, 67, 94, 116–118, 158, 166; *see also* Murdock, Matt
Daredevil (comic) 161; *Daredevil* #182 129
"Daredevil and the Death Penalty" 155, 158
Daredevil and the Punisher in Child's Play 21
DC comics 4, 52
Deadpool 2, 81, 88
Death (character) 69

"The Death of the Author" 92
Death Sentence (1975 book) 50
"Death Sentence" (1975 comic) *see Marvel Preview #2*
Death Wish (1972 book) 49; *see also* Garfield, Brian
Death Wish (1974 film) 2, 50, 158, 168; *see also* Winner, Michael
Deleuze, Gilles 56
democracy 28–30, 65, 127
Detective Soap 5
The Devil 38–41, 44, 69
The Devil as Muse 44; *see also* Parker, Fred
Dick Tracy 161
Dillon, Steve 42, 53
Dirty Harry 2, 49; 50, 158, 168; *see also* Siegel, Don
"Disarm" 98
Ditko, Steve 51–52
Dixon, Chuck 56, 140–141
Dr. Brattle 160
Dr. Death 142
Dr. Doom 115, 160
Dr. Faustus 2
Doctor Octopus 16, 161
Dr. Strange 15
dogs 56, 96, 99–100
Don Cesare 56
drugs 23–24, 55, 109, 129–130, 133–134, 142, 159, 166
Duterte, Rodrigo 58

Earth-616 49, 56, 65, 115
Earth-928 86
Earth-2992 75
Earth-200111 49, 56
Eastwood, Clint 158
Ebert, Roger 50
Einstein, Albert 30
El Borak 160
Elektra *see* Natchios, Elektra
Eminem 2
Ennis, Garth 7, 9, 35–38, 41, 52, 56, 93, 96, 102–103, 110, 144–146, 162
Escobar, Pablo 58
The Executioner 2, 49, 139, 155, 157; *see also* Pendleton, Don
exile 28–29
extremism 2, 22, 106, 166

Face 6
family 8, 77, 85, 103, 137; and death of 2, 5, 29, 42–43, 54–56, 62, 70, 85–86, 88, 94–96, 98, 116, 120, 125–126, 131, 133, 137, 142, 165–166, 168; *see also* Castle, Frank, Jr.; Castle, Lisa; Castle, Maria
fanfiction 8, 91–94, 96–100
fanzines 91
fascism 23, 50, 67

Index

Father Angus 22
Faust, Heinrich 40
FBI (Federal Bureau of Investigation) 4, 63, 95, 155, 159; *see also* CIA (Central Intelligence Agency); law enforcement; New York Police Department; police
female gaze 8, 93, 96, 99–100
femininity 130, 133, 166
feminism 7, 93, 105, 167–168, 172
film *see The Punisher* (1990 film); *The Punisher* (2004 film); *Punisher: War Zone* (2008 film)
Firebase Valley Forge 39–40, 42, 144
Flattop 161
"Frank Castle Just Wants to Sell Coffee, Dammit!" 92
Franken-Castle 55
Frankenstein 44
Frazer, James 28
Freud, Sigmund 30
Full Metal Jacket 103, 109
Fury, Nick 66–68, 141, 161

Galactus 49, 69, 71
Gallows, Jacob 5–6, 86
gangs 55, 86, 116–117
Garfield, Brian 49–50; *see also Death Wish* (1972 book)
gender 7–8, 75–83, 85–88, 93–94, 103, 107, 165–172, 174–175
General Padden 39
General Ross 3
Ghost 68
Ghost Rider 2–3, 24, 49, 63
Giacoia, Frank 129
Giap, Colonel Letrong 145
Girls in White Dresses 41; *see also* Campbell, Laurence; Hurwitz, Gregg
Gnucci, Ma 4
God 21–22, 35, 55
Goethe, Johann Wolfgang von 40
Goetz, Bernard 158
Goldbug 20
Goldilocks Syndrome 78
Good Housekeeping 93
Goodman, Alicia M. 8
Goodwin, Michael 48, 144
Goodwin, Steve 43
Gorman 59
Gossett, Louis, Jr. 159
Graine, Rex *see* Mr. A
Grant, Steven 55–56, 59, 62, 139
Greece 27–30
Green Beret *see* U.S. Army Special Forces
Green Goblin 161
Grimm, Ben
Guggenheim, Marc 5
guilt 42–45, 85, 95
gun control 165, 169
gun rights 166, 169

gun violence 7, 9–10, 83, 155–156, 163, 173–175; *see also* violence

Haley, Sarah 130
Hama, Larry 139
Hammerhead 1–2, 161
Harnett, John 7–8
Harper-Mercer Chris 156
Hauley, Mike 138
"Heaven Sent the Saints Down (Hell Sent Them Up)" 97, 99
Hegel, G.W.F. 31
Hell 38
Hell's Kitchen 20–21
Hinckley, John 162
Hitler, Adolf 160
the Hitman 133, 138
Hobbes, Thomas 7
Holloway, Matt 95
Hollywood 163
Home from the War 128
The Hood 4
Horak, Matt 53
Howard, Robert E. 160
Hoyle, Curtis 7, 119–121, 123, 166–167
The Hulk 16
human trafficking 52, 108–110
humanism 17
Hurd, Gale Anne 95
Hurwitz, Gregg 35; *see also* Campbell, Laurence; *Girls in White Dresses*
Hussein, Saddam 160
Hydra 62, 65, 67–69, 71

individualism 33, 51, 167
Indochina 125–126, 129, 131, 144
institutionalism 15, 17, 108, 167
Iraq 7, 63, 109, 119–120, 122, 134, 160, 169
Iron Heart 77
Iron Man 20, 68; *see also* Stark, Tony
Islamophobia 108
Iwo Jima 127

The Jackal 1, 50, 129, 157
Jackman, Hugh 93, 99
Jameson, J.J. 138
Jane, Thomas 1, 6
Janson, Klaus 55
Jendrzey, Elizabeth 8
Jigsaw 4–6, 55, 161
Joanau, Phil 6
Jones, Jim 58
Jung, Carl 8, 38–40
Junior 141
justice 3–4, 6–7, 9, 16–17, 19, 21, 36, 54, 65, 86, 99, 102, 137, 142–143, 146, 163, 165, 169, 171

Kanayama, Kelly 9
Kane, Gil 50
Kent, Miriam 9

182 Index

Kenyon, Burt *see* the Hitman
Kersey, Paul 158
Kierkegaard, Soren 59
kill count *see* body count
King, Rob E. 9
The Kingpin 22, 64, 160–161
Kyle, Chris 169

Lady Punisher 85
Larosa, Lewis 56–57
Las Vegas, Nevada 157, 172
law enforcement 5, 16–17, 94; *see also* CIA (Central Intelligence Agency); FBI (Federal Bureau of Investigation); New York Police Department; police
League of Nations 30
"Learn to Live with the Unimaginable" 99
Lee, Jim 57
legalism 17, 19
Lemon, Mike 9
LGBTQ community 92
liberalism 2, 7, 29–33, 119, 167, 169, 173
Lieberman, David *see* Microchip
"Lifeform" 161
Lifton, Robert Jay 130
Lightfoot, Steven 119
Lincoln, Abraham 30
Litsey, Ryan 7
Loan, Nguyen Ngoc 58
Locke, John 30–31
Lomax, Don 141–142
Loot the coyote 56
Los Angeles 56
Lundgren, Anders 8
Lundgren, Dolph 59, 159

Madani, Dinah 167
the Mafia *see* organized crime
Mahoney, Brett 117
male gaze 93
Manhattan 18, 53, 158
Manson, Charles 58
Mantlo, Bill 55, 60
Marcum, Art 95
"Mark of the Executioner" *see* skull
Marvel Cinematic Universe 116, 118–119, 121–123
Marvel Comics 125, 136–137, 139, 142–143, 155, 158–159, 165
"Marvel Comics and New York Stories: Anti-heroes and Street Level Vigilantes Daredevil and The Punisher" 155
Marvel Knights (comic) 56
Marvel Knights (team) 8
Marvel Knights Double-Shot 22
Marvel Knights 2099: Punisher #1 75–76, 78, 82–83, 85
Marvel Preview #2 54, 131, 136
Marvel Super Action #1 57, 139
Marvel Two-in-One 115

Marvel UK 18
Marvel Universe 2–3, 15, 49, 58, 70, 91, 115, 117, 134, 160
Marvel's Daredevil (series) 32, 91, 94–99, 116–118, 122–123, 155–156, 166; "New York's Finest" 117
Marvel's Jessica Jones (series) 167–168
Marvel's The Punisher (series) 6, 9, 29, 32, 48, 58, 94–97, 99, 119, 121–123, 134, 155–156, 165–174; "Bang" 116; "A Cold Day in Hell's Kitchen" 118; "The Judas Goat" 119, 121; "Kandahar" 29, 120; "One batch, two batch, Penny and a dime" 32; "Resupply" 121; "3 AM" 119, 122; *see also* Netflix
masculinity 9–10, 35, 85, 102–108, 110, 133, 165–170, 172, 174
mass murder 4, 9, 58, 108, 126, 134, 155–157, 159, 163, 170, 172–173
mass shooting *see* mass murder
Mateen, Omar 156
Max the dog 56
Mayor Abe Beame 53
McClancy, Kathleen 9
McEniry, Matthew J. 8
Melians 30
Mephisto 69, 71
Mephistopheles (literary) 40
mercy bullets 54
Michaels, Lynn 85
Microchip 2–3, 5–7, 19, 23, 32, 45, 55–56, 64, 159–160, 166; *see also* sidekick
Miller, Frank 21
Mills, Pat 76
Mr. A 51–52
Mr. Kurtz 39, 45
the mob *see* organized crime
The Monkey 140
Moon Knight 24, 64
Moore, Jason R. 166
morality 8, 36, 48–49, 51, 62, 71, 94–95, 98, 126, 129, 132, 146, 166, 174
Morrow, Lance 104
Moss-Bachrach, Ebon 166
Mother Russia 107
Motor Psycho 126
movies *see* film
Mumbles 161
Murdock, Matt 17, 20–21, 24, 91, 97–98; *see also* Daredevil
Murray, Doug 139–140, 142
Muscle & Fitness 93
My Lai Massacre 126–127

The 'Nam 139–140, 142; "The Long Sticks" 140
The 'Nam: Final Invasion 141–142
Natchios, Elektra 2, 75, 99, 156
Natchios, Franklin 76, 82
Negative Zone Prison 20
Nelson, Foggy 98
Nelson & Murdock 98–99

Index 183

Netflix 1, 6–7, 10, 144, 155–156, 167, 171; *see also Marvel's The Punisher* (series)
New Jersey 23
New York City 53, 67, 71, 94, 158–160
New York Harbor 23
New York Police Department 85–86; *see also* CIA (Central Intelligence Agency); FBI (Federal Bureau of Investigation); law enforcement; police
The New York Times 105
Newsweek 105
Nietzsche, Friedrich 41, 55–56
Nintendo Entertainment System 161
Nintendo Gameboy 161–162
Nirvana 161
non-lethal 23

objectivism 51–52
O'Brien, Kathryn 106
Odin 69–70
Odysseus 127
Ogami Itto 44
optimism 17
organized crime 3, 18, 23, 36, 49, 54, 56, 102, 116, 125, 131, 159, 165
origin 2, 32, 115–118, 126, 171
Orlando, Florida 156
Osgood, Charles 160
The Other Side 144; *see also* Aaron, Jason

Paddock, Stephen Craig 157
Page, Karen 7, 97–98
Parker, Fred 8, 45; *see also The Devil as Muse*
Parker, May "Mayday" *see* Spider-Girl
Parker, Peter 22–24, 98–99; *see also* Spider-Man
Parlov, Goran 37, 42
Pasahow, Meredith 8
patriotism 2, 17–18
Peloponnesian War 30
Pendleton, Don 2, 49, 54; *see also* The Executioner
People's Liberation Front 138
Persian Gulf War 160
Peter Parker, the Spectacular Spider-Man 130–131
"Peter Parker's Home for the Wayward Villain" 99
Petrie, Doug 116, 156
Petrov 66–67
Planned Parenthood 156
Plato 7; *see also The Republic*
police 5, 23, 86, 117, 159, 166; *see also* CIA (Central Intelligence Agency); FBI (Federal Bureau of Investigation); law enforcement; New York Police Department; police
politics 7, 9–10, 16, 165, 168–174
Popeye 52
post-9/11 20, 102, 104, 106, 108, 110, 115–116, 144

posttraumatic stress disorder 123, 130–131, 165–166, 168, 174
Price, Lee 62–63, 65, 71
propaganda 160
prostitution 109–110
Pruneface 161
PTSD *see* posttraumatic stress disorder
Pulliam-Moore, Charles 58
The Punisher (comic) 50, 55, 85, 116, 126, 140, 155, 160–161; *Circle of Blood* 126; "Double Edge" 161; "Eurohit" 55; *Intruder* 22, 59; *The Punisher #1* 136
The Punisher (1990 film) 6, 59, 159
The Punisher (2004 film) 6, 16
The Punisher (videogame) 161
The Punisher Armory 50
The Punisher: Dirty Laundry 1, 6
"The Punisher Invades *The 'Nam*" 140
"*Punisher Invades The 'Nam: Final Invasion*" 141
The Punisher Magazine 50
Punisher MAX 7–9, 35, 42, 52, 56–57, 59, 102–106, 110
Punisher MAX: Barracuda 52, 56
Punisher MAX: Bullseye 42
Punisher MAX: Frank 94
Punisher MAX: The Platoon 9, 48–49, 109, 117
Punisher MAX: The Slavers 52, 108
Punisher Noir 53
The Punisher: Return to Big Nothing 59
Punisher: The Platoon 37, 39, 144–145
The Punisher: The Ultimate Payback! 161
Punisher 2099 6, 76, 86
Punisher: War Journal 50, 57, 85, 140
Punisher: War Machine 50, 116
Punisher War Zone (comic) 50, 57, 85
Punisher: War Zone (2008 film) 6, 95, 98; *see also* Alexander, Lexi
Punisher: Year One 16

Quang, Ly 145
The Question 51–52

race 165, 167–170, 172, 174–175
racism 5, 57, 140; *see also* white nationalism
Rambo, John 132, 141
Ramirez, Marco 116
Rampage 5
Rand, Ayn 50
rape 53, 59, 85, 105–106, 127
Rawlins, William 32–33, 106–107, 110, 166
Reagan, Ronald 132, 139, 165
Recoil 4
Red Hulk 2
Red Leader 2
Red Skull 161
redemption 5, 28, 63, 65, 70–71
religion 59, 161
The Remasculization of America: Gender and the Vietnam War 104, 133

184   Index

The Republic 7, 30; *see also* Plato
the Rev 161
revenge 2, 5–6, 85, 126, 155, 163, 165, 170–172
Rhodes, James 66, 68, 71; *see also* War Machine
Rice, Boyd 60
Richards, Reed 19, 115
Riverdale 24
Robertson, Darick 40
Rogers, Steve *see* Captain America
Romanova, Natasha *see* Black Widow
Rome 28
Romita, John, Jr. 57
Romita, John, Sr. 4, 50, 137
Roof, Dylan 156
Rook, Frank 55
Rosa, Vincent 36
Rosenberg, Matthew 58, 66, 70, 72
Rucka, Greg 15, 134
The Russian 4
Russo, Billy 7
Ryker's Island 56

Sage, Vic *see* The Question
Saigon 109, 138, 141
Salick, Roger 140–141
San Bernardino 156
Santora, Nick 95
Saudi Arabia 109, 160
Scarlet Witch 19
Schmitt, Carl 7
Scorsese, Martin 138
Secret Empire 65
Serbia 108
Sergeant Dryden 45
Severin, John 35–36
sex trafficking *see* human trafficking
Shatan, Chaim 130
She-Hulk 19
S.H.I.E.L.D. 64, 66
"sic semper tyrannis" 120
sidekick 2, 4–5: *see also* Microchip
Siegel, Don 49; *see also* Dirty Harry
Signore, Don 22
Silver Surfer 69
Skinner, Tony 76
skull logo 3, 6, 78, 87, 102, 140, 169
The Sniper 4
Sontag, Susan 105
Southeast Asia 136, 140, 142–144
Spartans 30
The Spectacular Spider-Man 55
Spider-Girl 77
Spider-Man 1–3, 17, 22–24, 54, 64–65, 71, 91, 94, 125, 127, 129, 131, 136, 138, 157, 161; *see also* Parker, Peter
sports 80–81
Stark, Tony 20; *see also* Iron Man
Statue of Liberty 138
Stenkov, Galina 107–108, 110

Stevenson, Noelle 4
Stewart, Jim 160
Strauss, Leo 7; *see also The City and Man*
super-criminal 20
superhero 10, 15–16, 20, 56, 66, 75–78, 94, 128–129, 140, 165, 167
Superhero Registration Act 20
Superman 77
SuperVet 132–133

Tam Ky 122
the Tarantula 133, 157
Taslitz, A.E. 155, 159
Temple, Claire 98
terrorism 123, 158
Tet Offensive 48, 53, 126–127
Thanos (character) 49, 69, 71
Thanos (comic) 69
Thanos Annual Vol. 2 #1 71
Thompson, Flash 62–63
Thor 78
Thor Girl 78
Thrasymachus 30
Thucydides 29–30
The Thunderbolts 2, 63
Time 106
Tombstone 64
Torrance, Sergeant W.J. 40
trauma 170–172, 174
Trojan War 127
Trump, Donald 169–170, 172
Tuohy, Tim 145
The Tyger (comic) 35–36, 42
Typhoid Mary 64

Uatu the Watcher 70
The Unbeatable Squirrel Girl 24
U.S. Army 23–24, 63, 87, 95
U.S. Army Ranger School 87
U.S. Marines 84, 116, 136–137, 141, 144, 168
U.S. military 32, 36, 94, 102, 109, 116, 118, 128
U.S. Navy Seals 87
U.S. Patriot Act 20
U.S. Special Forces 84, 87, 137, 141

Valhalla 69–70
Valley Forge Valley Forge 41
van 94
Vendetta 86
Venom 2, 62–65, 70
veteran 2, 6–7, 9, 18, 42, 49, 62–63, 94, 116–123, 125–128, 130–132, 134, 138–139, 141–142, 166, 172, 174
videogames 161–162
Viet Cong 141–142
Vietnam 9, 18, 20, 37–40, 42, 44–45, 48–49, 53, 57, 103, 107, 109–110, 116–123, 125–134, 136–146, 157, 160–161
Vietnam Syndrome 139, 141
Vietnam Veterans Memorial 132, 139, 142

vigilantism 1, 9, 15, 17, 24, 50–52, 58, 82, 96, 98, 102–103, 116, 136, 143, 146, 155, 157–158, 170–171
violence 16, 51–53, 78, 81–83, 85, 95–96, 106–108, 116–117, 120, 127, 129–130, 132, 139, 143, 155, 157–158, 160–163, 165, 168, 170, 172–174; *see also* gun violence
Von Doom, Victor *see* Dr. Doom

Wacker, Stephen 15
war journal 19, 86
War Machine 62, 66, 70; *see also* Rhodes, James
War on Terror 9, 20, 108, 116, 121, 123, 134, 165
Washington, D.C. 19, 132, 139
Wayne, John 127
Webb, Jeremy 121
Webber, Daniel 9, 166
Wein, Len 138
Wesley, James 97

What If ... Venom Had Possessed the Punisher? 8, 64
White House 102
white nationalism 23, 169; *see also* racism
Williams, Riri *see* Ironheart
Wilson, Lewis 120–123, 166
Winner, Michael 50, 158; *see also Death Wish* (1974 film)
witzend #3 51
Wolverine (character) 2, 24
The Wolverine (film) 93
Wood, Wally 51
Worcester, Kent 7
World War I 53
World War II 18, 38, 115, 127, 134

Yakuza 159

Zeck, Mike 59, 139